PRAISE FOR *HIDING PLACES*

"A work that stares into the abyss of genocide, but also a work that finds the resilience, spirit, and humor of a people who refused to be vanquished."
—Samuel G. Freedman, author of *Jew vs. Jew: The Struggle for the Soul of American Jewry*

"I loved the warmth and energy and honesty. . . . *Hiding Places* touched me deeply."
—Anne Roiphe, author of National Book Award finalist *Fruitful* and *1185 Park Avenue*

"A daring book—often funny . . . finally frightening and moving."
—Peter D. Kramer, author of *Listening to Prozac*

"Deeply moving, very powerful, written in a fine American vernacular."
—Hugh Nissenson, author of *The Song of the Earth*

"A sumptuous, generous book where revelation follows upon revelation."
—*Providence Journal*

"As a love story between a father and his children, it is wonderful, warm, witty and achingly touching; as a story of personal development and maturity, it rings of truth; as a search for 'roots,' it has validity; as a sheer detective story, it is exciting; as post-holocaust literature, it is a worthy, factual addition to the genre."
—*Jewish Book World*

ALSO BY DANIEL ASA ROSE

Flipping for It

Small Family with Rooster

DANIEL ASA ROSE

HIDING PLACES

A Father and His Sons Retrace Their
Family's Escape from the Holocaust

THREE RIVERS PRESS
NEW YORK

Published by Three Rivers Press, New York, New York.
Member of the Crown Publishing Group, a division of Random House, Inc.
www.randomhouse.com

THREE RIVERS PRESS and the Tugboat design are registered trademarks of
Random House, Inc.

Originally published in hardcover by Simon & Schuster in 2000.
Printed in the United States of America

Library of Congress Cataloging-in-Publication Data
Rose, Daniel Asa
Hiding Places: a father and his sons retrace their family's escape
from the Holocaust / Daniel Asa Rose.
p. cm.
1. Rose, Daniel Asa.   2. Jews—Connecticut—Biography.
3. Children of Holocaust survivors—Connecticut—Biography.
4. Holocaust, Jewish (1939–1945)—Influence.
5. Connecticut—Biography. I. Title.
F105.J5 R67 2000
974.6'004924'0092—dc21   [B]   99-086348

ISBN 0-609-80915-6

10 9 8 7 6 5 4 3 2 1

First Paperback Edition

pour les enfants

CONTENTS

AUTHOR'S NOTE

This is a work of nonfiction. I've taken pains to tidy and pace the narrative, to conflate some of the characters in order to lend focus to the structure, and occasionally to imagine details in an effort to convey the deepest sense of the sagas recounted herein. When I have departed from the literal truth, my aim has been to remain true to the essence of both my own childhood as well as the larger family history. Names, locations, and identifying characteristics of a number of individuals have been altered in order to protect their privacy. All the details of the Holocaust atrocities, sadly, are factual as described.

You shall teach these words to your children,
speaking of them when you are sitting at home
and when you go on a journey. . . .

from the V'ahavta of the Shema

1

STARFISH

*T*he jet's crowded. Stopping and starting, we're slowly making our way down the aisle to our seats.

"Is this one?" asks my seven-year-old, lunging at the under-sized coat closet.

"No," I say. "Sorry," I tell the passenger behind us, a natty businessman who wears an impatient Gallic pout as Marshall steps on his lustrous black shoes.

"Is *this* one?" Marshall asks again, jumping to the galley's refrigerator compartment.

"No," I say. *"Pardon,"* I say to the French nun in front of me, as my overnight bag bangs into the back of her knees, eliciting a vinegary expression of tolerance.

"Marshall, let's wait till we get to Europe before we think we're finding the hiding places," I suggest. "We haven't even left Boston yet."

Marshall puts on a thoughtful look as if resolved to turn over a new leaf and ask only suitable questions from here on. But two aisles later, he can't contain himself. "What about *this?*" he cries, flinging himself to the carpet to inspect a cargo space beside the exit door.

It's an action that proves too much for his twelve-year-old brother. Alex drops his pretense of being unacquainted with us to shake his head disgustedly. "Dad, could you tell him that our relatives from World War Two did *not* hide on an Air France Boeing Seven-forty-seven jumbo jet?"

"Relax, Alex. Your brother's just excited."

"Yeah, Alex! At least I want to go on this trip!"

"I never said I didn't want to go," Alex says.

Marshall and I look at him.

"I just said I'd rather stay home."

Our seats come into view. They're located in the middle of a bank of five, between a Parisian model and an overweight Arab with one glass eye who doesn't feel like standing. I climb. The boys jump, slide, wiggle, and wedge. Before long we're in place.

"Want to know what a geek Hitler was?" Marshall asks the model beside him. "He wanted only blond people, and he had black hair. What a geek! We're going to Belgium."

"Yes? That's OK," she says.

"We're going to see J. P. Morgan, maybe. Not the real one, though. This one's an uncle."

"J. P. Mor—?"

"We're going free, because Daddy has his magical media pass."

"Magic . . . *quoi?*" asks the model.

"He's just enthusiastic," I tell the model in my broken French. To Marshall I say, "You want to pipe down so the whole plane doesn't know our business?"

Which Marshall takes to heart. He tries not to show it, but his face looks injured, like a dented hubcap. Seeing the extent of the damage, and not wanting to start the trip on an unhappy note, I open my arms wide. "Here you go," I say. "Have some of my strength."

A ritual. Marshall opens his arms and clutches me hard around the neck, inhaling with satisfaction. As he hugs me I can feel him soaking it up: calm, power, goodness, whatever he needs in order to take leave of his mom for a month and be with his dad on an odyssey whose strangeness he can't yet plumb.

"All better?"

A smile like sudden sunshine lights Marshall's face. He's vitalized: if he had a pelt it would be shiny again. But not altogether; a capillary of worry still twitches on his face.

"What if we run into bad guys in Europe, though?" he says. "Those Nazis?"

"The Nazis are long gone," I assure him. "They all got beat at the end of the war."

"But there are plenty of new ones," Alex points out helpfully.

"Are there, Dad? Because I'm too young to see them."

"Don't worry, you're not going to see them," I say.

"But maybe just to peek at them would be OK," Marshall adds.

With a sigh, Alex levels one more withering gaze upon his brother before he puts on his earphones and attends to Eartha Kitt.

I close my eyes against the plane's most intimate sounds: kitchen locks snapping shut, closet doors bolting closed, the tidy thrum of engines whirring fast and slow. Air streams down over our heads, but otherwise all is sealed. For some reason the sounds make me feel both invisible and bold, and I remember my father asking me, during the custody battle, why I wanted to share the kids halftime, why I didn't just let my ex-wife take them and I'd visit every other weekend.

I had no answer for him. I had no answer because it wasn't even a question for me. Maybe it was a generational thing. Maybe men of my father's generation didn't bond as deeply with their offspring, or maybe they bonded in a way I didn't understand. For me, the only response I could come up with was one that was too obvious for words. Because I did, that's all. Because they wore a look of expectation; *they* expected me to and *I* expected me to. The world was too sad and lively a place not to. The sadness and the liveliness glued me to them.

Besides, I think, what about all those parents from World War II who never had the chance to—

But I feel a poke in my rib cage. Marshall's taken dominion of my body again.

"Is *this* one?" he asks quietly. He's pulled apart the ashtray compartment and is peering inside.

Alex shakes his head. "Great, Marshall. Like that's really going to fit a bunch of Jews hiding from the Third Reich."

"But it *could* be a hiding place, couldn't it, Dad?" persists Marshall.

"How do you mean?" I ask him.

"Well, if they weren't hiding their whole selves, but only a part . . ."

"Hmm," I say. "You mean like a lock of their hair?"

"No! Like a memory!"

"Oh."

"Or like if part of me loves my rabbit, and I put that love there, to keep it safe."

"I think I see. . . ."

"They could hide part of themselves in one place, and another part someplace else. Couldn't they?"

It's a preposterously precocious thing to ask. But then again, if anyone has it in him to be precocious, it's my dalai lama child, my mystic clown with a laugh as bawdy as that of any whore-monger in Caesar's army. But how to answer?

"I say yes," comes a voice to my right. It's the model, resting a delicate hand atop Marshall's head. "In that sense a hiding place could be very big, or teeny-tiny small, as the boy says."

"It depends what you mean by hiding place," puts in the Arab to my left, fixing us with his glass eye and kicking off his shoes so that the smell of rotting lumber fills our space. "What's an ashtray to one person may be a hiding place to another. Who's to say what isn't a hiding place?"

"See, Alex?! They even said! There could be a hiding place in my pocket. Or in my hand. Or in my head."

Alex, the resident cynic, sputters with disdain. "How could a hiding place be inside your head!?"

"Couldn't it, Dad? Couldn't a hiding place be inside your head? Didn't you have hiding places inside your head, when you were our age?"

The Arab looks at me, waiting. Light winks off the lacquered surface of his bad eye. The model also waits. She has beautiful teeth, straight and sharp, and the cleanest scalp I've ever seen. Her fine hair is pulled back tightly so I can see through the strands onto the moonscape of her crown: white, calm, and ghostly. It gives me a strange sensation, like swimming out from shore in water so clear that I can see the starfish at my feet. It makes me feel I can see anything. I am thirty-eight years old and I can see the front of my life as well as the back, the future of my children as well as the past of my parents.

"Fasten your seat belts," says the stewardess, wriggling down the aisle. The Arab and the model do as they're told, concentrating on finding the right clackers to click. But Alex and Marshall stare at me expectantly, awaiting my reply.

"You heard the lady," I tell them. "Fasten your seat belts. We've got a lot of ground to cover."

2

HIDING PLACES,
SOCIOLOGY OF

*M*y mother was reading me Grimm's fairy tales from a faded green book with gold lettering on its cover and almost 900 pages inside. People were always hiding in these tales. In deep wells. In tall trees. In bags of white flour and buckets of pine cones. People were hiding to wait for the ogre to go away. Then just when they thought he was gone for good, he'd leap out and gobble everyone down with his horrible black tongue.

My mother would sit between me and my big sister (my "elder" sister, in the parlance of these stories) and read us these stories from the green book that smelled of almond cookies. Sometimes she'd let me sit in the middle so I got to hold the book, and its weight made a pressure in my lap that seemed to sharpen my senses and give the world an extra pleasant focus. (Later in life, as an adolescent, I'd feel the same pressure when I'd sneak one of my father's heavy psychoanalytic tomes on sex out of his study, and sit with it in my room. It was wonderful to get my central European mythology, Grimm's as well as Freud's, with a dose of erotic tension thrown in.)

"Once upon a time," the fairy tales began, then went on to talk about trolls who bathed in milk and cabbages that turned into donkeys and wolves that would eat a lump of chalk to disguise their voices so they sounded like a human mother. Magic cloaks whisked you wherever you wanted to go. Kissing snakes made you invisible. You could eat the hearts of dead birds and thereafter know how to walk through rocks. You could tap on a bed and have it descend into the earth. Loaves of bread had blood leaking out of their crust. Fish said thank you for saving them.

"Thank you," my mother would say in a high squeaky voice that made me love her, pretending to be a fish who'd been saved. Then she'd put some saliva from her tongue onto the tip of her forefinger and rub it against my chin where cake frosting had dried. Her saliva smelled both bad and good, like sour strawberries.

This was the early 1950s when a new kind of tale was filtering into the world, and my mother told us some of these, too. They were like Grimm's fairy tales, updated, with people hiding in laundry hampers and haylofts and wood sheds until the ogres went away. To my ears, these fearsome new ogres were called Not-sees, and instead of having double heads or an eye in the middle of their forehead, they had blond hair and shiny black boots. That was how you knew they were bad. Everyone else had raggedy shoes or no shoes at all, and the Not-sees had shiny black boots. Maybe the boots hid cloven hoofs, or webbed feet like the devil. No one knew. They looked like normal people, but they weren't normal at all.

The name I heard, Not-see, said it all: they didn't see things normal people saw. They were incapable of seeing that other people wanted to live just as they did, that mothers and children wanted to be together, not torn apart. But the name had a second meaning: You wanted them to not see *you*. You wanted to hide in as black a hole as possible. The stories my mother told were all about hiding from the Not-sees. A mother was hiding and her infant daughter started crying and the mother had to smother the infant to keep from being found out. A man lived in a chimney all winter and people dropped food to him down the smokestack. Hearing these stories, my sister and I had the sense that the world was aglitter with peril. Danger sparkled all around. Magic was on the loose, not just something to be found between the covers of a book.

And here was the clincher: the people in these updated fairy tales were cousins of my mother, actual aunts and uncles who had experienced these things just a few years before my sister and I were born. They weren't beautiful princesses from the long-ago but flesh-and-blood relatives with names like Shasha and J. P. who had survived the Not-sees and were still hobbling around Europe with backs crooked from bending and with hearts broken from smothering their babies. I wanted to ask my mother if maybe someday I could go see Shasha and J. P. and the others? But no, this was too terrible a thought. I never wanted to go to that land where Not-sees had once laughingly thrown candy to children before machine-gunning them.

Seeing how much these stories thrilled and scared us, some-times my mother was sorry that she told them to us. But she couldn't help herself. She'd escaped the Not-sees, too! She'd gotten away just before they could get their hands on her, and the tales seeped out of her by accident. Other times, though, she excused her slips by saying these were tales we ought to know by heart so that we wouldn't be fooled into thinking the world was the safe and kindly place our naive American teachers told us it was. This seemed reasonable. If ever I had children, I thought, I'd teach them the same stories so they wouldn't be fooled, either.

◆ ◆ ◆

My mother first told them in the kitchen one day; I felt my breathing go strange and my brain get an inside-out feeling, as if I were being subjected to a series of small electric zaps. My sister asked why she sometimes started sobbing out of the blue and she told us. I stared at the pantry door that was covered with Christmas cards while she spoke of a starving child's hand sticking out of a cattle car and a villager putting a grapefruit in it, guffawing because it was too big for the hand to bring back in; of Nazi soldiers going through a maternity ward and, for sport, dropping newborns out the windows onto the bayonets of their comrades below. My mother told us these stories and then she dried her eyes and lined them with mascara and went to be gay at the cocktail parties of the art gallery she owned. At one of these openings she once poured champagne down the shirt of a formidable art critic, and the man turned to my father looking as though he were going to clobber him and instead he embraced him and told him what a lucky man he was. My mother would sputter and be joyous at these parties, happy and quick-witted, and the only time she let her grief show to the outside world was once a year, at Christmastime, when the Booths and the Lawlesses and the McDougals and all our other good neighbors would come up our driveway to carol us, and my mother would run upstairs to her bedroom and lock the door. This seemingly well-adjusted Connecticut socialite was a little girl in Antwerp, hiding from the Christian mob again.

(I say "again," but when did she learn to fear Christian mobs? No Christian mob had ever come down the street in Antwerp during her time there or even after she left, when the war was at its fullest. Could she have had a cultural memory of an earlier time in Poland or Russia, when on Christmas Eve religious revelers would put on horns and riding whips and take to the streets looking for Jews to hound? But this was Fairfield County, Connecticut; my sister and I always made up for her absence by joining the carolers with extra cheer.)

In my mind, the Grimm's tales and the tales of the Not-sees melded. People tried to escape the ogres the same way they tried to escape the Not-sees. Mostly they did this by procuring small magic things that could help them in times of trouble. In Grimm's, it could be a bean so you could climb up a beanstalk and get treasure and stop being hungry anymore. But usually in

Grimm's it was gold, little pieces of gold laid by magic hens or offered in the beaks of sparrows, concealed in a secret pouch, sewn into trouser seams, or buried beneath the floorboards. Gold was what saved you.

In the real-life stories of the Not-sees, it was diamonds. Diamonds bought you freedom. My mother's relatives in the diamond business of Antwerp smuggled their diamonds in the false tops of nail polish bottles and in wax behind their fingernails. Then they'd parcel them out to people so they could hide in their barns and attics. This was important, because my mother's cousins in Belgium couldn't fight the Not-sees any more than the peasants of the Black Forest could fight the ogres. You had to use your diamonds to escape and hide, then maybe later you could find a magic sword and plunge it through the ogre's heart.

◆ ◆ ◆

If it was Grimm's that first made me want to get hiding places of my own, I soon came to see that all the best folks had them. Peter Pan. Batman. Zorro. (Years later I had a stint as a restaurant reviewer and so enjoyed the idea of not revealing my identity when I visited restaurants incognito that I gave myself the pen name Zorro, and would leave green peas on my plate in the shape of a Z.) Also Anne Frank. When I was small I had a crush on Anne Frank because her tender musings about love and sex were loaded issues for me, too. I wondered if when they opened the door to find Anne and her boyfriend in their hiding place, did the air pour out like the air after a junior high school dance, so hot with erotic tension it quivered, the girls flushed, the boys with dazed expressions and sweat drops in the soft spots of their faces near where they were starting to shave?

Hiding places made me wonder about such things. Hiding places had *prana,* the Hindi word for breath and spirit. People invested them with more energy than they did ordinary spaces. You breathed a little differently in them. Your voice had more respect. It was as though you imagined your words were being recorded on the air, as though the hiding place itself had consciousness. Maybe the walls could read the sort of person you were and were registering your soul.

An etiquette was called for. Hiding places were so special I needed a different set of rules on how to conduct myself. They weren't places to be silly, for instance. Not always, but sometimes, I felt hushed in them, on my best behavior, as if I were trying to impress a teacher I really respected. It wasn't a pretend behavior, because I was genuinely capable of such respect. I just didn't exhibit it elsewhere.

Sometimes it was like being in a church or temple, and the person I was trying to impress was God.

Was I ascribing too much magic to hiding places? But these places knew us more intimately than any other places. In keeping our secrets, they helped us form who we were. Even if they didn't save our lives, they allowed us to reveal ourselves more fully than anywhere else. That was the wonderful paradox of hiding places. Not merely dark holes of concealment, they were also places of revelation.

◆ ◆ ◆

As an adult, one midnight when I was being driven through the ancient capital city of Ecuador, I saw a homeless man and woman copulating on the street. The act resembled nothing so much as a slow-motion dog fight. Their arms swung about as if in distress, their legs rocked awkwardly. This was in a bad section of the city where, at that hour, throats were routinely cut. My companion and I rolled up the window of the cab and looked away. The couple lacked grace. They lacked discretion. What they lacked, most egregiously, was hiding.

Adolf Eichmann in his glass cage, too, was sorely in need of hiding. O. J. Simpson getting the word that he'd been found not guilty and making his craven little wave, a rumpled Truman Capote coming on live television in the middle of a two-day debauch to boast drunkenly about how many people he was in the process of bedding—they also suffered from a hiding shortage. When you're overexposed to the world, but no privacy is available to you, this is a condition that in modern terms could be called hiding place deficit.

The need for hiding places is universal—as necessary to Asian warriors as to fundamentalist Christians. One has only to think of the Vietcong's network of tunnels through which they survived an entire war, cooking, plotting strategy, even raising their families; or to pick up a snatch of a hymn on a Bible Belt radio station out of Okeechobee some starless night to know how global it is:

> There is a hiding place
> where you can go
> when you are sad and weak,
> King Jesus will know . . .

Hiding's a need shared by our species since our first appearance on this planet, long before the Bible had the babe Moses hidden by his mother so the Egyptians couldn't kill the future savior of Israel. Barbara Ehrenreich, author of *Blood Rites: Origins and History of the Passions of War,* speaks of how Homo sapiens "are always in big trouble morally when we forget the helplessness and the weakness that we came from. . . . Our view of our own species has been too triumphalist—an image of striding out from the forest, stick in hand, and suddenly being the boss. We have to revise that and understand how much time our species has spent hiding and cowering and trying to fight off the leopards. . . ."

And Marshall was right: down through history, hiding places *could* be in your head. Renaissance philosophers said it's as important to conceal as to reveal. They preached keeping mystery alive by not having all the answers. It's a point upon which both East and West agree: Eastern religion has always fostered the art of not knowing; while the European poet Keats held that the real poet must cultivate what he called "negative capability," the ability to entertain "uncertainties, mysteries, doubts without any irritable reaching after fact and reason." Not even God was immune: Hebrew theologians spoke of *"hester panim,"* the temporary "hiding of God's face" as an explanation for why He didn't protect His people during periods of persecution.

Arguably, however, the world has never needed hiding places more than during World War II. Spying and smuggling, both specialized forms of hiding, were cranked into high gear. In the frantic espionage of the war years, my Belgian relatives weren't the only ones to go in for smuggling. British scientists working on penicillin hid mold spore under their lapels so they could take it with them if they had to flee. Diamonds and rust, as the singer said. Marquises and mold spore . . .

After the war, many surviving Jews were still in a state of psychological hiding. After all, when you go into hiding from something that massive—from something that makes all the prior woes of your five-thousand-year history piddling by comparison—at what point exactly do you emerge? When the shooting stops and you crawl out to dust yourself off? When your eyes have adjusted once again to sunlight and your nose can sniff fresh air? Is that emergence? Or is that just the head of a frightened animal, who keeps most of his body in shadow?

For me, a Jewish child of the 1950s far from the field of battle, as well as for my Christian neighbor children, the need for hiding places seemed great. They were places to not understand everything, to celebrate nothingness and thereby replenish the soul. They didn't have to be places no one ever went to; they only had to be places where I could count on not being found, so that I could be most myself or most unlike myself, depending on my mood. Hiding places allowed me to hide or expose the best part of myself, and by doing so, preserve it. If they didn't have the revolving panels of Zorro's hiding places, they did have the two ingredients necessary: mystery and sacredness. They were inanimate spaces, but I invested them with the power to protect me. They were timeless.

We were average children, all of us kids who hid in Rowayton. We kicked balls. We swapped baseball cards. We threw snow-balls. We chased squirrels. We volleyed and we slam-dunked. We tagged and tackled, we homered and stole home. We cap-sized, we checkmated, we crossed the finish line. We made the nanny jump half a foot off the floor when we shot a cap gun at her from behind the door.

Most of all, though, we hid. Hiding was what we did as children; our career and great passion. We played hide-and-seek and capture the flag and go fish and all the other games of child-hood that have concealment as their central feature. We hid in tool sheds from older siblings. We hid in coat closets from mean teachers. We hid in off-season baseball dugouts, luxuriating in the sensation of feeling safe. I wish I could say I always spent a minute of silence before departing these places, like the Russian custom of saying a secret grace before taking leave of a place. But I did no such thing. I was too average—an average boy in an average place, as special as any anywhere.

If not Nazis, what were we hiding from, my Christian pals and I? The same things humans have been hiding from, under various names, since the beginning of time. Bad guys. Good guys. Boogie men. Guardian angels. Our worst nightmare. Our better nature. Ogres, in a word: both those on the outside and those on the in.

3

CRASH COURSE

*I*n all of Brussels, Marshall is nowhere to be found.

"Marshall, are you *here?*" I ask, pulling back the heavy velour curtains of the hotel suite's windows that look out onto a roofline jutted with cathedral spires. A billboard across the street shows the painted face of Goldie Hawn twelve feet high, her features subtly changed—nose lengthened, expression a bit more wry—to make her appear Belgian.

"Are you *here?*" I ask, looking under the king-size bed.

"No," comes Marshall's voice from behind me, his excited tittering muffled by clasped hands.

"Dad, he's in the closet again," reports Alex, munching from a bag of frozen peas and looking up from his dog-eared paperback of *The Rise and Fall of the Third Reich*. "If you try *looking* instead of *pretending* to look, you'd see his feet right under your pants there."

"I don't think so, Alex," I report after an inspection. "I'm pretty sure Marshall's feet were wearing yellow socks on the plane today, and those in the closet are wearing blue ones."

Right on cue, the toes wiggle theatrically inside their bright blue socks.

Alex sighs with long-suffering dismay for the way I mollycoddle his brother. It's his bitterly held contention that Marshall's had an infinitely easier time of it than he has. The way he sees it, he's been the pioneer son, carving out new son territory, breaking me in as a father. According to him, on my first go-round as a dad with him as guinea pig I had been domineering, overbearing, unyielding, tyrannical, and power mad—making him wear a seat belt, for instance, and eat his asparagus. Now I was mellow, and Marshall reaped the benefits. Even though I still insisted Marshall wear a seat belt and at least *try* the asparagus, my attitude was better this time around.

Despite my improvement, however, it's painfully obvious to Alex that I still need work in several areas. Giving them stars for good behavior, for example: how cheesy is *that?* And going on this trip, for another. Every other father with an ounce of sense gives their kids a drum set with a chrome-plated cymbal suspension cage for a bar mitzvah present. Not Alex's. Alex's father is giving him the Holocaust. And *why?* What earthly reason could a father have for dragging his sons along to find the places where their ancestors hid during World War II?

"Where am I?" asks Marshall.

"Marshall, would you Auto S?" Alex exclaims—family shorthand for shut up. "You're embarrassing yourself with this infantile behavior."

Dejectedly, Marshall emerges to join us. That makes three of us sitting around in underpants and socks. The mood is down, but immediately comes back up again. "Dad, if you were locked in a garage with a car turned on, would you smash the garage?"

"Why're you thinking that, Marshall?"

"I'm just thinking of ways to escape," he says. "Can we call Mom?"

"Hey, I've got an idea: Let's see what's on cable," I suggest.

"We get cable for free, too?!" he exclaims.

"We get everything for free," Alex informs him world-wearily, tossing back another mouthful of peas. "The magical media pass strikes again."

(About that pass: It's nothing more than an ordinary everyday press card. But it's magical for me, because with this card I manage to make my way around the world scaring up lodging, airplane rides, and everything else I need to live life as a fin de siècle travel essayist. Meaning I get paid to visit outlandish places for free, eat extravagant food for free, have preposterous adventures for free, *and* complain about it. It's one of the few perks available to late-twentieth-century American writers who are, as a rule, underpaid and overexploited. I don't see it as a rip-off. I see it as reparation.)

I snap the TV on, then shut myself into the adjoining bedroom to think about why I'm exposing my kids to material that had so frightened me as a child. Oh, I know what I always tell myself. First and foremost, it's a chance to spend time with my favorite companions. Alex the coffee-drinking prodigy, Marshall the freelance court jester.

Alex: sober atheist, strict prohibitionist, logical problem solver. I'd penciled on his nursery door Alex the Imperious, and my ex had changed it to the Impossible. Years later, it seems prophetic. He has the contrary nature of an artist, with a need to isolate himself that's almost physical. (Indeed, his left eye will turn inward when he needs to mull.) Now he's contracting the pissiness of the preteen: he sulks, he broods, then has flashes of insight so dazzling I'm blinded.

Marshall: so sweet his mother's girlfriends call him Delish. When it was time for him to be toilet-trained, I suggested, he consented, and that was that. Never another word on the subject. And generous: when his team won the T-ball championship, an event he'd been dreaming about all summer, he withheld his joy long enough to go console his pal on the losing team. Only after he'd made his pal feel better did he permit himself to roll on the ground in sheer joy.

If Alex is phobic, Marshall's intrepid. If Alex is always famished, Marshall's a monk. If only Alex's drawing pad reveals what's going on under the surface, Marshall's very skin shows every nick and scrape of life, his scarred legs documenting the history of his childhood in cuts and bruises. And despite the fact that Alex's toothbrush has Thai letters squiggling down the sides and Marshall until recently clutched a Mount Cook Airlines quilt as his security blanket, neither of them has ever been west of Michigan or south of Washington, D.C. They're parochial as only American kids can be—meaning they consider the smell of Chicken McNuggets the finest on the planet and almost any other smell cause for alarm.

On the whole, I couldn't have dreamed up kids more devilishly fun than these: squabbling, certainly, but in the nature of birds, building a nest. What father wouldn't want to spend time with them?

All this is what they know already. And all of it makes perfect sense. But what are my deeper reasons? What could lead an assimilated Jew, recently divorced from a Midwestern WASP, to risk traumatizing his children by taking them to visit the Holocaust?

Reason the obvious: The Holocaust is their history. I want them to see the real thing up close, where it'll mean something. A museum's fine as far as it goes, but I've seen children at Holocaust museums snapping their gum and rolling their eyes and whining, "Can we go now?" I don't want Alex and Marshall to gaze passively at plaster castings but to smell the pigsties with their own noses, to hear the bone-dissolving wail of European police sirens with their own ears. Then if they snap their gum I'll allow it, but at least they will have been there.

Reason the personal: We have to do it for our own private reasons. Shell-shocked by divorce, splintered into a joint custodial situation, we need an experience that will forge us into a unit. Lacking connections with anything larger than ourselves, we need to collect a memory greater than the three of us and see ourselves in a new light. By introducing them to my mother's people in Europe, I hope to reclaim our roots and plant them deep. The boys will solve their dislocation and feel connected. Then we might all be at peace, or, if not at peace, at least *in context*.

They need it at least as much as I. In their short lives they already experienced loss: they'd been wrenched from me in tears as our home was dispersed. I'd felt as all parents do in divorce, like I was trying to hold my babies above my head while I myself was drowning. Ours was a tragedy, but a tiny one, a lowercase holocaust. Maybe it will help to see the real Holocaust to understand how puny our woes really were.

Perspective, that's what we're after. By throwing our woes against the larger relief of World War II, we might regenerate ourselves and become a family again, against a backdrop of loss. We'll look to our history for healing.

I stretch on the bed, feeling a touch of the old asthma I had as a kid while I wonder whether it's blasphemous to put it in those terms. Is it in bad taste to call such a mundane occurrence as my divorce a "lowercase holocaust"? Am I trivializing the great subject of the Holocaust by making my own petty middle-class American connections to it? But these are the only connections I *can* make: this is all I have to go on, to make sense of something so massive. The alternative is not even to try, to see it in an airless exhibition hall and not make the essential *click!*—that this material lives with us as part of the air we breathe day after day.

I know—the critic T. W. Adorno has said that poetry after the Holocaust is barbaric. The documentary filmmaker Claude Lanzmann says it's obscene even to attempt to comprehend the Holocaust. Silence, according to these gentlemen, is the only correct response to horror of such magnitude. Art manages only to violate the suffering of the victims.

Yeah, but hey. This is our planet, too.

I take a deep, asthma-free breath to absorb the truth of that (for truly, the only thing worse than triviality is sanctimony). What I want is a time to attend to ourselves, not to make light of issues or put a happy spin on things but to feel the sadness, to explore the grief of being alive and in this way to honor the grief in ourselves. It will be a chance to talk to my sons with a new voice. Our everyday horsing-around voice is fun and sunny and works well for us, but for the next four weeks I want to try for something better—my most sincere voice, straightforward and settled, the voice from my sober heart. It'll be a voice they'll hear better and a voice, I hope, that will resonate inside them and last.

There are a lot of other reasons, too, that will reveal themselves in the fullness of our quest. I don't need to know all the reasons right now. In the deepest sense, the trip is about finding out why I want to take the trip. But for now, these reasons are enough.

Except for this. Dare I admit it? I *do* want to traumatize my children. As I've been traumatized, hearing about World War II. As we've *all* been, learning what the human animal is capable of. The world will singe them anyway, that's what the world does; I consider it my parental duty to touch their hands to the flame myself—there! now it's done—and be there to kiss the pain away afterward. Or forget flames—think of vaccines, a small dose of badness to build immunity. It'll be on the order of a polio shot, an inoculation of evil so they'll build antibodies against evil and know how to fight it off when they encounter it again, in whatever guise. Or think ogres—it'll be a crash course in ogre spotting, to teach them how to deal with them when they run across them in the future, when I won't be around to help.

My foot's asleep. The bottom line is, I don't really know why we're going, other than to say I'm looking for something bigger than ourselves, something with which to make *us* bigger. Amplitude, in a word. We'll go to find the hiding places in our history; perhaps we'll also find the hiding places in ourselves.

At the close of the millennium, then, I seek to bring my children face-to-face with the bloodiest event of the bloodiest century on record, and to make them stronger people for it, kinder people, braver people, better people. "Once upon a time," I think, "a father took his sons to visit the land where the Notsees roamed. . . ."

◆　◆　◆

Marshall's tapping on the door. He has the divorce orphan's Morse code, the nervous habit of tapping on anything, anywhere: through hotel walls, against bathroom stalls. I swing my feet to the floor.

"How's the TV?" I call into the other room.

"Boring," Marshall calls back. "It's click click boobs. Click click boobs."

Sure enough, I find Alex deep into an X-rated film.

"You were gone four minutes twenty-one seconds," Marshall reports, squeezing the fleshy white petals of the hospitality tulips provided by the hotel.

"It's good to know you're keeping track," I say, snapping off the TV and spying a letter written in crayon scrawl. "Been writing to your rabbit again?"

"I just don't want her to get homesick without me," Marshall says. "She's very delicate."

"I'm sure your mom's taking good care of her," I say.

"Yeah but isn't boobs a kind of bouncy word, though?" he says. "Boobsy boobsy boobsy—"

Alex and I make eye contact to ignore this line of discussion. The allegiances among the three of us are ever shifting and as Byzantine as the court of Marie Antoinette. As Alex goes around the room lifting various lamps, judging their weight, I see that he's written the phone number of the hotel on the back of both his hands, *just in case.*

"Gentlemen," I say, "let's go see some diamond smugglers."

Heaving himself back and forth in an overstuffed armchair, Marshall is making it pitch like a rocking horse. "First let's hear a story about when Dad was growing up!"

"Yeah, Dad," Alex chimes in, "tell us what it was like to be the only Jew in Connecticut!"

4

THE COSSACKS OF CONNECTICUT

I didn't grow up the only Jew in Connecticut: it only felt that way sometimes. Mine was one of the few Jewish families in the WASP lobster town of Rowayton, which lay across the river from "Aryan Darien," the proverbial anti-Semitic hamlet of *Gentleman's Agreement*. Rowayton in the 1950s was half lobstermen who would finish their labors by noon every day and half advertising execs who would ride the 7:02 to Grand Central every morning and the 7:14 back every night. There was also a smattering of poets and painters who through luck or good sense could afford to live by the water. These were my neighbors, and I felt closer to the children of these lobstermen and admen and artists than I did my elegant pale cousins in New York who went to *shul* on Saturdays while we were out hunting for horseshoe crabs to kill with our bare feet.

It would be only partly correct to call Rowayton a suburb. In the '50s it was a scruffy little town not unlike a small rural town in Minnesota, say, where everyone knew everyone else: you knew which girl had scallion breath at dancing school, which boy had the guts to take the Test at Bayley Beach or venture near Heart's Castle. The only difference from a scruffy little town in Minnesota was that from Rowayton's beaches you could see the spires of Manhattan twinkling in the blue haze forty miles down the shore. The capital of the universe was one hour away.

Rowayton in those days had world-class WASP icons. The Man in the Hathaway Shirt—that distinguished-looking gent with the black eyepatch—could frequently be spotted at the helm of his ketch puttering up the Five Mile River. The yacht club around the corner from my house fired off its cannon each day at sunset. At Miss Hunnibell's ballroom dancing school both girls *and* boys had to wear white gloves. Charles Lindbergh was forever flying overhead to his estate across the river, and when our grade school principal Mr. Cunningham rattled on at assembly about how much he appreciated the verse being published by Lucky Lindy's wife, he failed to mention the fact that Lindbergh was what was most charitably called an "isolationist" at the beginning of World War II—as if all Lindbergh did was advise us to stay out of the war, not visit Germany numerous times while Hitler was in power and express his admiration for the Germans' way of life.

And of course there were the lobstermen. If I were looking for people to call enemies—and I was, I was—I could imagine that the local lobstermen were the Connecticut version of Cossacks, the cavalrymen who'd so terrified my antecedents under the czars. Full of pomp and swagger, they were out on the river before dawn boisterously setting their traps, then spent the rest of the afternoon rather meekly playing checkers on a couple of weather-beaten benches by the docks. The braggadocio that started out so fresh at dawn was, by lunchtime, more than a little faded, in the way that I imagined Cossacks would be faded by the middle of the day when they had to come home for lunch. The lobstermen of Rowayton were almost but not quite dashing in the way that the Cossacks of Russia were almost but not quite dashing, cutting a glamorous figure from a distance, standing tall and proud in their stirrups or the cockpits of their lobster boats, posting to the galloping plains or waves, but up close they both smelled pretty bad (booze and horse in the one case, booze and fish in the other). If any pogroms were to take place in Rowayton I pretended that they'd be the ones to conduct them; alas for my dramatic sense of persecution, however, the rowdiest they ever got was to occasionally stray, drunk and harmless, through the halls of our elementary school, the squeak of their moist rubber boots on waxed linoleum making them sound not so much like fierce warriors as tardy school-boys, bashful and wet, and perpetually at a loss to find home-room.

I never witnessed any out-and-out anti-Semitism in our cosmopolitan hick town. I was well liked by teachers and class-mates both and everyone took pains to protect me from the faintly off-color secret that I was different. In my presence, the grade school teachers referred to Moses as a "Hebrew." To spare me embarrassment, Mrs. Seiffert in current events class once referred to Israel as being inhabited by "people of the Hebraic persuasion"—in the same way that assimilated Poles in the 1800s used to call themselves "of Mosaic denomination." They indulged me my Judaism the way they'd forgive a mascot his limp so it was hardly noticed anymore. If there'd been a grade school yearbook they might have named me "our Jew," the way some Czech or Romanian villagers were said, in centuries past, to have grown fond of the few Jews in their midst.

Rarely did someone in Rowayton not know I was Jewish, and on those occasions the information was received with amazement. "Really? A Jew?"

"Sure," I'd reply, shyly. "What'd you think I was?"

"I didn't think you were anything!" came the reply.

They were right: I wasn't. My instinct was to wince and blush. I felt apologetic, for no reason I understood. In school there was sort of an unofficial don't ask, don't tell policy. I wasn't trying to pass—that would have been shameful—but neither did I want to push anyone's face in it. We had a mezuzah on our house and I deemed it proper to have one, but I wished we could've had it on the back door where it wouldn't be so visible. It was right that we didn't celebrate Christmas but that didn't stop me from feeling self-conscious that Mr. Bradford the garbageman saw no boxes of discarded glittery wrapping paper down by our mailbox the morning after.

It's like what they say about native Israelis: hard on the outside, but on the inside, very hard. I was embarrassed on the outside, but on the inside, very embarrassed. Being Jewish was like having a shoe fetish. We were part of a special group, all right; I just wasn't sure it was anything to boast about.

The world wasn't like it is today. Park foresters didn't advise tired hikers that a certain trail was a "schlep." People like Howard Stern didn't exist, or were at least kept muzzled by their communities. Bagels had not yet become America's pet ethnic food; Dunkin' Donuts didn't sell "bagelitos" in the barrios. In this nonhomogenized world, I lowered my voice when singing the chorus of the Beatles song "Hey, Jude." I was mortified that the license plate on our family station wagon had the letters *YD* in it, thinking the DMV had us pegged. On those unlikely occasions when I happened to look up something Jewish in a card catalog, I'd leave the file open to a different topic so the next person wouldn't suspect what I'd been perusing, the way an overweight person will push the weights back before stepping off a scale.

I wasn't merely embarrassed. I was also aware that I was supposed to be proud. Even while blushing at photographs of Hasids, I was conscious that there was a sense of honor integral to being Jewish. I tried to do it both ways. At High Holiday services, conducted in a borrowed church, I'd fantasize how I'd save "my people" by throwing myself on a grenade some anti-Semite might toss in the window, but at the same time I wore an earphone that snaked down into my suit jacket pocket where my hidden transistor radio was tuned to Cousin Brucie on

WABC, so while the rest of the congregation was singing the Kol Nidre, I was humming to Herman's Hermits under my breath.

In twelve years of growing up in Rowayton, whatever anti-Semitism I encountered was of the most mild generic sort. The mother of a friend, a kindly watercolorist with bangs in her eyes and an interest in books, asked me with genuine anthropological curiosity if my family ate "bajels"—as if our snack food *sounded* beige as well as looked it. I never saw it firsthand, but I heard of another neighborhood mother who routinely offered her family their choice of two kinds of bread: "white bread or Jew bread" (rye). The only discourtesy I ever received at the hands of my classmates took place where most American children learn their first hard lessons, at the junior high school bus stop.

Ours was made up of the same two knots of people all school bus stops were: the girls, talking decorously among themselves with round little puffs of white breath, and the boys, stamping their feet against the cold and making valiant stabs at scatological conversation. And although the circle of boys always seemed to be staring at me every morning as I walked the long block toward them toting my clarinet case, these were the locals I'd grown up with since first grade; there was a genuine effort at trying to find things we still held in common and could agreeably talk about. We thought ourselves rough and tumble, but we were basically all good little suburban gentlemen and the idea of singling someone out because he was different, or even using the word for his difference in a disparaging way—was unthinkable. Which was why it was so odd when it happened.

It was prompted by a foreign boy, significantly, the only actual foreigner among us. Hulking Grady Hartog had come over from Holland in second grade and immediately set out to destroy any group memory in us that he wasn't a local, even going so far as to take on the quintessential American nickname, Hotdog. My mother, who was from the Low Countries herself (she escaped from Belgium in 1939), had been instrumental in getting his family out of Europe in the mid '50s, and had hired his mother for a few months to help clean our house. Maybe this was humiliating to his household; maybe Hotdog had picked up talk around his dinner table about "those rich Roses." (We weren't really rich, just different: My father was a psychoanalyst on the faculty of Yale, we played marbles on Persian rugs, Pablo Casals could be heard blasting out of our windows on Sunday.) But Hotdog was the one who used the word at the bus stop that morning, the only time I ever heard it used in a negative way. Referring to the shop teacher, he said, "Oh, he's such a Jew." There was a general murmur of assent around the circle, then an audible intake of breath as they remembered; then a pause, followed by a torrent of apologies as they blinked at the kid who stood there clutching his clarinet case. "Not you, Danny," they assured me, "you're a *good* Jew."

So this was a new thought. There were good Jews, apparently; what did that make the others? I accepted their apologies like the good sport I was and we all went back to stamping our feet. But for the first time I thought: Ah-ha.

◆   ◆   ◆

(And of course there were no blacks. A few years before, the UN ambassador from an emerging African nation had briefly moved his family to the unfortunately named Witch Lane and had been forced to put up a twelve-foot-high fence against townspeople dumping their garbage on his lawn. Things weren't that bad by the time we got there, though the only blacks to be seen were at the bus stops in the dusk when maids and domestics and housekeepers—"help" was perhaps the nicest euphemism—waited to ride home to the tenements of South Norwalk. My mother once caused a stir when she brought "our Juliette" to the beach; prior to that there'd never been a nonwhite at Bayley Beach. Art Chace, the eternally bronzed and muscular beach tender, stared but said nothing to us, maybe because he'd been there the week before watching Jackie Robinson play a tournament match at the adjacent Bayley Beach tennis courts, the only time a nonwhite had ever stepped foot on that clay surface. Weren't we becoming tolerant! To this day I shame myself by startling whenever I see a black person on any beach.)

◆ ◆ ◆

Discomfort made me rash. I wasn't like the good children described by Helen Epstein in *Children of the Holocaust*—piously dutiful to make up for my parents' suffering. I was rebellious and confused and ferocious, even though I melted in the company of people I sensed were truly kind. I was the picture of paradox: hot-blooded, thin-skinned, quick-tempered, strangulated by the world's injustices and full of get-even schemes, but ever ready to dissolve into a puddle at the slightest word of warmheartedness from a stranger, which came not infrequently. My loyalty to that stranger would thereafter be iron.

Perhaps the most noticeable thing about me was my proclivity for recklessness. This made perfect sense, though I didn't grasp for a couple of decades that my specialty of hiding was intrinsically cowardly so I compensated by exhibiting bravado in other areas. I dangled from the top of backstops with one hand, jumped across roofs, talked back to teachers, played pranks on policemen, rode ice floes around the harbor. I studied how close my sled could come to the back wheels of moving cars. I alarmed friends by how long I stayed underwater.

Not that I was invulnerable. Far from it. The tree limb frequently snapped, the ladder fell, the teacher flipped. I cracked my teeth, sprained my ankles, broke my leg and then broke the cast racing a friend on crutches and had to have the leg set again. By the time I was twelve, I'd fallen through the ice on Long Island Sound four times, and calculated that if I continued in this fashion, I'd be falling through every third winter for the rest of my life. I was to get into a total of thirteen car accidents.

Actions like these and a dozen others convinced people around me that I was an intrepid fellow. I wasn't. I resorted to such foolishness because I couldn't do the one truly brave thing that is asked of any human being, and that is to be who he is.

◆ ◆ ◆

To the limited extent that I defined myself as a Jew, therefore, it wasn't through positive associations but through negative. We didn't go to church. We didn't hang lights at Christmas. Instead of pride at my heritage I felt shame at a mother who beneath her gaiety was brittle as a piece of buttered matzo, shame at the little skullcaps that seemed like embroidered bald spots, shame at the phlegmy Eastern European accents that made me once run out the front door screaming, "I want to burn everything in this house that's Jewish!"

Not that there was much Jewish to begin with. My mother owned an art gallery and our cardboard palace, our subdivision McMansion, was filled with West African bambaras and Eskimo soapstone sculptures and pre-Columbian figurines, a very cosmopolitan mix in every sense except one. There was no Jewish art. My parents weren't trying to hide their Judaism exactly; they just considered themselves emancipated from all that. "Liberated" was the word they used, as though centuries of tradition had enslaved their forebears; my parents felt enlightened beyond God. Of course this brought with it an inborn set of paradoxes and none, it seemed to me, was greater than this: neither of my parents believed in God, but they'd met at a Zionist camp. But even this was a classically Jewish paradox. The state of Israel itself struggled with issues of secularism. And on those occasions when we did identify as Jews, it was meant to be comical. If my father and I were hopelessly bungled up in a mechanical project, for instance, we'd call ourselves the Rosenzweig boys. Later, when I got my first car, my father gave me an emergency road kit containing not only flares and jumper cables but also a prayer book and yarmulke. It was tantamount to a mock anti-Semitism: we got the drop on our foes by being the first to poke fun at ourselves. My father's joke definition of anti-Semitism, in fact, was "hating the Jews more than absolutely necessary."

Given this ironic mind-set, this almost postmodern self-consciousness, perhaps we were less assimilated than "acculturated"—doing our best to accommodate ourselves to the mongrelized environment around us. In our home we ate rice pilaf rather than noodle pudding, put a "dollop" of sour cream on our crêpes rather than a "schmear" on our blintzes. At school assemblies I soloed "Edelweiss" on my clarinet. I was known to be one of the fastest hunters at neighborhood Easter egg parties. To delight my buds I would go to some obnoxious neighbors to solicit for my own private DAR Fund, capitalizing on the fact that I shared initials with the Daughters of the American Revolution, the starchiest WASP society in the New World, which urged FDR to let World War II run its course with no meddling from us. The result was that when it came time to study for my bar mitzvah, I could sound out the Hebrew letters only if the vowels were added, beginner style, not like real Jews who could skim through text without the aid of such training wheels.

It was my parents' prerogative, of course, to abandon a belief system that was stultifying to them—the trouble was they didn't replace it with anything. As a result, I was vowelless with regard to more than Judaism. Lacking the *a*'s and *e*'s that fleshed out an inner life, my soul was a kind of shorthand I couldn't read, all consonants that couldn't help me decipher the words of my situation. I continued to make do, knowing that the Jewish year was 57-something only because Joe DiMaggio was number 5 and Mickey Mantle 7. But though I was moved by the music to "Sunrise, Sunset," my girlfriends were blond and blue-eyed as a matter of course. Jewish girls, though beautiful in a heartbreaking way, seemed too sisterly. Make out with my relatives? *Right.*

I turned to the Christian world for the sex appeal I found lacking in Judaism. I considered my parents' hard-drinking

Christian friends glamorous, friends like the old *New York Times* Moscow bureau chief who'd drive up from Manhattan in his soft-top Spitfire and twirl his fiery Italian countess wife out of the passenger seat on the driveway—he was very light on his feet, with his seersucker suit and pallid eyelashes—and the two of them would waltz to the back of the car and pop the trunk open, revealing a tumbler of martinis, nicely shaken by the drive up the Connecticut Turnpike where one in six drivers was said to be riproaringly smashed out of his gourd. To be a drinker was to trumpet one's non-Jewishness loud and clear, it seemed to me, and I was pleased with the hard-drinking social whirl my parents were in the thick of, throwing loud jazz parties where, as bartender, I would serve fisherman's punch and scotch and sodas. Rowayton was a series of fizzy fascinating cocktail parties where world-renowned architects in Fijian shirts would stuff the bathroom full of balloons so no one could squeeze in, and middle-aged heiresses would plunk down on the floor next to the Labrador retriever and teach the dumb dog to beg, and famous TV news anchors would pass out on the Castro convertible in my bedroom, which doubled as the guest room. They were giddy, racy, boisterous parties and my parents would let my sister and me have a glass or two and encourage us to mingle, then afterward report how Mrs. McKissock declared us to be charming; and we were, in the Connecticut manner, despite the fact that I wore that earphone, and the whole time I was mingling I was listening to Cousin Brucie and the Good Guys.

◆ ◆ ◆

I was living in a WASP town and going to WASP parties—not so much assimilated or acculturated, perhaps, as thoroughly *mingled*—but at the same time I also had two righteous greatuncles named Yudl and Velvl forty miles away on Manhattan's 47th Street. To these gentle souls, worldly diamond-dealer brothers of my mother's father from Belgium, we were Connecticut outlaws. They didn't care how many celebrities and professionals we showcased, to them we were rabble-rousers, we were Christmas carolers, we were that most frivolous goyim thing: glitzy. Every so often these great-uncles would show up at one of the parties, an anniversary or a graduation. They didn't drive, it was out of the question, but every so often they took the New Haven Railroad and the expression on their citified faces when they emerged at the Darien station, hot and dusty, said what they thought. They thought: *This is the Wild West*. They thought they'd taken the stagecoach to Dodge City. The suburban split-levels and cardboard palaces of Darien and Rowayton were Red River Gulch to them. Where were the newspaper hawkers? Where was the local bakery? When they got to the house they stood in their gray flannel pants, fidgeting the diamond pouches in their pockets, and they'd look out at the balloons filling the bathrooms and the heiress barking on the floor and the news anchor giving me a noogie because I'd put tonic in his scotch instead of soda, and they'd think, *For this we escaped Hitler's Europe?*

Or we'd drive them to a barbecue at the beach—the spiritual heart of our seaside town. We'd pick them up at the station in their pinstripes and ties and they'd sit in the back, leaving the passenger seat empty, as if riding in a cab. It wasn't rudeness—they just didn't know suburban car etiquette, that you fill up the front first. We'd drive to the beach and it would be like out of Tolstoy, the urban dwellers coming by locomotive from St. Petersburg to visit country cousins in their provincial dacha, getting bundled in muffs and wraps to travel miles in a sleigh over snow-covered barrens. We'd deposit them on the sand and they'd look on as the kids played touch football with the package of hot dog rolls and the parents stood in the water up to their knees, sipping martinis. Disdaining the *schmutz* beneath their soles, staking their claim to the beach blanket and not venturing off except to make an occasional foray to the snack bar, they'd tramp gingerly across the wasteland in their Old World sandals (barefoot? go naked in front of strangers?!) to order a Sanka and produce blank stares from the high school help who only knew how to process orders for Cokes and frozen Milky Ways. An impasse. There at the snack bar the Cossacks would stand staring at the Jews with their shirttails tucked inside their baggy bathing suits, their black socks pulled halfway up their celery white calves, and the Jews would stare back at the Cossacks with their necks sunburned leather red around their dirty T-shirts, and eventually the first camp might loosen up enough to chuck them a Coors, and the second camp might let their hair down enough to *sip* the Coors, while munching on a roasted shrimp with two fingers only, the other three fingers remaining kosher in the air, figuring that they were already transgressing by finding themselves so deeply among the goyim, a little two-finger transgression wouldn't hurt. . . .

And yet they were my conscience. Yudl and Velvl would look at me mingling with my fisherman's punch and know me for what I was. Reading me with one glance they'd know the awful truth, that I was a crypto-Jew, a chameleon Hebrew, a modern-day Marrano right there in Fairfield County. The look from my New York relatives told me what I already knew, that deep down it was really my Connecticut family who were the Cossacks—not the hapless lobstermen, not the innocent Christmas carolers—but we ourselves who were beating back our blood history, brutally crushing our own traditions. After the party was over and the news anchor was poured into the back of his Mercedes for the ride home, I'd collapse on my bed with the whirlies, only to realize that he'd puked in my wastebasket. That's when it would stink to me, all that glitz, his celebrity puke mixed in with the furtive cigarette ashes I'd deposited there; I would know it all for the emptiness it was, and I'd be sickeningly aware that I had nothing whatever in my teenage life to hold on to. There was a hole right in the center, a gaping lack where there should have been bedrock. Writhing nauseated on my bed, peering up at my bookshelves upon which my bar mitzvah books were buried beneath tennis magazines, I'd try to cling to the image of my parents, my family, some kernel I could grab hold of. But there was nothing there. There was only a desperate mingling of too many conflicted selves instead of any true sense of self—a frantic fraternizing instead of a deep and systematic knowing who I was. I was rooting around for social acceptance instead of driving my roots deep. What roots? I had no code, no key to understanding myself, as unpronounceable as the vowelless Hebrew words I struggled to decipher. What was I? I had no c*nt*r. I had no cor*.

5

HUGGING AUDREY HEPBURN

*O*ne was said to have escaped with her jewelry by wearing it all at once so the Nazis thought she was a whore displaying her baubles. Another hid in the circus, stashing grenades under his cot and using oil from sardine tins to clean his guns. There was even supposed to be a widower somewhere in Europe who'd changed his name from Jacov Pesach Morganstern to J. P. Morgan and smuggled diamonds inside chocolate bonbons and in the hollow stems of bread knives.

These were great-aunts and second cousins, and there seemed to be dozens of them. The New York branch was a patriarchy headed by Yudl and Velvl, who in appearance and habits would strike you as not unrelated to computer nerds except that they were in diamonds. Diamond dorks, if you must, but in the best sense possible: they were elegant eccentrics, obliviously resting their glass teacups half off their saucers, stubbornly closing one eye when crossing the street against traffic instead of troubling to get a new eyeglass prescription, ceremoniously leaning into the light from the window to read the Sunday *Times* rather than waste electricity by flicking on the lamp. Eternally bemused and with bottomless tact, they were at the same time cosmopolitan and deeply insular, with equal amounts of delicacy and certainty in their movements. You imagined they pressed their pj's and went to sleep with their watches on; and none of your digital watches but choice old Swiss timepieces on leather bands, genuine calfskin bought at discount. For all their wartime exploits (though they didn't see them as exploits—they saw them as *mishaps*), they weren't phys-ical folks. If there had been a Morganstern family crest the leg-end would say: Be Cautious in All You Do . . . and yet by escaping the Nazis they pulled off one of the most audacious feats of the twentieth century.

There's an image in Isaac Babel that jumped out at me in col-lege: "the philosophers who cut diamonds." This they were: courtly, mild-mannered burghers who saw in diamonds not only order and geometry but also an aesthetic to live by and even a moral code. With due modesty they saw themselves as philosophers entering into a dialectic with each stone, bringing out the argument inside; as scholars, studying each stone's indi-vidual makeup; as artists, like Michelangelo sculpting forth the soul of each diamond from the rough. In discussions with my father, the shrink, they even allowed as how they functioned as diamond psychiatrists, bringing to the surface and grinding away centuries-old imperfections. Gentlemen diamond dealers, in a word, who were gratefully out of sync with the late twenti-eth century, so old school that with Victorian disdain they re-garded the stock market and movies and even soft drinks as vulgar; who reluctantly owned maybe one television for select educational programs only. Did people who speak six languages watch *Cheers* with the rest of America after dinner? They did not. Did they read fiction? "Not lately," they'd say, meaning not for the past thirty years. Instead they studied: history, religion, philosophy, mysticism. They learned ancient Greek so they could read Plato in the original. They read Maimonides in bed, or Baudelaire if they were feeling frisky—the only people in New York to consider *Les fleurs du mal* foreplay.

Still, their smiles were a wonder to me. Their faces were in-formed with subtlety; their humor was restrained; their wit was

dry. *(Why don't Jews drink? It dulls the pain.)* So long as a joke
was low-key, preferably of a jewellike clarity, their mouths
would pucker to smile, then when you were least expecting it
erupt in a silent laugh with a shocking display of long horselike
yellow molars. But even when not smiling their faces contained
a mysterious flicker of self-mockery; what was *that* about?

It made you want to hug them. But so breakable did they
seem, thin and brittle as though their bones were made of
Limoges porcelain, it'd be like hugging Audrey Hepburn. And
just as you can see a glow through a piece of Limoges if you
hold it up to the light, so too could you make out a faint glow
behind their faces, an ambient kindness, an aura of goodness
that permeated their features and raised the temperature in
your heart half a degree.

◆ ◆ ◆

Their shoulders were their most eloquent feature. As a child I'd
always assumed my great-uncles' Jewish shoulders were timid.
They held them in graceless positions, awkwardly lifting them
in attitudes of supplication, dropping them, shrugging them. If
I could translate one message from these shoulders it was of the
ultimate diffidence: *"Why me?"* But as I grew older I started to
discern a whole rhetoric to these shoulders, and it was hardly
one of timidity. With great power and precision they com-
plained: *Who can do anything about it?* They ranted: *What good is
it? You try! Go do it if you want! Sure, go, what do I care?* More
than merely express resignation, the shoulders could flirt, could
stonewall. Who knew Jewish shoulders could be tough and
merry at the same time? But they had enough nuance to be
worthy of a weekend course on body language. The shoulders, I
came to learn, were a function of their owners' discretion,
telegraphing a range of emotions their owners were too but-
toned-up to voice.

But sports? Baseball? The great American outdoors? Having
Yudl and Velvl as my models, for years I thought being Jewish
meant being sedentary. It would be several years before I got my

ass routinely whipped by a bunch of Jew boys on a college tennis team and revised my opinion on the subject of Jewish mo-
bility. But in the years of my growing up I'd make my sisters
giggle by asking them, at the most inopportune times, to picture
Yudl on water skis, or Velvl roller-skating. My uncles were beyond unathletic. They were unathletic *on principle*. With them it
was more than a matter of never having mastered the art of riding a bicycle (OK, maybe they did master that high-wire bal-
ancing act, but the handlebars would wobble as though they
were coasting down a hill of cobblestones). No, in the manner
of *ideologically* unathletic people, it went beyond a lack of sheer
physical prowess; it extended beyond those unimaginable occasions when they might be called upon to throw a ball, to the fur-
thest reaches of their lives. Driving, for instance: Exiting a
garage one afternoon, Yudl had put a borrowed car in forward
instead of reverse and deposited himself in the kitchen of the
super's apartment. Even manipulating a seat belt into place
taxed their abilities. They were unathletic standing woodenly in
line for ballet tickets, daring to pet a cocker spaniel, passing a
loaf of French bread at the table and then sweeping the nuggets
of bread off the linen tablecloth into the cupped palms of their
long hands, there to be prized and nuzzled like the sugar nuzzled by a skittish thoroughbred.

At a wedding reception I once made the mistake of offering
to bet one of these uncles that the Yankees would win the World
Series.

"World Series, what is?"

"Baseball. You know. The sport of baseball."

"This is a sport, that they take turns sitting on their tuchases?
Look, I'm sitting on *my* tuchas, no doubt I too should get six
hundred thousand dollars a year."

But also in the way of certain unathletic people, there was a
nervous elegance to them. They compensated for their unphysicality with polished urbanity. They were possessed of an almost
occult gentility, putting their fingertips to their lips if they dis-

agreed with you on a point about Rimbaud, and placing their fingertips on the table before them if they disagreed violently. They had the low-key manner of, say, an English prince consort, folding the carbon copy of a delicatessen bill neatly so the waitress could throw it away, or the self-deprecating aplomb of a 1940s radio detective, so that even the act of clearing the throat sounded apologetic. But they were never so refined that they lost their peasant roots. It wasn't beneath them to squeeze out their tea bags or wipe their grandchildren's noses with their fingers.

And discreet! "Whom do you favor to win the election?" you might inquire. (With anyone else you'd bellow, "Who ya votin' fer?" but the formality was contagious.)

"Well, this is information I can't divulge," would be the answer—the only people in America to insist upon the secret ballot.

So reserved were they, in fact, that it wasn't until my twenties that I learned there was an appreciable prejudice against Jews for being coarse. Not till after college did I see that there was a sufficient number of crude Jews in the world to constitute the basis for a whole subset of anti-Semitism. Growing up, I'd always assumed anti-Semitism was a reaction to our overcultivation. (Of course there's that prejudice, too. Anti-Semitism is nothing if not adaptable.)

But my great-uncles didn't come by their courtliness only through their Jewishness. They weren't Jewish as Israelis are, for instance, with a bluster that seemed a little *brut.* No, their poise was the poise of European gentlefolk. And the bottom line was they seemed to me more like ancestors than elders. That's how I thought of them, as my Venerable Jewish Ancestors. They were of that peculiarly dated upper-middle-class school that still recites telephone numbers using the prefix word (as in ENdicott 3 instead of 363), that still navigates the curbs of the Upper West Side with varnished canes and a quarter-inch of starched hankie running across their breast pockets, taking tiny steps in their rubber galoshes as their diminutive wives clutch their wrists. When these old souls are gone, what will the modern world know of finish? Of manners? Of the sort of refinement that, if they stumble into a parking meter, makes them say, "Excuse me"?

Tall and stately and hunched, these ENdicott Jews were civilized to a fault. It was the noisy Americans who lost out in the manners game. Conversations with my New York relatives didn't proceed at a normal American clip; they loped along, stopped mid-sentence, and were attended by something almost unheard of in American discourse: thinking. You'd ask a question; they'd pause before responding. The pause could last twenty seconds. They were polling their intellect prior to fashioning their replies. Such reflection could often be disconcerting, mistaken for reticence. If you were a typically impatient American, your instinct would be to forge ahead and fill in the embarrassing blanks. In this manner you could conduct an entire conversation without ever actually hearing from them—an unfortunate outcome because their responses, when finally phrased, would always be salient and frequently droll.

My father, the American, a Harvard Jew who'd met his share of bullies growing up brainy in Boston and who cultivated charm to cope but who nevertheless always struck my great-uncles as suspiciously Jamesian (Jesse, not Henry), once asked my great-uncles how business was going. The two brothers looked back and forth at each other for some time.

"Not bad," they finally said.

My father bided his time. "That good?" he asked at last.

Mirth was occasioned. My great-uncles arched their eyebrows. They liked this snappy rejoinder so much that they raised the corners of their lips and smiled, showing the barest tip of tongue.

"Now he's catching on," they congratulated each other.

It was as demonstrative as two Southern boys letting rip an Apache yell and high-fiving their beer mugs in the air.

◆ ◆ ◆

For a professional life of over half a century's duration, the brothers Yudl and Velvl sat across from each other at two cheap gunmetal desks shoved together in their seedy office above 47th Street. It was the best marriage you ever saw. In gray smocks over their handsome tailored suits and muted ties, they were like a Flemish Smith Brothers, staring at each other over a collection of cough drops, each with 228 perfectly polished facets. The Watson and Crick of 47th Street, perfecting the double helix structure of diamond crystals . . .

But they were like no one so much as the brothers Wilhelm and Jacob Grimm, who collected Germanic folk tales and published them as *Grimm's Fairy-Tales* (1812–1815). Like Yudl and Velvl, Wilhelm and Jacob were together all their lives. As children they'd slept in the same bed and worked at the same table; as students they'd had two beds and tables in the same room. So too were my great-uncles joined at the hip, though in one respect the Morganstern brothers did not resemble the Brothers Grimm at all. The Grimms were described as "sharp nosed and sensitive nostriled." The Morganstern boys had schnozzles. It used to scare me studying genealogy in high school biology, especially when learning that noses continued growing one's whole life, after the other features had stopped.

The next thing you'd notice would be their hands: long and so white as to be almost blue, pale and veiny, the big sensitive mitts of a concert pianist, with fingers capable of reaching an octave and a half. Too strong to be called fine, they were mazurka-trilling hands, working jeweler hands, diamond smuggler hands that were always doodling diamond shapes on the top of a menu or the back of an envelope: intricate cutting angles, circumferences, radii. It was rumored they even doodled diamond shapes in their dreams.

Was it their great-hands and great-noses that made my great-uncles so avuncular? But photos of them as *toddlers* showed them looking avuncular, with mischievous hooded eyes and a sorrowful wise mirth playing around their mouths, the germ of that self-mockery with which their maturity would be stamped. Already at age five, as well, the frugality could be seen a city block away. Not stinginess—*frugality,* the virtue of getting full value from life. Frugality was the discernment to see that paper towels, when dried over the toaster top, could serve just as well a second time, that just because rubber bands were broken didn't mean they'd outlived their usefulness. Frugality was the knack for keeping the same bottle of Chivas for two decades sitting on Yudl's shelf (a shelf, not a cabinet! Liquor is so important it needs a cabinet to itself?) and polished twice a week by "our Lulu" for twenty years till it shined like a topaz. Once in a blue moon the schnapps would be broken out and a thimbleful disgorged. What could merit such extravagance? Your engagement, perhaps, your once-in-a-lifetime engagement (frugality alone would forbid them to countenance a second engagement—the waste of divorce! The sheer squandering of emotions!). So that after twenty years the Chivas, that unlikely Yiddish-sounding scotch, was still two-thirds full.

Item: Sir Morganstern

Family legend has it that in Belgium the father of Yudl and Velvl, Bonpapa, was once offered a chance to buy a title. Imagine that: the founder of the family diamond business could have been Sir Morganstern. Bonpapa turned down the honor, reportedly for the same reason my great-uncles dismissed out of hand the idea of fixing their noses: a certain strength of character that bordered on antivanity. But knowing my family as I do, I've long suspected another reason. The title might have been a little on the high side.

Not only were they Jewish, after all. They were also Belgian. Belgian frugality was so mythic that it was said the

Belgian army didn't shoot at the Germans when they invaded because they were intent on saving their bullets.

So I made fun. They were of such unassailable dignity—even the shoes of my aunts were hallowed by dint of how out of fashion they were—that I had to snicker. What else could a Connecticut kid do with victims of the worst war in the world?

On the drive from our home to a Passover seder in New York, the Rambler station wagon was filled with lacrosse sticks, ice skates, football helmets. I was trying to make a 7-Up last the ride, but no longer than the ride because I knew my New York family wouldn't approve of my bringing soft drinks into their home any more than they would comic books. Leave America outside! In the backseat I'd turn to my siblings and present them with a palsied fish hand, trembling from the wrist, and mutter, "Good *yontov*." I was making fun of a great-aunt who in the winter of '43 had jumped out of a cattle car and lived in a pigpen for four months; soon on this balmy spring evening of 1962 she was due to greet us at the door with a hand that felt like soggy mattress filling, and say in a trembly voice, "Good *yontov*," her eyes filling with tears at seeing such healthy American cheer.

"Good *yontov*," I'd say in the station wagon, fluttering my eyes with mock joy. "Vant some Chivas?" Scandalized, laughing despite their best efforts, my siblings thought me cruel. I did, too. But cruelty is rarely such a simple matter.

Coming off the Henry Hudson Parkway onto 96th Street, we entered what amounted to a Moshav West Side—four branches of the family in one building. The mosaics in the lobby were crumbling. The white marble walls were yellowing. Julio the doorman had seen better days: his uniform's stitching was coming apart, the velvet rubbed through. So too the elevator man. The elevator had been automated for years but my uncles had kept Gus on for security, they said, but really it was loyalty; thus did their well-guarded sentimentality emerge. Ascending with him in his tiny walnut-paneled cube that seemed to have soaked up decades of suffering, with dry cleaning hanging in plastic bags from a hook, Gus never sat, never chewed gum. Would Yudl chew Wrigley's Spearmint gum, or wear Robert Hall suspenders of garish green? Then why would his elevator man?

Inside, the apartment was like a mini Versailles, a hallette of beveled mirrors and abbreviated chandeliers. It was opulent but not stiflingly so: the function of the opulence was to give. We were aggressed by generosity: crystal bowls of raisins awaited us, silver platters of walnuts, pale tea in gleaming glass tankards. Every inch of the huge apartment was crammed with books in German on Russian icons, books in Hebrew on French Impressionists. And paintings: sixteen paintings on a single wall was not unusual—all abstract oils of the mid-century Bourgeois-appreciates-Bohemianism school. Up-at-the-heels modernism that shows true struggling but not such struggling as to be judged unsafe by academics. *Approved* struggling art. With maybe one or two seventeenth-century Flemish masters in gilt frames thrown in for good measure. It was as prescribed that the rooms of these Upper West Siders should contain these works as that a coffeehouse in LA feature black-and-white photos of the undersides of iron bridges.

And always, at the center of every apartment, was a dining room table with an embroidered tablecloth upon which sat a bowl of waxed fruit—apples with a perpetual dull sheen, grapes that never got gnats. These were the waxed version of my relatives with their squeezably pale skin, their soft-hard flesh, their manner that was both resilient and resistant at the same time so you felt that if you seized their elbow to keep them from falling you'd leave a full set of fingerprints. Even their blemishes seemed wax-perfect, etched in for show. Their warts, their wens, their kempt or remarkably unkempt eyebrows, were almost too superrealistic to be real. The only jarring note were those six watery blue numbers etched on their arms. Why would the manufacturer leave the lot number there?

Waxed Jews . . .

Into this atmosphere we charged, young bulls from the country: Fairfield County ruffians, Ivy League hoodlums. (In truth, we weren't the only ones to have infiltrated the Ivy League, but what had Herschel done with his four years among the exclusive eating clubs of Princeton? Founded the Kosher Kitchen.) I accepted a cup of tea and in my brash innocence plunked both lemon and cream into it, then nonchalantly pretended that I preferred it curdled.

The gentlemen diamond dealers had their smocks off now to reveal their French linen shirts; the smell of cooked cabbage clung faintly to their V-neck cashmere sweaters. Here Yudl and Velvl were at home, and as awkward as it had been to see them on our turf among the lobstermen of Bayley Beach, so was it illuminating to see them on their own, the wife needlepointing Vasarely, the husband using a diamond loupe to read the fine print on a matchbook instructing him to keep the cover closed when striking. They chipped their butter from the top, instead of oafishly taking a slice from the end; just a little chip, and then another little chip, why waste a speck? They were diamond cutters at the table, wielding their words as they wielded their butter knives, managing both their badinage and their bread sticks with an economy that was dainty, good-natured, occasionally even ribald, but ribald in the most virginal way, so that any dirty words that happened to pass their lips sounded squeaky clean, like an experiment in phonetics only. Here Velvl was at ease, and his dignity was never so overbearing that some adolescent wisenheimer of a grandson couldn't stand behind him as he presided over the table, twaddling his earlobe . . . for minutes on end! And Velvl would just sit there taking it, doodling to himself and smiling mysteriously with that twinkle of self-mockery on his lips.

I couldn't suss them out. All the ENdicott Jews—the women as well as the men—were both more formal and, paradoxically, more gay than we were. It occurred to me that our Americanism came too cheap. We hadn't quite earned it. We were spontaneous but they were tolerant. Their laughter bubbled forth from a deeper place in their chests. Their sorrow was sorrier, their joy more joyous. Yet they maintained such a scrim of fineness that they were forever blushing for us, forever lowering their eyes, and giving off such a sense of sweetness that I felt wicked in their world.

One still held his nose when he sneezed, a holdover from hiding days when his life depended on not being heard. Another who built apartment buildings on the side couldn't bring himself to go into an underground parking garage. Yudl himself was unable to straighten up completely, the result of spending four months doubled over in a chimney. Yet another whose eyes were shadowed with kindness and fatigue was for a medical experiment given the option of having his neck vertebrae fused up or down and chose to have them fused upward, the better, as he said, to spit in God's eye; and if you thought that sacrilegious, if you thought perhaps he should have spit instead in the eye of a Nazi he would reply with precise gentle diction that he wanted to go to the head Nazi and that was God. No false piety for these survivors.

You could spot the women who'd spent time in concentration camps: their eyes watched you while their faces were affectless. Their effervescence was removed, like the 7-Up I hadn't quite finished and was going flat on the floor of the station wagon. One who was so wispy she looked as if she was going to vaporize on the spot, had been pregnant when she arrived in Auschwitz and Mengele let her have her baby, only to learn that she was part of an experiment to see how long it would take to starve the baby to death. Another was lugging a suitcase full of ammo with a few leaves of basil on top to disguise the smell when she was stopped by a German who asked her what she was carrying. "It's full of ammo!" she said, and thinking of course that she was joking, he helped carry her suitcase. Yet another was said to be quite beautiful in her day. She used to lure

German soldiers to ride bikes with her through the park, where they'd be ambushed. *Kilt! Kaput!* Old ladies in Adidas running shoes who harbored terrible secrets, these were the wary ones, and like birds too wounded to fly south for the winter, they watched and waited, not trusting the world that had changed around them too many times.

Seeing such people at home in their element, you realized that a more docile and less presumptuous group of individuals would be hard to find. And you realized something more. Sitting in their drawing rooms, watching them stutter gracefully and tinkle their glasses of sparkling cider and with great spunk maintain their veneer of stateliness against all the depredations of the twentieth century, you knew that Hitler's targeting of them to exterminate was not some higher social ideology, no advanced philosophy based on questions of genes and race. He'd merely picked on the meekest people he could find. He wasn't a political scientist, a social architect with a comprehensive *Weltanschauung*. He was a schoolyard bully, picking on those least able to defend themselves.

◆ ◆ ◆

Nevertheless I snickered. I cackled. I persevered in my ridicule. Later in the seder, when it came time to go round the long table reading, I made my siblings laugh by putting my finger over the lines they were supposed to read. I planted whispered images in their ears of Velvl on a Harley-Davidson or Yudl going over a mogul at Stowe. I tittered beneath my breath about a Low Salt Holocaust Diet and muttered jokes about a Holocaust aerobics class. But the best part came when the room fell silent to allow a small second cousin to stand on a chair and sing the Four Questions. He was named Little Henry, in distinction to an older devout Henry nicknamed God's Henry, and I couldn't help but snortle. On and on went his singsong voice as the bright-eyed boy gazed about the room eager to please as I got my brother and sisters to snortle, too. Giggling, sputtering, trying to avoid each other's eyes, staring hard at a piece of chipped plaster on the ceiling to take our minds off the syrupy-sweet singing, till we'd catch each other's eyes and erupt, shooting our hands in front of our mouths, ashamed, at last, of our glee.

But here was the thing that truly shamed us. Little Henry's parents would keep smiling, their eyes shining with pride, as their son kept singing. Little Henry's parents had been married before the war, to other people. They had each lost their spouses and children at Birkenau, at Dachau. Penniless, dazed, wandering Europe after the war, they'd met in a refugee camp, gotten married, had a son. A miracle. Out of the ashes, a baby boy. That boy developed leukemia and died at age five. Though they were aged before their time, they mustered the courage to try again. They had a second miracle: another boy. This boy was standing on the chair now, singing the Four Questions.

Unlike most of the other grown-up men in the room, Little Henry's father was not well off. He dealt not in diamonds but in diamond dust. Diamond dust is necessary because only diamonds can polish other diamonds, and diamond dust is the thing to do it. But it's not the most glorious part of the business. It's the most humble, and Little Henry's father would come to the basement of Velvl's apartment building to grind some of Velvl's leftover stones into dust to make his living, an act of charity that was never spoken of. Little Henry's father would lose his wife in a few years but he would remain close to his son. Little Henry would grow up to be a renowned neurosurgeon, always rushing off to do important operations. As an old man Little Henry's father's eyes would fill with tears, his eyelashes glittering with diamond dust, when he would report that no matter how busy he was, Little Henry would still call him once a day at five, every day, like clockwork. Later still, six months after Little Henry's father died, Little Henry would die of prostate cancer at age forty-one, never having married, never having furthered his race, a sweetly bitter man, eager to please till the end.

But for now, Little Henry was on the chair, singing the Four

Questions. His parents' eyes shone, the candle glow reflecting on their smooth cheeks as they mouthed the words in time with his singing. All their attention was focused on their pride and joy. It didn't matter to them that we laughed. They forgave us. God had been generous with them by giving them this boy, and they could afford to be generous with the privileged children from the countryside, the sons and daughters of Connecticut.

Afterward they smiled warmly at us, pretending to share in our laughter, as though the whole time we'd been laughing at how nice it was. This was their most generous gift of all.

Why didn't Little Henry's parents slap me across the face? Why didn't they rip the shirt from my body, pull my pants down right there in front of everyone and spank the smugness out of me?

They did better. They tolerated me. They let me live with it for decades until I came to understand.

◆   ◆   ◆

At Passover, the Haggadah tells the story of four sons. It is a very simple and profound story. The first son, the wise son, asks what Passover means. The second son, the wicked son, asks what it all means to you—to you and not to him, for he removes himself from the group. The third son is dim and just says, What is this? The fourth son does not know how to ask.

What it took me half a lifetime to understand was that I was not that wicked son. Though I thought the Holocaust happened to them and not to me, though I mimicked my stuttering relatives who survived their exodus from Hitler's Europe and parodied the ones with such severe Parkinson's the numbers on their saggy arms shook, still I was not that wicked son. I was a different son, a fifth son who had been damaged.

It took me half a lifetime to understand that for this damaged son, making fun was his way of metabolizing the Holocaust, of filtering the horrors through at his own speed; that he had to have sons of his own and take them to see the tragedy of his people in the land where it happened, before he could pay for his blasphemy, and redeem himself.

The trip I took in my late thirties with two sons to find the hiding places where our ancestors survived was not only a trip to reconstitute ourselves as a family after our divorce, not only a chance to heal and to get in touch with our deepest selves, in a land where our people died for being Jews.

Reason 14b. It was, above all, a trip of atonement.

6

UNLIKELY HEROES

*I*n the Brussels elevator, the boys' watches go off in sync as they ready themselves. Wearing a T-shirt that is both backward and inside out, Marshall manages to wrestle his way into a Harris tweed sports jacket that's already buttoned. Alex fastidiously combs his hair, using the dented aluminum wall of the elevator as a mirror. Tourist warriors, I think, with oversized sunglasses propped on their noses and cameras cocked—where'd they get this Banana Republic notion of what it means to travel?

"Alex, what'd you put on yourself!" exclaims Marshall, sniffing his brother.

"Some stuff."

I sniff, too. "How much cologne did you put on?"

"Just half."

"Half what?"

"A bottle . . ."

We descend to the hotel lobby carrying the tulips from our room. In the peach champagne–colored foyer a piano is playing; the chanteuse, a Buffy Sainte-Marie clone warbling Piaf, cocks an eyebrow at my sneakers; the tinkling of piano keys blends pleasantly with the buzz of computer printouts from the cashier's desk. Very tasteful hotel, the Metropole; I can see why it served as the headquarters for the Gestapo during the war.

Outside, the Grand Place is like a boy's model of a central square, filled with homey touches. I watch a second-floor window where instead of a monarch bestowing munificence upon his subjects, a cleaning lady is watering geraniums from a Coke bottle. Alex lifts Marshall so he can rub his hands along the bas-relief of a brass Madonna reposing with a greyhound. Its surface has been burnished to a dark gold by generations eager for luck.

"There you go, Marsh," Alex says. He puts his brother down and strains to lift me, too, but he's not strong enough. I step out of his embrace.

"Don't you want some luck yourself?" he asks me.

"This is how I get mine," I say, rubbing both their scalps at once.

Handing me a gum wrapper and an empty film canister (my pockets are their pockets), Marshall takes my hand. Alex finds the sight so repugnantly tempting that he arranges to take his father's hand by grabbing me and saying, "We got him prisoner! We're bringing him to jail!"

And that's how my children start holding my hand, during what I know will be the last summer they'll be young enough to do such a thing.

It's one of the nicest walks in years. The sidewalks are slanted, the morning moon hovers above the orange triangles of roofs at every corner. With a boy at each hand we're romanced into a family again. Two black men pass, holding hands in the African manner, their fingers cupped gently in each other's palms, followed by a trio of hookers right out of Daumier, with pocked skin and beaked noses.

"Hey, someone pinched my butt," Marshall says. "Let's do that again."

But Alex is insisting that we go into a novelty store that specializes in plastic french fries, ice cubes that break your teeth, alarmingly real dog turds that would emanate from dogs larger than the miniature schnauzers the natives favor. While Alex appraises the goods, Marshall purchases a pair of World War II aviator goggles and walks me outside to watch street workers perform the painstaking work of replacing cobblestones in tangerine-colored sand. Putting the goggles on in the sunlight he reports, "I can see old."

"What do you mean?"

"Everything looks like the way it was a long time ago."

I try them. Indeed, framing the view with these leather strap-ons of scuffed glass does lend the contemporary scene an old-timey look, the way films from a few decades ago look ancient by dint of random scratches.

When Alex joins us we continue our stroll under June leaves. Marshall keeps up a steady stream of chatter, a babbling free verse that's as pleasant to listen to as a brook in the background.

> You don't sip beer
> You guggle it
> But Dad? You know what's so sad?
> When you die, you don't have anything to do.
> You just lie there
> Till it ends
> And you just get sick of it.
> Do you think there's an end to the galaxy?
> Maybe we're in a black hole. Can I
> Have an Orangina?

We've only a rough idea how to get to the address we're looking for: the apartment of a great-aunt who's invited us to a family tea. But for some reason all three of us sense we're on the right track. "We're getting warmer," says Alex, passing a Sikh with a turban standing at attention outside an Indian restaurant.

"No, colder," says Marshall, the pint-sized swashbuckler bouncing two steps ahead and, as usual, needing to pee. "We ought to turn right."

We make a unanimous decision to turn right, then left, just like three ducks in a pond, steering ourselves as one unit. Before long we find ourselves on a bourgeois boulevard where the well-heeled apartments front a triangular sward of green lined with chestnut trees, under which little girls in school blazers play monkey-in-the-middle. The buildings are elegantly blackened brick with wrought-iron grilles protecting windows of Belgian lace. *Fake* lace: real lace curtains would be a thousand dollars a pop these days. Between the curtains, wide-angle mirrors enable the nosy inhabitants to keep tabs on the street scene without having to crane; a dachshund pokes his face through the lace to fix beady eyes on us as we step up to number 214.

Brass name plates indicate that several branches of the Morganstern clan live here, headed by the matriarch Shasha. Inside the apartment I see it's family, all right, the same mini Versailles school of design, the same extravagance superimposed upon the same economy. They won't turn on lamps; the green glass cloth appears nearly blue in the available light, the Persians appear purple. Yet they push walnuts and pitted olives on us with a generosity that's almost violent. Everything's either diamond-glinted or chocolate: chocolate wafers, chocolate biscuits, classic Belgian chocolate bonbons. Great-aunts dither about in a prism of diamond-blue earrings and red manicured nails, their upper arms as vanilla-fleshed as flan—caramelized aunts—but burned into the custard are the watery blue numbers. 211834. 355240.

"Such dashing eyepieces!" Shasha pronounces.

Marshall faces Shasha with glory. "They're my time goggles!" he tells her. "I can see the past with these!" And rears back to sneeze so hard he makes the strings of the grand piano vibrate.

"May God bless you and keep you," says Shasha, startled. "What a splendid sneeze."

She sniffs in sympathy, then holds her nose aloft. "What is that heavenly scent?"

"That's my Old Spice," Alex says half proudly, thrusting the tulips out as an offering.

"Very compelling," Shasha says, pouring the wine. "May we offer you a sherry?"

"Better not," Alex cautions. "If Marshall gets drunk, he'll show you his penis."

If anyone's put out, they're not showing it. "You strike me as the type of gentleman who remembers being a sperm," says the diamond dealer introduced as Izick, arching his chin to stare languidly at the ceiling and pull ruminatively on a long gray hair from his Adam's apple.

"I *do* remember!" says Marshall, taking a chug as his brother rolls his eyes. "There was a girl sperm racing next to me, but I beat her to the egg, and that's why I'm a boy."

"And quite a boy you turned out to be," Izick agrees. "What are you going to be when you grow up?"

"Industrial designer. But my backup: baseball player. Third base for the Red Sox. But my backup before that: asset manager for Smith Barney."

"Why not?" Izick shrugs, pursing his lips thoughtfully. "Pick up some extra smackers."

Everyone in the room concurs. "Extra smackers couldn't hurt."

"What about the stock market?" asks the diamond dealer Chaim, nonchalantly fingering a flesh-colored mole above his lip. "Think it's going to be a bull for the rest of the decade?"

To their credit, the boys know when they're being set up for a gag. They clam up. Besides, why should Alex share his theory of where the Dow's headed?

A mule-headed wit named Schmuel is cranking himself up for a joke, so zealous he's physically sputtering. "I also wanted to play baseball," he puts in, tittering with anticipation. "But my position was Left! Out! Get it? The Jewish position: Left! Out!"

Marshall has jumped off the couch and is busy admiring the

pale numbers etched into Shasha's upper arm. "Boy, you *really* don't want to lose your phone number!" he exclaims.

She laughs comfortably. "That was courtesy of the Germans," she says.

"Wow, so many wrinkles," Marshall says admiringly, turning his hostess's arm around to inspect her elbow. "Are you rich?"

"Jesus, Marshall!" cries his offended brother.

"I'm proud to say filthily, disgustingly rich!" Shasha says gamely.

Marshall picks up on the tone of irony. "But you *are* Belgian?" he probes, climbing back atop the sofa and carefully situating ten olives on ten fingertips.

"I was born in Poland, and educated in France. So on balance, yes, really I am Belgian."

This provokes merriment with much nodding of heads and wagging of double chins. "On balance," repeat the sensitive-lipped Jews, chuckling heavily. *Clink! Clink!* go their glasses. I get the first of many red wine stains on my wrist.

"Do you get along with the *real* Belgians?" Marshall pursues.

"We get along," Shasha enunciates, "with everyone but the Germans and the Arabs, who we suspect are really Germans in human form."

"Ha-ha." More toasts. The chocolate is going to people's heads.

"How do *you* like Belgium?" Marshall is asked.

"Belgium kicks butt!" he hollers with such energy that two of the olives go flying around the room.

The cake comes right on time.

❖ ❖ ❖

Half an hour later, things have settled down. The white tulips are on the sideboard along with Marshall's goggles. The cake, dotted with lacquered cherries and layered with kiwis in cream, has been dispatched. We are deep in conversation.

"What I don't get, why did the Germans invade Belgium in

the first place?" Alex is asking. "Belgium didn't do anything to them."

"To use your word? They were buttheads," Izick says.

"In fact," says Chaim, limpidly blinking his large luminous eyes, "do you want to know exactly how pleasant these Germans were? The day before the invasion, the German ambassador came to see the Belgian king to assure him personally that Germany would respect Belgium's neutrality."

"But as soon as the war came," asks Alex, taking a chocolate stick the diameter of a knitting needle out of his mouth, "why didn't everyone leave?"

"We didn't believe it," Izick says. "It was illogical that Hitler would be as virulent against the Jews as he was. His Reich was supposed to last a thousand years; who thought killing Jews was at the top of his To Do list? That's why we studied *Mein Kampf*—to try to get a handle on this madman."

I find this fact amusing. "You helped boost Hitler's royalties?"

Chaim licks the mole above his lip. "There was no time to lose. J. P. even put his copy in a brown paper bag and read it in temple. And this, of course, was an Orthodox synagogue."

"About this J. P. . . ." I begin, but am interrupted by Alex asking, "Are you still Orthodox?"

"Let's put it this way. The *shul* we don't go to is Conservative," Izick says, to appreciative chuckles all around. "The *shul* we *used* to not go to was Orthodox, so you see we've liberalized to a certain extent."

"He!" Shasha says, "was always liberalized. In the war, a counterfeiter par excellence!"

Izick shrugs owlishly, spearing another slice of pickle.

"You know what he would do? He would write to the city halls that he knew were blown up, asking them for verification of his birth date. They would write back that all the records had been destroyed, but no matter to him. Now he had the city seal on their stationery, to forge false papers to cross borders."

Izick shrugs again to show it's forgotten history. But not quite forgotten: he lets out a little self-satisfied burp.

"Oh, he was an artist with a potato, that one!"

"A potato?"

"How else could he counterfeit? You think he had rubber stamps and tools? He would cut a potato in half, wait till it dried out, then etch his counterfeit stamp into the meat of the potato."

"Have potato, will travel," Izick says.

"Wasn't it dangerous?" Marshall wants to know, nibbling the edges of his chocolate macaroon.

Shasha answers for him as Izick mildly waves his hands "so-so." "Only if you call being tortured and shot dangerous," she replies. "But this one, he was so brave. Physical brave, I'm talk-ing!"

Izick sits back with a self-congratulatory pat to his belly. "That's only because I had never been hoit in my life. Had I known how much a hoit could hoit, I never would have dared, believe me."

This sends them into titters. Talking with their mouths full, these garrulous Jews fracture the table talk into a melee of six separate conversations in German, Flemish, Yiddish, Polish—laughing and choking, coughing and wheezing as flying bits of kosher pastrami and crumbs of tongue color the air. *Clink! Clink!* More wine on my cuffs. Was ever a people more guile-less, more innocent than these, with their protected upbringings and bourgeois sensibilities? And yet these were the diamond smugglers, the escape artists who outfoxed the Nazis. History called upon them to act and they did—moles and all.

Shasha reads my thoughts. "Unlikely heroes," she says. "And we were the young generation! You should have seen our par-ents! If you could have seen my in-laws in their fur coats and top hats, trying to figure out which was the head of a bicy-cle. . . ."

"But now you can't say *head*, you know," points out a sparrowlike old lady with two hearing aids. "For the youngsters already *head* is the word for sex!"

"Shut up with you, please! It's true?"

"Oral head! I read about it, sure!"

"Shut up again! Our guest will tell us if it's true for oral head! Daniel?"

But I am saved from elucidating this by a sleepy Marshall, coming to claim my lap. Removing my foot from my knee, he primps and flattens various of my limbs to his liking, climbs aboard, and settles into his private throne. Also depleted by the talk, Alex needs to check out for a while. He surreptitiously puts on his Walkman—a chip off the old block—but you don't get away with inattention in this crowd.

"What do you think of all this, Alex?"

He snaps out a nod. "Interesting," he says.

An eyebrow is raised. *"Everything* is interesting," he's reproved. *"This,"* he's informed, "is fascinating."

Alex takes off his Walkman.

◆   ◆   ◆

Fascinating it may be, but when I ask for details, I hit a dead end. "Were there any hiding places around here?"

"Some were in barns, some were in churches, it's too long a story. Nobody wants to hear about them."

"Oh, we do," Alex says. "We want to *find* them!"

Izick looks less than pleased. He breathes through his nose soberly, squeezes the end with his fingertips for a minute. "You know what it'd be like? Like trying to find a pin in a haystack."

The prospect seems to tire them out. "It's boggling." Chaim nods in conclusion, his eyeglasses flashing sunlight. He doesn't need to say *mind*-boggling: With these cerebral folks, the mind is assumed.

This is the moment when we're supposed to move on to a new subject: the wall tapestries at the City Museum, perhaps. To stay with the subject is to risk impudence.

"Still, we'd like to do it," I insist.

Stiffening visibly, the heads slowly revolve on the fragile columns of their necks.

"Impossible."

"Why?"

"Number one," Izick says, making his points on fingertips that don't correspond with his points. "Most of the people are dead. It's a half-century ago, yah? Number two, those people who are alive, they're very secretive. It's the silence of the survivors. They'll shy away from you."

"Why?"

"Who knows why anyone's shy?" puts in Schmuel, sputtering again with wit. "They're looking to find the gene for shyness but it keeps hiding behind the other genes!"

I pursue Izick as Schmuel goes, "Get it? It keeps hiding!"

"But seriously," I say. "Why won't they talk to us?"

"They're suspicious by nature, A. And B: They don't want to relive those days. It makes them jumpy." Izick pauses. *"You'll* make them jumpy."

"Anything else?"

"Yes, number three: the world has changed too much, there is nothing recognizable to see. And so I conclude, it is a goose chase." He serenely takes off his glasses to wipe his rheumy eyes with the point of his handkerchief, then stuffs it back in his breast pocket with an Old World flourish. "You are wasting your time."

Subtext: wasting *our* time. Subject closed. If I'm so obstinate as to pursue further, I'll be relegated to the third person. Left! Out!

Yet when they do resume talking, there is a spark of hope. Almost as an afterthought Shasha says, "Well, they might want to try J. P."

A dismissive wave. "He'd never talk to them."

I nod to myself. "So we really do have a relative named J. P. Morgan?"

They smile enough to show their teeth, a reserved form of

chuckling. "He thought changing his name would make him fit in better. A wild one, him. A real rabble-rouser."

"What made him so wild?" I ask.

"He read Spinoza!"

Right. A radical in my family is not someone who mails letter bombs but who reads Baruch Spinoza, whose philosophy was thought scandalous by the Jews of Amsterdam in the 1600s. But the subject of J. P. seems to spark them to life again. The air is rife with rumor and counter rumor as they go down J. P.'s spec sheet, shaking their heads in amazement.

"A character, he was! And a Casanova! Don't forget that! A real skirt-chaser!"

"J. P. could charm the birds out of the trees."

"And an athlete!"

"Really?" I ask.

"Oh sure, he was a champion stone thrower. Could skip a stone on the water three, maybe four times in a row!"

"A regular Willie Mays," I observe dryly. "So does he still live in Belgium?"

Clucks of disapproval. "Here in Brussels, a neighborhood that has gone down. Better he should have stayed in the countryside somewhere, living as he did with Resistance fighters—"

"He fought in the Resistance?"

"Long enough to shoot himself in the foot—"

"To hide under the bed!"

"Maybe he was not such a war hero. He started out to be an artist, but gave up when someone painted swastikas on the back of his canvases—"

"But he was very artful about hiding—"

"Oy, a champion hider. At one point he was playing billiards with a Gestapo commandant to win his freedom at spa—"

"Not at spa, at a beach hotel somewhere, Hôtel de la Plage—"

"Where he slept with the commander's wife, if you believe

what you hear. You have to take everything with a grain of truth—"

"A grain of *salt?*" I ask.

They show teeth again. "He has the poetic license," they explain.

"And also," adds Izick, tapping his head, "he has the nerves."

"What's the 'nerves'?"

"Some of us who hid, we have more nervous disorders than those who were in the camps. We suffered more from always looking over our shoulders. . . ."

"Is that why J. P. never married and settled down?"

"Oh, but he *was* married! His first wife—a heart attack, early in the war. With twin daughters he traveled through Belgium and France, trying to escape anywhere he could, saved at one point by a Christian named Pelican. . . ."

"Pelican?"

"He never talks about it—"

"And then after the war, he had another child, a son—"

"To him he doesn't speak one word—"

"Who converted. Lives like a *goy* in Paris—"

"What do you expect with such a father? A swindler, and so cheap! A tightwad!"

"How can you say that? He was a *maven*—"

"A *macher*—"

"A *mensch*—"

"*Meshugeh*—"

Shasha turns to me, my interpreter through this cacophony. "Who can parse the poetry from the truth? But what's for sure is he never got over his lovely little daughters being lost—"

"Lost how?" I ask, cupping my hand to my ear.

"*Tragique,*" they say, but that's all they say. They convey, with a shake of the head, that it'd be bad taste for me to pursue the matter. *Fini.*

By now everyone's in a time warp. The tabletop is a collection of peach pits, cherry stems, and diamond earrings on small plates. The tablecloth has smudges from the boys' chocolates. Marshall is asleep, nestled into my shirt, his arms draped over me like someone clinging to a buoy. It's his pattern: the louder his surroundings, the deeper he sleeps, snoring his triple-toned snore. How could such baroque sounds emanate from such a small body?

Izick's nurse comes in—such is the protocol that we're not introduced—and there's a whole range of leavetaking negotiations in French. Izick exits in a wheelchair; Chaim limps out on a cane; great-aunts take their leave on many-pronged walkers. I had forgotten they were old.

"As for you," Shasha says, watching me stroke Marshall's head after everyone's left, "you are an unlikely hero yourself."

"Come again?"

"To do this. With them. It is heroic to take your boys like this."

It's the first time I've blushed since high school. "I've had girlfriends who say I'm a jerk for spending so much time with them."

Shasha walks us to the door. "Ignore the nay-sayers, all of them," she says, clasping both my wine-stained wrists in her hands. "This is a small world you are dealing with—a world of Jews who know each other or *of* each other. Now, about J. P. . . ." She presses a benediction in my hand, the back of an envelope on which she's scribbled a list of names and addresses. "But watch out," she says, waving a hand over my boys, "don't give *them* the nerves. . . ."

7

CARS WITH ALLERGIES

*I*t was a small world in Connecticut, too—and an even smaller one in Kew Gardens, Queens, where I began life. My mother walked us every day to a playground not far from our apartment building, a tar oval ringed by concrete water bubblers. One day, when I was two and my sister three, we meandered out of my mother's sight, up a small hill behind the playground to the forest beyond.

The rest is what my sister and I swear happened, and no one's ever believed. We kept walking. The woods smelled of resin. We came across a giant shoe, like an old lady's lace-up boot: bigger than a swing set, smaller than a telephone pole. Children were playing around the shoe, climbing through the eyelets and sliding down the laces. An old woman was supervising them, carrying an old-fashioned straw broom.

Hand-in-hand, my sister and I watched, hidden in the brush. But somehow the old woman saw us. She started running after us, swinging the broom and squawking. We could run faster and we made it out of the woods. We told my mother. We told everyone. No one believed us.

Rational explanation: maybe it was a Catholic school rehearsing for a play. The shoe was a giant prop, the nun-director didn't want us peeking. But it doesn't really matter if we saw a giant shoe or not. What matters is that my sister and I were infatuated with the adventure. It confirmed our sense that the world was resplendent with hidden things. Sorcery was afoot.

My mother's combination of Grimm's and Not-see tales infused my first years with a mythical aspect. My grandmother standing on a street corner in a long black fur coat and, up above, the tops of the trees moving in a fluid motion. The deathbed of my grandfather, hushed and solemn, and my sister and I rolling a marble back and forth along a groove in the top of his dresser drawer. Someone shaking a colander of egg noodles, the steam whorling upwards into the sunlight streaming through the kitchen window. Holding on to a wire fence as we walked along a street, and the witchlike head of a woman appearing in a top window of a house to scream at us. Pressing the red button on our early-model TV to make our fingertip glow radioactively red, rimmed with dirty nail. The saintlike maid Louise, with her smooth milky brown skin and her honey voice, taking something out of the top shelf of the hall closet where it had been hidden all year: a silver menorah.

I loved my sister Renee, with her cascade of Egyptian-black curls. The Grimm's stories frequently featured a brother and sister, often orphaned, always lost and resourceful and utterly devoted to one another in the face of the world's dangers. One afternoon at an aunt's wedding all my older girl cousins in their white crinoline took my breath away but most beautiful was my sister, the flower girl, tossing rose petals to left and right; I had to be restrained from climbing out of the pew to throw myself around her neck in adoration. Another afternoon my sister and I came out from our lunchtime nap and our mother was nowhere to be found. Her purse was there, but where was she? The radio was on, the coffee cup still warm. We looked all through the kitchen—not there. We ran into the living room— not there. When she still wasn't in the kitchen, we started crying. Had the Not-sees captured her? But then she popped up from behind the kitchen desk, in the dark space where she stored paper bags. "Peek-a-boo!"

There were the same gray-blue eyes I cherished, the same big crooked nose. My chest heaved with love. Ah, there is my mother . . . She was the woman tenderly cupping a candle in an oil-darkened Vermeer painting, or stepping with infinite grace across the cracked orange surface of a Greek vase. Mommy . . .

But she had a frown on her face. We children played hide-and-seek, she said, peevishly; couldn't *she* sometimes play, too?

But this was breaking the rules. I needed her to be there in the light. When she realized that, she hugged us and told us not to cry. She didn't mean to scare us. Hiding was sometimes only a game. We had won the war and the Not-sees had been beaten and wouldn't capture anyone anymore.

Perhaps, I reasoned, some people had gotten so used to hiding that they were still in the habit.

❖ ❖ ❖

My first memory is of my mother trying to make an upside-down cake. She prepared it carefully, melting brown sugar in a skillet with butter, whipping eggs, opening a can of pineapple chunks, and shaking a jar so small it was like a toy: a baby jar of vanilla. She placed the batter in the oven, then later gingerly lifted the spongy cake with its sweet billowing swells of heat off the oven rack. It was so soft it would flake apart if you breathed on it wrong. Maybe it would even "perish"—my favorite word because it started off with a puff of life and drifted to nothingness like the black wisp of smoke after my mother's yahrzeit candles had burned out.

She was a relatively new cook, and she squinted at her creation critically. Her nose sniffed it approvingly. She lavished brown sugar icing on the cake, swirling it and flattening the waves with a broad knife. Then at the moment of truth she flipped the cake over and it fell on the floor. She burst into tears and I burst into tears with her.

What I didn't understand at the time was that she was sobbing not for the upside-down cake but for her mother and father who'd escaped Antwerp but had no energy left for their remaining years in America. She was sobbing for one of her neighbors who'd become a prostitute to the Gestapo in order to survive, for her classmates who'd been gassed. I sobbed with her, thinking that a fallen upside-down cake was the worst suffering anyone ever experienced. Once I came to realize that my crying didn't lessen her grief, I felt impatient and eventually alienated and finally numb. If there was nothing I could do for my mother, I wouldn't even try. But that was later.

At the time I attended to her bereavement. I watched her light her yahrzeit candles and take care not to blow them out with her sour strawberry breath. Then afterward, preparing to go to a suburban barbecue in her jazzy '50s sandals, I watched her laughingly open a capsule of nail polish the color of a Bloody Mary and paint the nails of her toes that were like the toes of all the old European Jews I knew—crabbed, like something out of Grimm's.

"I have a lot of rage in me," she once confessed.

"Why?" I dared to ask.

One word. "Hitler."

◆ ◆ ◆

We moved to Texas for two years. My father had to fulfill a medical residency for the Air Force. It was so hot you could spit on the arm of the lawn furniture and it would disappear while you counted to five. There was a bush in the backyard with castor beans so dangerous you could die if you ate them. One time in the woods behind our house I sighted a cowboy and a cowgirl on horses like Roy Rogers and Dale Evans, which everyone seemed to find plausible, though to me it was on the same order as seeing the old lady and the shoe. Another time my father pushed me on a bicycle and I went riding into the white bedsheets hanging on the clothesline. To celebrate my learning to ride, my father took me to a toy store to buy the kickstand I'd been coveting for a month. It was a special outing, just the two of us. We passed a Mexican on the road and my father stopped and put me on his burro and the Mexican took a picture. (I have the negative still: my father holding the reins protectively, our heads leaning in to each other with unbearable tenderness.) At the store my father told me to wait and not touch anything while he went to find a salesclerk. I did so until I spotted the most mesmerizing gun. When I pulled the trigger, neon squiggles shot through the plastic barrel.

Suddenly my father was snatching me by the elbow. Hadn't he told me not to touch anything? I was at a loss to explain my behavior. Instead of buying the kickstand, he yanked me out of the store and we drove home in silence that had all the crushing weight of my father's disapproval inside it. I was crestfallen, because I'd crossed some irrevocable line. Fifteen minutes earlier our heads had inclined toward each other for an historic photograph. Now and ever after I was someone who'd disappointed the father I loved.

Shortly thereafter we moved to Connecticut. The reason made sense—my parents wanted to be halfway, sort of, between my mother's family in New York and my father's in Boston. But I couldn't pronounce the state's name. It stuck in my throat like the word *kickstand*. I was starting kindergarten and all the other kids were able to say it but I was tongue-tied because of what I feared most: that I was not now and never would be the boy my father wanted me to be.

Nevertheless, the world was starting to make sense. As small pieces of the puzzle fell into place, each had the immediacy of a revelation. It was about this time that I understood that clocks were not merely wall hangings but actually had a function, and that if your sister read the words in comic books aloud to you you'd get a lot more out of them than if you just scanned the pictures. Drawings weren't something you merely had fun do-ing; for some reason grown-ups also liked to look at them *after* you were done. (But why did some kids draw *lightly?* My draw-

ings were always dark, hard, vivid—sometimes too vivid for my
own good, as witnessed by the broken crayons and wax grime
on my bitten fingertips. Years later, when I tried Prozac, it was
like becoming one of the kids who colored lightly.)

I kept endeavoring to get a reading of my mother, the subtlest
person I knew. In the way that some computers can read thousands of colors, she could detect thousands of gradations of
expression and gesture, language and mood. With her six languages (French, Flemish, Yiddish, German, Spanish, and English), words meant more than one thing at a time. Meanings
overlapped and fused and took on new shades. How happy she
could be, when she wasn't sad! She delighted in primitive paintings and autumn leaves, for the sheer color of them; she turned
the car radio to Spanish stations because she adored the joy she
heard there. Yet when my sister and I tried on her rhinestone
glasses, the world tilted so we felt we'd fall forward through
space. At first it was fun and we'd understand why she liked her
parties so much. But soon everything became wavy to a sea-
sickening degree. It was like the inside-out feeling I got when I
thought about Not-sees, a feeling which got bad enough for me
to be taken to the pediatrician, where I described it as "sparks in
my brain," but he and my father just lifted their eyebrows to
each other, two medical men at a loss.

Our first winter in Connecticut coincided with the mythic
flood that hit New England in 1955. I was five and my mother
took my sister and me across the railroad tracks to downtown
Norwalk to see the destruction it had left. We stood on a bridge
and watched a house float down the river and sink. Even more
amazing was a six-story apartment building that had been split
down the middle to reveal a cutaway view. Everyone's private
places were exposed to the light of day. A bedroom was pink,
above a yellow kitchen. A toilet was a festive blue, and there was
another just like it three stories below. Had the occupants
known they shared the same color toilet? A poster on a wall was
curling up at the bottom from being moistened by the open air.

A green kitchen table set for breakfast was perched on the precipice, one of its legs dangling over the edge. A broom closet was split in half, exposing the heads of mops like a race of wild people. We could see the interior of people's lives, and from this perspective, their lives seemed as plain as ant farms. How pitifully unsubtle were the lives they made for themselves: the primary colors and flesh tones, the attempts at cheer that had ended in this humiliating exposure.

Years later, I saw a photo of a building in Dresden that had been bombed at the close of World War II. It had suffered the same inversion of private things suddenly made public: toilets exposed, women's nighties flapping in the rain. I wondered: Did the German occupants feel as these people in Norwalk must have?

◆ ◆ ◆

Magic was in the air. (Indeed, *Magic* had been the code name for the American code-breaking machine just a few years before in World War II.) I layered my own magic in as I continued to make sense of the world. The following summer my mother took my father back to Belgium to see what had become of the homeland she'd fled sixteen years earlier. They left my sister and me with our father's family, an uncle and aunt in Providence. We had a baby sister by then, and it may not have been wise for our parents to leave her, a six-month-old, for a whole summer. But for us two older children, aged five and six, the interval was one giant fairy tale come to life. There was a laundry chute behind a latched door on the second floor that would send us down to the basement. Even better, my elder sister slept with me in a room under a ceiling that had an elongated bulging stain, which we decided was an ogre's footprint. By so naming it, we multiplied the mystery, for then we had to figure out how an ogre's footprint came to be on the ceiling. One night in bed, while contemplating the problem, I happened to get a cherry pit caught inside my nose. I'd been idly experimenting to see if it would fit, and after several minutes of trying in vain to negotiate its release, I panicked. Would I sprout a cherry tree inside my nose? Fighting off an asthma attack, I ran downstairs to my uncle, who extracted it with a tweezers. Thereafter the incident always reminded me of a homemade Jack and the Beanstalk: the ogre's footprint looming above us, and me in danger of germinating a magic bean.

Each day that summer my sister and I were given a metal lunch box and put on a bus and sent far into the countryside to day camp. Each day the ride was pandemonium. Screaming kids ran up and down the aisle, the dirt roads bumpy enough to knock the remaining kids out of their seats. Finally we turned down a trail through blueberry bushes so lush they scraped against the side of the bus, and arrived at the site of the camp. It was the summer Davy Crockett was all the rage, and I felt conflicted about holding on to my sister's shirt while wearing my coonskin cap. But I didn't dare let go. With my parents away, I needed my sister more than ever before or since. She was like the big sister protector in Grimm's: a mother dove whose downy feathers could hide me so that wherever I found myself with her, I was home. But at camp they wanted us to separate. Renee would walk me to the center cottage that smelled heavenly of all the sandwiches slow-cooking in their waxed paper before she ran off to be with her friends. I'd spend the rest of the day mooning for my sister: sad, scared, skeptical, refusing to go in the pond or use the swing set, but never quite so desperate I'd remove my coonskin cap.

The climax of that summer came the night before our parents were due back from Europe. For a final send-off our uncle and aunt took us to our first amusement park. We did the usual things. We gnawed our way through a plume of cotton candy, gamely pretending there was more to it than there really was. We went on bumper cars that were so much fun I would later try to re-create the sensation on public roads after I got my driving license. Then my uncle and aunt walked my elder sister and me up to the platform of a barnlike structure where a kind of trolley cart was waiting on a set of tracks. A bored burly man snapped a metal bar over our middles, my aunt waved the arm of our infant sister good-bye, and we were jolted into darkness.

Maybe it was called a Tunnel of Terror. I only knew that we left the real world behind. In darkness the cart lurched us into a chamber where a trio of pigs cowered against a black-lipped wolf blowing off the straw roof. The cart lurched us into a chamber where a green witch with gluey eyes flew straight for us on a broomstick. We plunged deeper into a complex cata-combs of red fog and swooping monsters. I tried to hang on to the logic of my life, but as we banged through chamber after chamber I soon went into a trance of doubt that I'd ever emerge.

At the end, of course, the tracks disgorged us into summer twilight. There, backlit by the floodlights, were my aunt and un-cle with my baby sister waving hello, as the man lifted the metal bar to release us. My sister and I did what generations of amusement park vets have done for years. We blinked grate-fully, begged halfheartedly to go back in, walked away on un-steady legs. But as we wobbled off through the parking lot, a part of me wondered. What if this outside world, with its black crows pecking at popcorn, its bulbous basset hound on a chain leash, was just another of the tunnel's chambers that rolled out with seeming infinity before me? By getting out of the cart and walking off through this extended stage set, might I be straying so far I'd never find my way back?

◆ ◆ ◆

I made up friends to guide me: lamps, chairs, rugs. What did I care that grown-ups were so self-important, so vivocentric, that they assumed we human beings were the only ones who *felt?* As in the more primitive Grimm's tales where a sewing needle or a millstone was animate, I endowed dozens of my belongings with names so I could converse with them. Each could be ac-cessed via a special code, so I could summon the attention of Howie the kindly strong house, for instance, by tapping on the wall five times. It so happened that all my Things were Jewish: my shy wristwatch Timmy, my debonair and somewhat over-sexed pillow Coyote, most of all my beloved and ever-loyal bike Tommy. Things outside my ken were not Jewish—the slide at school, for instance, was definitely not—but Things that belonged to me were, theoretically, at least, persecuted: if anyone knew of the existence of wristwatches and bikes that happened to be Jewish, they'd probably be mad at them. I was their theoretical protector, telling no one about them, speaking to them only when no one was around.

My loyalty to them was immense, and especially to the underdogs of the inanimate world—chipped marbles, carpet pads, undershirts that rarely got to see the light of day—the unsung and disenfranchised crowd that labored without complaint to make the lives of the privileged animate run smoothly. No one ever thanked them, so I made it my business to.

In this manner the world was very alive. Rocks had appetites. Cars had allergies. Scissors had preferences for what they liked to cut and individual pieces of paper had distinct opinions on whether or not they *wanted* to be cut. All were invested with a spirit that I assumed, with a naturalness theologians might admire, was divine. No biggie—godliness just resided in everything.

I don't remember experiencing loneliness as a child.

◆ ◆ ◆

(Studying anthropology in college, I discovered I was an animist just as primitive peoples were, investing inanimate objects with holy attributes. Why, I wondered, was monotheism universally considered to be an advance from that? Why wasn't it just as good to regard all things on earth as having souls? They always talked about Judaism's contribution to the world being the idea that there was one God, but why was that an improvement? The difference between animism and monotheism seemed the difference between a Navajo tribe and a superpower, between bootleg liquor and Seagram's Corporation. Why was the larger bureaucracy superior?)

◆ ◆ ◆

There was an additional benefit to having Things be my friends. I was always protected by them. My childhood bedroom was downstairs, separated from the rest of the family by two sets of stairs and a dark hallway with two right-angle turns. If a Notsee or an ogre hiding in a bucket of pine cones came to get me in the night, the rug would trip him or the lamp would blind him. Howie the house would do something to foil his efforts. Things lent me themselves to hide in: an abundance of secret places with make-believe elevators and hidden passageways. Most protective of all were Things that were blue and white, because these were the colors of Israel. No one from the outside world had a clue, but I had a private pact with anything blue and white that kept me from being lost in their presence and them in mine. That the state license plates had white characters on a field of dark blue was a secret comfort to me, and meant that even some of the hot-rodders buzzing around with "glass" (fiberglass) mufflers were in cars that were in some sense Jewish, and thus shared a secret kinship with me, whether they knew it or not.

But for real protection I needed superpowers, and these I had in spades. I could activate X-ray vision by pressing on the side of my temples. I could invoke the ability to make wishes come true simply by using the word *wish* or *hope*. These powers also happened to be Jewish, and were so potent that I hoarded them zealously. In fact, with my hereditary sense of thrift I was vigilant never to use them but to keep them in reserve for some black night when I might really need them.

Unfortunately, no superpowers could save me from my mother's grief, which came and went with no order I could understand. Her grief hung in the air the way the smell of chemicals might hang in the air of a family who lived atop a dry cleaning shop and didn't notice it until a breeze blew it the other way. Someone or other always seemed to have died; when she wasn't going to parties, my mother was always commiserating on the phone or writing condolence notes. In her persecuted penmanship she crossed them out and scrawled them again with her smelly blue fountain pen—no modern American ballpoints for her. (In grade school, I was always hesitant to ask her to write me an absence slip because the ink in those pens smelled like used dental floss.) Her condolence notes littered my childhood. On the back of a report card was the rough copy of one. On the soft covers of my children's books were the indentations of another. "Giselle, dear, I was saddened to learn . . ."

It was too much for me. When she sat next to me at the dinner table and then got up to answer the phone, I'd push her chair a few inches away. When she offered me a taste of her endive salad, I was careful not to let my tongue touch her fork. And when she kissed me I'd be quick to wipe the strawberry sourness away. I was repelled by her tears and would slam my door against the sounds of her sobbing that seemed to rekindle itself out of thin air. Wounded by this, she'd retaliate by alternately neglecting me and railing at me, giving me a wide berth until something set her off. "You're impossible!" she'd scream. Later, when I learned a vocabulary with which to defend myself, I'd rage back, "I'm not impossible! I'm *improbable!*" And we'd both back off, snickering. But as a child I didn't know any better than she why I acted as I did or what it would take to heal either of us. Which was why after one raging fight I dreamed she was putting a Band-Aid on my finger. The cut was on my knee, but it was a start.

◆　◆　◆

She was saddened to learn. She was grieved to hear. She was shocked to understand. A second cousin would die and her grief would start up dirgeful and messy and loud. Her wailing had a momentum and a cadence, with periodic seizures like vomiting or worse—it was an unbearably intimate thing to witness, full of excess that made me cringe, but that also fascinated me because she was giving the deceased so much attention. Later, it occurred to me that one of the reasons I married my WASP wife, the boys' mother, was because she cried *silently*. But at the time my mother's weeping embarrassed and scared and excited me and I spent a lot of time thinking about dying and wishing sometimes that I could be dead so someone would pay that much attention to me.

I wasn't a particularly precocious child, but when I was small I'd seen enough of her grief to ask my mother when people cry at death, are they crying because they feel sorry for the deceased because they lost their lives, or are they crying for themselves because they don't have them around anymore?

My mother looked over at me with eyes red from weeping and seemed both proud and alarmed that a child of hers should think such a thought, that the Holocaust had caused someone to ask such a question who wasn't even alive when the Holocaust occurred.

And she couldn't, of course, answer me.

◆ ◆ ◆

No wonder I wiped her kisses off. She flavored her cakes, she scented the bedrooms with her tears. I was resentful of the shine of blue under her eyes, of the damp running down her indomitable nose, rolling off and being absorbed and rolling off some more, her face hard and soft at the same time, like the face of an ancient and infinitely subtle sea animal.

"Thank you," my mother would say in a high squeaky voice that made me love her. Every now and then, as I grew older, I still glimpsed a woman cupping a candle in a Vermeer painting, or stepping across the surface of a Greek vase, and had the fleeting thought—ah, there is my mother—before the thought slid away again. But she had told me tales that made my armpits ache, that made my heart sore inside my throat. My mother was the war. When I wiped away her kisses, I was wiping away carnage. I was wiping away the crying of children under the bleating of machine guns, the mischief of blood-lust and the flirtatiousness of death.

So yes, I may have dreamt that she was putting a Band-Aid on me. But it'd be years before I had it in me to dream what it was my destiny to dream: that I was putting one on her.

8

THE SHOULDERS SPEAK

*T*he cuffs on my shirt are hardly dry from the wine stains when we ascend from the Brussels metro in an updraft of cellophane cigarette wrappers. J. P.'s neighborhood feels like a different country from Shasha's. Arabic lettering festoons the tobacco shops. Arabic music wafts from falafel stands. An old Arab with leathery skin holds his cigarette with four fingers while unfolding flower-colored rugs on the street. Shops hawk incongruous combinations: clocks and sneakers, grapefruits and Firestone tires. Even this main thoroughfare is so teeming with idle men that it has the flavor of an alley.

But around the corner the side streets are even smaller. Here it's not Arab but black enough to be the Belgian Congo. Instead of the little dachshunds of Shasha's elegant neighborhood, the sinister face of a Doberman snarls out of one doorway. Double-parked so as to block the street, an antique VW bus exhales a great plume of blue smoke before stalling out, and two Africans, their skin as luminously purple as eggplants, slide out from beneath it on a dolly, licking lemon Popsicles.

A slinky black woman with beautiful skinny arms is leaning on her elbows out a first-floor window, smoking a Turkish cigarette and watching us. We come closer to her, go past, back up, and finally ask, "Do you know where there's an old man who's lived here since World War Two?"

An expulsion of Turkish smoke. "World War *quoi?*"

"The Second World War. Y'know, Hitler, Auschwitz, six million . . . ?"

Flick of the ash: She never heard of any of it.

"Do you know where number Fifty-two is?"

"Chez moi. The Restaurant Ubundu."

J. P.'s building now houses an African restaurant on the first floor, a little cave of a private eating club from Zaire. The proprietress's name is Maudeek and she lets the boys peek in her window. The sole customer, an Idi Amin–sized man in a sheeny gray suit, seems amused by the boys' faces in the window, sitting there flossing his teeth with a frozen silent grin. It's dark and cool; Coltrane is playing quietly and the mood is one of alert languor—a place of shade out of the African sun.

Unhurriedly, Maudeek moves to buzz us in the front door. We walk through the lobby, the boys' sneakers squeaking across the tiles the way they always seem to do in Europe, as though all the Continent is one giant stone church and we are rubberized Americans. Closing the rickety gate of the tiny elevator, we start to go up when Maudeek shouts through the lobby: "Keep your hands inside, a child lost her arm last week!"

On the fourth-floor landing, we knock. Standing outside J. P.'s door, even the air seems to vibrate to a cultural rhythm different from the street scene below. The cool torpor of the Restaurant Ubundu is gone; the hall is a heated, intense space, thick with mental busywork from the resident within. I don't know how I sense this; maybe it's the crazed paint on the door, a complexity of tiny cracks and cross-hatching. The reek of boiled socks hangs in the air.

I clear my throat nervously. It echoes down the line from Alex to Marshall. The locks clank open. And as usual, it's the shoulders that speak to me first. *Nu?* they say, half hoisted, suspicious but ready to deal. *What menace is here now?*

I introduce the three of us, prompting J. P. to cock his shoulders belligerently. *Nothing doing!* they say, moving to nudge the door shut in our faces.

"Wait!"

Not giving an inch in the doorway, J. P. squints at me through eyes that are half closed but as alert as those of any small hunted animal in the forest. This was the radical? The diamond-smuggling athlete? The Casanova skirt-chaser whose charm could knock a bird out of the sky? He's dressed in polyester brown leisure pants with a deep permanent crease running down the middle to the orange socks that he wears with no shoes. His fly is half open. A bit of cottage cheese trembles on his upper lip. His chin is sweating from the exertion of eating; that we've interrupted his lunch is apparent from the fork in his hand that has harpooned several strands of egg noodles and is dripping butter to the linoleum floor as he fidgets.

"Have we caught you at a bad time?" I ask. "Maudeek downstairs was kind enough to buzz us in. . . ."

But before I get her name out, I realize my mistake. Maudeek? He has no more truck with Maudeek and her Zairian eating club than she has with him and some ancient event called World War Quoi. "Should we come back later?"

J. P.'s shoulders are noncommittal, neither hostile nor inquisitive, merely tilted slightly as though weighing the odds: whether to flee or finish shutting the door against us. *Who wants to know?* is what the shoulders are saying.

I address this question as directly as if it had been spoken aloud. "We're family from America," I explain. "We got your address from Shasha and we'd like to ask some questions about how you managed to survive the war."

"How you didn't die like a sheep!" puts in Marshall.

Startled, J. P. focuses his attention on the boys with half-closed eyes. It seems to pain him to take in their presence. J. P. remembers the fork he's holding aloft, and surmounts the saliva in his mouth to speak out loud for the first time. "I don't want my banquet to get cold here so I am keeping on eating," he apologizes in a voice that's surprisingly fine for such a rough figure.

"May we come in?"

Impatiently, the shoulders say: *Of course, what are you waiting for?* Obsequiously, they say: *Sure, why not, let me get out of your way.* Defiantly, they say: *If you think I'm gonna give you squat, you got another think coming.*

Still, they give way.

Inside, we case the joint while our eyes adjust. As we'd been warned, the one-room apartment is poorly lit because he's a cheapskate who doesn't believe in wasting electricity during daylight hours. Even in the gloom, however, it's apparent that my mother's second cousin doesn't subscribe to the same school of interior design as my great-uncles do. Not for him the shelves lined floor to ceiling with leather-spined classics, the oak-paneled walls plastered with abstract oils. No. For him a swimsuit calendar is plenty, with a round tag glued on the front: *"Réduction de cinquante pourcent!"*—apparently it's one of J. P.'s ploys to save four dollars by waiting till March to buy. A clunky black rotary dial phone, circa 1938—all models since the war deemed too extravagant. A 1940s-model typewriter on which he pecks out his shopping lists the old-fashioned way, with *t*'s that don't quite line up with *z*'s, with *b*'s and *q*'s whose cavities are shaded. A space heater hooked up in front of wallpaper the shade of grandfathers' pajamas. Only thirty seconds into the apartment and our main impression is one of dire and irremediable miserliness: threadbare Persian rug, grimy gray windows, a film of profound and defiant parsimony over all.

But—blink!—everywhere there are diamonds. Little heaps of them in the maw of a green cast-iron safe squatting in the fireplace. Tiny mounds of them in the pan of an antique balance scale propped on the radiator. From soft crinkly paper pouches on every available surface spill forth cascades of diamonds sparkling carelessly in the dim light, glittering on the place mats like puddles of desiccated fire. In the middle of all this dinginess such dazzle, like an oyster producing hundreds of pearls.

Without a word, J. P. scuttles back to his chair with small shuffling steps as though he's placed newspaper pages on the floor and is stepping them forward in order to soak up a dog's piddle. He hunches before a mini TV propped on two telephone books in the middle of a card table. On *Oprah,* Arnold Schwarzenegger is playing drums, quite atrociously, pursing his lips and closing his eyes with concentration. The volume is turned down low, another money-saving measure, no doubt; J. P. likely figures it uses less electricity to have the sound so he can barely hear it. From a distance of six inches he studies its screen like the Talmud, sitting with tufts of white chest hair poking through the buttonholes of his undershirt while he resumes slurping his egg noodles a little nervously. And this nervousness is the only concession he makes to our presence. No invitation to sit down or join him in his meal taking. Yet I am not put out. I find J. P. both more schnooky and more powerful than I imagined. He radiates energy, and it's a rascally energy besides. I'm charmed. He's not good-looking, surely some of his women must have admitted he looked a little like a bullfrog with dandruff, but there's no discounting the allure, irascible but fascinating, with eyes that are in equal parts shrewd and soulful so that when you think you're going to fall for the latter, the former keeps you on guard. Yes, I can see how he could seduce the wife of a Gestapo commandant. In his own schleppy, skinflint way, he's mesmerizing.

Standing there in the flickering TV dusk, the boys and I raise our eyebrows to each other. And as usual, it's the seven-year-old who gets the ball rolling. "Did you really shoot yourself in the foot?"

"Oh, that's a whole kettle of fish!" J. P. mutters wearily, reaching for a freebie ketchup packet from McDonald's and squirting it into his noodles. His English uses only obsolete idioms and imbues them with a Yiddish flavor. "Kettle" comes out "kyeddle," like some sort of whole grain Passover dish.

I cut to the chase. "Do you ever speak of your experiences during the war?"

He sighs through his nose, making a chirping noise, and stirs the mishmash in his bowl before slurping it into his mouth. Clearly he'd rather relish his disgusting meal of pasta and ketchup than attend to us, and he gloomily watches Schwarzenegger laugh with Oprah, slapping his lips together as he chews.

Just as I look away to consider my options, he jabs me with a gnarly Old Testament finger—ouch! in the ribs!—and speaks.

"You can ask about Germany."

I'm startled. Is he really giving us permission to question him? "Germany?"

Still watching the TV he says: "Did you know more Jews died defending Germany in World War One than all Israelis have died in Middle Eastern wars to date? Did you know this? It is an historical fact. *That* many Jews were patriots to Germany. And still Mr. Hitler said we were traitors."

"I didn't know this," I say carefully.

"It is an historical fact."

He fidgets with the antenna, his lips working even after his words have stopped. And pokes me again.

"You can ask about France."

I'm getting the hang of it. "OK, France," I say.

"No other country cooperated with the Nazis the way France did. Not only did they write their own anti-Semitic legislation, they also provided French police to deport Jews from the south of France. Eighty percent of the French were on the side of Nazis during the war, then eighty percent claimed they were in the Resistance afterwards."

With his teeth he tears open a packet of sweet and sour sauce from KFC and drizzles that, too, over his noodles. "This is not strictly facts, it is some facts and some opinion thrown in free of charge," he concludes.

"Well, the French," I chime in, "you know what Saul Bellow says about the French, don't you? 'They are so wonderful, they are so disagreeable.'"

Oops. It's clearly not my place to express an opinion. This is *his* apartment! I'm using up all the talk! Fortunately he forgives me as he gnaws the inside of a cream cheese packet from Dunkin' Donuts. "You can ask about America."

So this is the secret to warming him up: let him take the ball and run with it. In electrical engineering they talk of a certain kind of oscillator being self-exciting—it makes itself go. So it seems certain Jews are self-exciters. "Shoot," I say judiciously.

"Two times American bombers flew over Auschwitz on their way to bomb targets five miles away and they couldn't spare a single bomb to close it down," he says. "In nineteen forty-two your media was carrying stories that two million had already been killed, and did FDR lift a finger? Even though ninety percent of American Jews voted for him. But your State Department was such a bunch of anti-Semites they turned away a boatload of Jews off the coast of Florida, they could see already the bathing beauties on the beach!"

"But of course there's no forgetting," I point out, "it was America who won the—"

"And now look," he says, pointing his middle finger to Schwarzenegger on TV. "Who is now your superhero? A Nazi!"

"Well, that's not quite fair," I say.

"So who is wanting to be fair?" he posits, with a look of mischief on his face. This is indignant mischief, I see, deep-grained impishness that hankers for nothing so much as a good fight, and it finds its truest expression in his shoulders, suspended long enough for me to read the addendum: *The world is so fair to me I have to be fair back?* And with that, he plunks the noodles in his mouth and chews happily, his lips not touching.

"So," says Alex, "you hate America?"

"I love America!" J. P. replies at once. "I hate nothing! People are only people doing the best they can—in Germany and France, too—and if they screw up all the time, like clockwork round the clock, this is merely the way we are made, God help us."

This declaration seems to fire him up anew, and now he takes a sudden shine to the boys, springing from the table and spreading his arms wide. "Hug! Hug!" he cries with his eyes closed. And what follows is one of the most astonishing sights of my life: this virtual stranger J. P., this mythic tightwad with his open fly and halo of dandruff, clutching my sons in a ferocious hug and exclaiming in a hiss: "I lost both my babies in the war!"

And so I understand at last. It hurts him to witness the health of my two sons. From the time we arrived at his door, he would have liked nothing more than to squeeze the stuffing out of them, but it would have pained him too much to feel their life.

In his bear hug, his glasses have slipped down his damp little nose, exposing his round blue eyes. "Strong boys! Strong!" he says, pulling himself away with an effort and popping his biceps in the boys' faces for them to squeeze. "I also am strong! Feel here!"

"Wow!" say the boys—and they wouldn't say it if they didn't mean it.

His arms are as sinewy as they are freckled. "Feel *here!*" he is saying now, inviting them to finger his gluts, his delts, his abs. "Not feel like a piece of glass, *punch!*" he says, and each boy delights in hauling back and punching this eighty-eight-year-old man in his gut. And now I see what I didn't before—that beneath J. P.'s reserve he's buoyantly, irrepressibly cheerful. It takes a cheerful man to live through what he's lived through: a sourpuss wouldn't have made it.

"OK, that's enough," I tell the boys, but am immediately overruled by all three.

"No, it's good!" J. P. says, for he's in his element. Why shouldn't he enjoy? These are his *kindelich* relatives and he's showing off. I get the feeling J. P. could survive any environment you threw him in. Hard-boiled American kids? No problem. Hong Kong terrorists? Not to sweat. The man is *wired*. If he were tossed in with cannibals, he'd come out king because no one would want his scrawny tough meat, while he'd eat every-body. White, black, Jewish, gentile—he'd be an equal opportunity cannibal. *Why* is he so strong? Simple, he tells the boys: he works out three times a week at the Yimcha.

"What's the Yimcha?" Alex asks, panting from the exertion of belting the old man, who is merely beaming.

"The Yimcha! Everyone knows the Yimcha. It's an American club *mit* branches."

"*Mit* branches?"

"All over the world. Different clubs you can go in sometimes downtown, sometimes the suburbs." He appears an inch before my nose to direct his ire at me. Breath, spittle, sinew: he was *born* to be in your face! "What kind of American father are you, you don't take your boys to the Yimcha?"

Dutifully, I furrow my brows. "The Yimcha," I say with caution. "How do you spell it?"

"Sure: Y. M. C. A."

And now, regarding me with his hooded glittering eyes so that he registers me for the first time, he pounces to sweep a moldering cardboard box to the side of the table with his bare forearm and gestures us to join him. "Come! Sit! Sit!"

As *Hogan's Heroes* comes on ("the most popular show in Germany today," he informs us), J. P. pivots to produce three bowls from a cupboard behind him and an enormous pot he's been hoarding out of sight till now. "You hungry want eat? Noodles and ketchup, delicious. I was going to freeze the rest but you can have?"

Noodles and ketchup? I don't think so. But Marshall is game

as always and in no time has dug in to his elbows, squirting packages of ketchup on his noodles and talking with his mouth full. "Dad, you ought to try it. It's great!"

J. P. beams at him. He's made a convert. He touches Marshall on the wrist. "You can ask about diamonds."

Even in the caloric upheaval he's undergoing, the seven-year-old is always open to his main chance. "Are they free to the family?"

J. P. winks at me. "A shrewd businessman," he says approvingly.

Marshall is dead serious. "Well, are they?" he pursues.

J. P. sidesteps the question. "These are nothing, tiddlywinks only. Better you ask: Why are Jews in diamonds in the first place?"

"I don't know. Why?" asks Marshall.

J. P. swipes at the sweat running down his sideburns, happy to divulge himself. "OK, I shall tell you. A diamond is not just a diamond. This is the first thing to understand. A diamond is a loaf of bread. For if you have a diamond you can buy a loaf of bread in a concentration camp. A diamond is also false papers, for if you have a lot of them you can buy papers to Spain, to Portugal, to freedom. Why do Jews put all their fortune in buying a diamond instead of for instance a grand piano? Because a grand piano you can't sew into your pocket and run through a sewer pipe to freedom," he says with a sly wink, patting his pocket. "So now you know something about diamonds you didn't know before, eh?" he says, and pinches Marshall's cheek.

Never before having been pinched on his cheek, Marshall thinks this is a game. He reaches out and pinches J. P.'s cheek back.

"Good, little one!" J. P. says. "Good spirit."

"But why do you always point with your middle finger?" Marshall asks.

"Oh, man!" says Alex, rolling his eyes.

J. P. isn't offended. "Why? Because I am old! When you are old, you too will point your middle finger."

"You smell like salami," Marshall notes.

"Marshall!" Alex says, but J. P. only gestures for Marshall to lean closer, as he delivers his reply in a stage whisper. "This also is because I am old. You want to know how we get so old? You just hold in there, and *plufff!* you're old!"

With a grimace, he pulls a tiny diamond out of Marshall's ear and puts it back on the place mat.

Marshall's eyes gleam.

J. P. pokes Alex in the rib cage. "You can ask about the Resistance."

"Okeydoke," Alex obliges. "Tell about the Resistance."

"We had the best Resistance in Europe, right here in Belgium," he says proudly. "Me, I was only a tiddlywink in the Resistance. My brother Schloime in Antwerp, *he* was the big shot!"

With another sleight of hand he produces a pair of old battle headphones from out of the moldering cardboard box. Also part of an old parachute, remnants of food rations, machine gun casings. He's living here in a kind of museum of war curios, playing soldier with artifacts from the underground. And off he goes again.

"My brother distributed an underground newspaper, he and two girls delivered it on foot every night. One time he was approached by Germans and he starts kissing both girls, and the Germans don't bother them. It was very good for him to be in the Resistance, always a chance to be *mit* girls."

"Did he French them?" Marshall asks.

"What is?" inquires J. P., his face big and round next to Marshall's.

"Of course he didn't French!" Alex snarls. "This was in Belgium!"

While I'm plotting how to rescue J. P. from this blizzardy conversation, I get another jab! in the ribs. Clutch! Grope! Grip! Grab! Every gesture he makes hurts.

"You can ask about concentration camps in France."

"In France?" I say. "You mean the ones in Poland, right? I never heard of a concentration camp in France."

"Sure in France. Sometimes they called them detention or transit camps, holding everyone till they went to Auschwitz. 'The little hell before the big hell,' they called them."

I look skeptical, which seems to put J. P. on a playful track.

"It wasn't so bad, really, we had a doctor who would carry an aspirin on a string. And if you were very sick, you would fold your hands behind your back and lick it once."

"Why'd you have to fold your hands?"

"So we wouldn't grab the aspirin and run away. Not that we'd get very far, but."

"What if you were dying?" Marshall asks.

"Oh, well this was a different matter. Then you get to lick it twice!"

The boys look at me for verification. I raise my eyebrows: *Don't ask me . . .*

"We had one bucket for eating," J. P. goes on, "and for crapping."

The boys pursue him without tittering. "You mean . . . the same bucket? How'd you wash it?"

"Ho-ho!" he says. "We didn't!" With the precision of small distances shared by all diamond cutters, he adjusts his dinner bowl half an inch and gestures again toward the box. "We had only one layer of clothes. We stuffed paper inside to keep us warm. No heat to sleep, no pillows. Only one blanket, *voilà*."

Flashing his palm to show there's nothing in his hand, nothing up his sleeve, he reaches into the box and withdraws a piece of blanket for us to feel. The touch is rougher than a horse blanket; it would rub like a hair shirt next to your skin. But we have only an instant to take this in before J. P. steers the conversation in a new direction. "Why did we hide and keep going, this is a good question to ask," he says.

OK, fine, I allow as how it's a good question.

"Oy, is that a good question to ask," he says. "Not because we thought we could get away, I'll tell you that. Not even because we wanted to, after a while, we were so heartsick. But we hide because we didn't want to give him the satisfaction, Mr. Hitler. We hide because it was the only thing we can do to say to him, fuck you, Mr. Hitler."

He points a tapered Old Testament finger to us, the nail as yellow as old glue, to show that he uses the curse with care. "You can ask why I call him *Mister* Hitler and I'll tell you why. Because it should not be forgotten he was a man. Calling him 'Hitler' sounds like 'Frankenstein,' ya? But he was not a monster. Thinking that is letting the human species off the hook."

"How'd you smuggle diamonds in knife stems and chocolates, that's what I don't get," asks Alex.

"You don't *get* because you don't *eat*," J. P. says, ladling Alex up with noodles. Hovering over both boys' plates now, making additions and subtractions as he tastes, he produces patties of fast-food butter and packets of mayo. Only fifteen minutes ago he wouldn't let us in the door.

"Dad, he's right, it *is* good," Alex informs me after one bite. "You don't know what you're missing."

But J. P. is placing gnarled rugged fingers to the roof of his mouth, now, and tugging. "Even in my mouth I smuggle," he says, popping off his front tooth. With a lisping gap in the front of his smirk he drops the tooth into my hand and points to the space inside it. Sure enough, big enough for a diamond.

"Always I was using something like Chapstick to stick it back on," he says, snatching the tooth back and wiggling it into place.

"They had Chapstick in those days?" Alex asks.

"And corn flakes and Chrysler cars, too! You think this is ancient Greece we're talking about?"

The boys have a million questions. "How long did you hide under the bed? Why did you play billiards with the Gestapo? When did you last speak to your son in Paris?"

J. P. puts up his hand like a traffic cop in the flickering light. "To answer all your questions would take as long as the war," he says. "Enough to say I was not only a diamond dealer. I was also a *mahar*, you know what is? A go-between, a finagler, someone who figures all the angles."

"An operator," I offer.

"Sure, sure," he nods, bored by my word. They have a technique for rendering you superfluous, these survivors. When they're struggling to verbalize a concept and you come up with the perfect way to do it, they turn dismissive on you. "Sure, a *mahar*! Someone who gets you bleacher seats to the Yankees when the Red Sox are playing!"

"Like a scalper," Alex offers.

His eyebrows bob flirtatiously. "A little bit scalper, a little bit barber, and I throw in a foot massage, too, free of charge. What's it gonna hurt? They used to say, during the war, that for every Jew the Nazis catched, another *mahar* was born. God help me, if that's the way Mr. Hitler was going to play it, I was going to become a *mahar*. And I did too! I was a *mahar* supreme, a *mahar* par excellence, I was the best goddamn *mahar* . . ."

Here J. P. sparks a fugue of self-congratulation so lavish we have to turn away. The spittle is flying as fast as he can foam it forth. I look over at my boys, who smile and shrug their shoulders as if to say, *Sure, let him go on, he's having a good time, what could it hurt?*

I try to bring him back on track. "Your Jewish star, what did you do with that?" I ask, noticing that I'm mixing up the syntax, Jewish style.

Closing his eyes, J. P. takes off his glasses and folds them in his hand, no doubt to preserve their focus. "It was the first way we disobeyed!" he says. "If you wore a star like the Germans told you to, you had no chance. If you put your star in your pocket, you had not much of a chance, but some." Fondly he pats his pocket, a place that apparently came in handy during the war. "Mine is the story of those Jews who did not do what the Germans told them to do," he explains. "Who put their stars in their pockets and vamoose!"

◆ ◆ ◆

And like quicksilver it's time to turn the tables. Enough with our questions, already. He has questions of his own. "So you are here to make a conquest of my hiding places," he says.

I'm surprised how fast it's been leaked to him. "How do you know this?"

He waves the air, a hand near his ear. "I know, I sense. On many matters I am an expert. Not only history, also psychology, parapsychology, popular mechanics, did I say this? Sure, it's a fact."

"We want very much to find your hiding places," I say. "Not making a conquest but a *quest*, I guess, if anything. Have you gone back to see what's become of them?"

He chuckles, not an altogether pleasant sound. "Why would I go to see them? I am happy right here"—he gestures with a sly glance to his apartment, to his secondhand toaster with the dial turned to extra light (pennies add up!)—"in my castle."

"Do you think they're still there? The hiding places?"

He raises his shoulders. Translation: *Who knows? If you can find them they're still there.* "Besides," he says aloud, *"this* is a hiding place."

"In what sense?"

He snorts at my obtuseness. "The physical sense, what else!"

Seeing my confusion, he elaborates. "Not for me, myself. But for my cousin Yudl, your great uncle. He lived here an entire winter, in that chimney there."

The boys are bug-eyed. "This is the chimney where Yudl hid?"

"The very one."

It's like meeting a movie star. Shyly I touch the mantel, the gray-painted brick, making its acquaintance.

"Sure. And that's the window he wiggled out."

"Yudl wiggled?! Out a window!?"

"When the Gestapo comes, you wiggle."

Lifting up the dusty Venetian blinds, Marshall peeks out the window. "But there's no fire escape. . . ."

"A drainpipe, yes?"

"Kind of," Marshall says. "But it's so shaky, the hinges are no good."

"It was either that or Auschwitz."

Leaning out the window, Marshall rattles the copper drainpipe to test its reliability, while Alex peers down four floors to the street below and whistles with new respect. I meanwhile feel that the wind has been knocked out of all the Passover jokes I ever made at Yudl's expense. Maybe he *could* windsurf. . . .

"So tell me," he resumes, grimacing and swiping his mouth, failing to get the bit of cottage cheese. "You are an anti-Semite?"

"No," I say, shifting in my seat uncomfortably. "At least, what do you mean? Would I be taking this trip if I were?"

"How do I know *mit*-out I ask?" he says.

Still surprised at the way this conversation has turned, I say: "I mean, I have problems with Jews like anyone else. . . ."

"You are a recovering anti-Semite, then?"

"You mean, like an anti-Semite in remission?" I say with a smile, but he's sternly taking the measure of me. "No. I want to take this trip to find out what happened to our people. . . ."

"And you are confident you can do this?"

"I'm the opposite of confident," I confess. "I'm in awe of this material. I pray for the clarity to do it justice."

He chirps through his nose, appraising. "Answer me this," he continues. "Your wife, she was a nice person?"

"She still is," I reply. "Just because she left doesn't put her in the past tense."

But he's waving away my words like so much bad air. What, I think life lasts forever that I should go on yapping so? We have important business to discuss!

"These beautiful children," he asks. "You have been gypped of them? Robbed of your family?"

The kids blink at me, wondering how I'm going to field this one.

"In some ways," I admit. "But in others, I've been able to cherish them more than I would otherwise. They're a gift I prize more profoundly."

J. P. grunts assent. This also he understands. "Answer me this," he continues. "You have girlfriends?"

"Sure."

"You expose these children to your girlfriends?"

"Sometimes I introduce them, you bet. This is the twentieth century."

If this is an impertinent thing for me to say, it seems only to enliven J. P. In fact, the subject seems to be one dear to his heart. He clumps his shoulders forward, the equivalent of a chuckle, and puts his glasses back on.

"I also am boinking the womens," he declares.

"Come again?" I ask, hoping I heard him wrong. The boys register disbelief and start to muzzle laughter into their hands.

"You know what I am boinking last year?" J. P. says, turning to the boys and slapping his thigh as though he still can't believe his good fortune. "A Christian Scientist! Sure! And the year before that, a cashier for a health food stores! Even in the war I am boinking the womens!" he tells the boys as he pats his pants pocket, the site of his favorite adventures.

He's demented, I decide, as he stares smiling at us, the light from the mini TV glinting off his glasses. But the boys are eating it up with a spoon. They love the male camaraderie, even if they're not certain of the technical end of things. J. P. giggles with them, his big magnified eyes glittering with perspiration.

"Eat! Eat!" he tells me. And such is my state of astonishment that I do. How do you like that: noodles and ketchup aren't bad, I decide. I'm laughing but I'm also wincing a bit. J. P. picks up on it.

"I see you are shocked," he says. "Even as you laugh you are thinking, sex in the Holocaust? This is not supposed to be said in the same breath, sex and Holocaust. Well, this is too bad. I am sorry to disturb you. You have a delicate constitution. But you came here to ask me and so I will tell you—"

"Yes?"

"You have the wrong idea."

"Excuse me?"

"About the Holocaust. The wrong idea! The wrong idea!"

"I'm sorry. What do you mean?"

He slams his palm down on the table suddenly, making the diamonds jounce, and fixes me with a fierce twinkling eye to burn this thought into our brains.

"Where did you get the idea that the Holocaust was a Disney movie?" he demands. "For everybody to cry boo-hoo and then everybody to feel better? Why do you think of it like a holy experience, so everyone has a nice cry and then blows their nose and forgets about it! That's why maybe," he says, and here he grips my knee with iron fingers, hucking up an angry wad of phlegm from the base of his tonsils—*hawk! hawk!*—"maybe you should go home! Maybe you should forget the whole business unless you can stop *mit* the boo-hoo—"

"Stop *mit* the—?"

"Stop *mit* the boo-hoo and talk about the *real* Holocaust, not the holy Holocaust but the one full of love and sex and passion because that's what it was! And hope and desire, too! Do you know in the refugee camps after the war, there was the highest birth rate in the world! It's a fact! Survival is not for sissies!"

◆　◆　◆

Silence in the dark apartment. We're quiet, the diamonds are quiet, even Colonel Klink on the TV is quiet. Only J. P.'s breathing is audible. But you can hear every verb in his breath. It's extravagant wrathful breathing, laden with pious obscenities that blue the air. The breathing of an Old Testament prophet who's been wronged.

And still he's got his hand on my knee. There's no release from the iron grip. The gesture is intimate and it hurts.

I'm blown away by his speech. Maybe it's perverted. Maybe it's wise. I don't know anymore whether he's demented or the sanest person I've ever met. All I know is that at this moment I feel confused and unworthy. Maybe the warning at Shasha's was right. It *is* a goose chase. I'm stumbling like a blind man through a room of folding chairs.

And then I look at my two sons staring at me, and I know that what I'm doing is sound. And so with gentleness in my uncertainty I tell J. P. this: I need to do this. I may louse it up, and I may get nowhere, but I'm doing it the best way I can because it's my responsibility to show them how some survived, when six million died. . . .

But at this J. P. looks as if he's been smacked in the face with a dead flower. He straightens up by degrees and slowly unclenches his hand from my knee. And grows an expression I never thought I'd see on his face: shyness.

Almost apologetically he says softly, "Here I have a problem." He studies his fingernails quietly. "Six million . . .

"You see, I don't know from six million," he says. "Six million is for me too big a number. Also a very common number. Both at the same time: too big, and too common. Do you know that the number of cigarettes smoked by teenager smokers each day is six million? Unbelievable, yes? But the scientists tell us so. On an average summer afternoon the number of people playing tennis in America is six million. Also unbelievable? But I read it in the paper. It is not such a big number when you look at it this way. It is not so special. Six million is cigarettes, is tennis players. Only in one way to me is it special. . . ."

And suddenly his face turns red, his eyeballs bulge and turn shiny for an instant, before he blinks twice and tries staring at the TV.

"It is my twin girls."

And an odd thing happens. Because he won't allow his eyes to fill up, *my* eyes fill up. I look over at my preadolescents and their eyes are filling up, too.

Still staring at the TV with his eyes filmy and red, he says in a thick voice: "So this is why I say finally, it is a good thing you are doing. To find my places."

"Yes? You approve?"

"Alex and Marshall, you are detectives?" he asks. "You have a head for clues?"

They nod vehement assent.

"Then help your father, together you shall find." He points his swollen-jointed finger at them, an injunction from the Bible. "So!"

And with that, he slings a book across the table to Marshall.

"What is it?" Marshall says. *"Berlitz Guide to French, Nineteen Thirty-Eight . . ."*

"You can use it maybe to pick up girls," J. P. says. "As for you . . ." he says to Alex, flinging an old leather notebook across the table to him with such violence the pages flutter. "This could maybe help."

"What is it, your journal?" Alex asks.

"Something like."

"Thank you!" I say, taken aback by the big black swastika across its front. "We'll make sure everything gets back to you in good condition."

"It doesn't matter," he says, yanking me to my feet suddenly and nudging me to the door. His shoulders slump. His hands wearily wave us ahead. Opening up to us has drained him. He can't afford to feel any more of what we make him feel.

Even without opening it, I see the journal is crammed with scraps of mail, old phone bills, expired pawnshop vouchers. The pages are scrambled out of order, with little spiderlike scrawls in a watery purple pen. Also a sepia print of two little girls, angelic and mischievous, which J. P. plucks back and puts in his pocket.

"What is, I mean, who are—?"

"Go now. It is enough," he says. He shuffles us toward the door in silence.

"Are those your—?"

With his finger to his lips, he keeps shuffling us forward as his shoulders, heaving softly, say something I'm too rushed to read. "Enough. Stop *mit* the boo-hoo," he says. "Good-bye."

It's only after the door is closed, after we turn in the hall and silently descend in the rickety elevator, that I understand. This the shoulders were saying, softly:

Let me grieve.

9

NOTHING BUT A
HOUND DOG

We settled into kickstand-sounding Connecticut. Ostensibly the location served as something of a halfway point between my parents' families. But given my parents' ambivalence, their mock anti-Semitism and emancipation beyond God, it was perhaps no coincidence that Connecticut was overwhelmingly Christian. We rented a house in a not-great neighborhood for a winter while we looked for a better one. Even at knee level, where my height stationed me, I could tell the neighborhood wasn't well off because the cellar windows had doily curtains. The garage foundations were cinder block instead of brick or stone. The little yards were cement instead of grass. The people, too, were more concrete than what I was used to, with a plainness to the grown-ups and a meanness to the kids, and no pretense to be otherwise. The neighbors were of different nationalities—Polish, Italian, Irish—but being Jewish I was more different from them all. So they had someone to band together against. Plus I was little.

In those days there were bunches of '50s hoods known to us younger children only as "bigkids." The term was synonymous with bullies, but "bullies" seemed too limiting, putting the person who used the term in the role of victim and denying the bully himself the chance to be more than a bully. "Bigkids" allowed more possibilities for them as well as us. In any case, they were powerfully malevolent and we called them bigkids with more reverence and fear than was ever inspired by the benign figure of The Fonz. (Maybe that was because The Fonz on TV's *Happy Days* was played by a Jewish actor, and as such never conveyed the menace that these junior thugs did. To me, bigkids could have been Syrian or German or Crusaders from the Middle Ages, for all the difference it made. They were anything but Jewish.)

One time a bigkid asked me if I wanted to see a match burn twice. I did, and he lit it—that was one—and blew it out and stuck it to my arm—that was two. I was surprised and puzzled. Another time a bigkid told me he had a valuable postage stamp and he'd give it to me if I'd hand over the money from my mother's purse. But I'd seen that same purple three-cent stamp with a Statue of Liberty on my mother's condolence letters and so I politely declined. I could tell he was trying to burn me twice. Another time a group of bigkids told me I could play with them if I ran home and spit on the cornerstone of my house. I wasn't sure what a cornerstone was, but I did it on a stone in the corner of the foundation. The sensation of spitting on my house was a strange one: it felt lewd. When I went back they laughed at me. I was five.

A nasty girl lived next door in a house that seemed to be the source of meanness. The mom was said to beat her with a clothes hanger; the plumber dad was worse. The girl's name was Kimberly, but privately my mother called her Catastrophe and my father called her Calamity. She was always pretending to like me, but it always turned out she didn't. She wore barrettes and I knew she had the potential to stick me with them. One time she told me I'd look nice if she painted my fingernails red. She was wrong. Everyone laughed. I hated her for many weeks. Then it was winter and I had no recollection of ever seeing snow, though I was told I had before I moved to Texas. Kimberly told me that the reason I'd never seen snow was because I was the devil. I don't know if she'd overheard her parents call us Jewish devils, but her calling me that coincided with my learning to pack a snowball. When Kimberly was running past my driveway, I hurled a snowball and it hit one of her legs. I couldn't believe my luck.

Thereafter I prided myself on my aim. It won me respect as a marbles player and kept me from becoming victimized. When a kid in my kindergarten class teased me by calling me Rosey, I threw a wild mulberry right in his open mouth. Hah! So this was a power I could have, but it wasn't reliable because I didn't always have things at hand to throw at my adversaries, so I came up with an even better power. I told Kimberly that she was nearly right about my being the devil. I wasn't the devil himself, I told her; I was the devil's best friend. She pretty much left me alone after that.

These powers made me feel I could do what I needed to do and it would be out there, a done thing. Shortly after I hit Kimberly with a snowball, my mother asked if I was big enough to watch over my sleeping infant sister while she took Renee out for some quick grocery shopping. I said yes but it got longer and then longer turned into later and then it started getting dark. The Mickey Mouse show came on. My back got itchy and I rubbed it against the scratchy plaster. My infant sister woke up and started to wail and I lugged her out of her crib, her knees hitting the sides, and held her in the living room to watch TV with me until she stopped. It got even darker and still my mother wasn't back. Then I heard a noise like thunder outside. I thought maybe it was a distant car accident and my mother had been killed and she'd never come back. Who'd take care of my infant sister then?

I figured out what to do. I propped my sister in the couch and put on my coat and went next door to Kimberly's house. It was dinnertime now and the neighbors had to snap on the porch light to see who was standing there. The mother came to the door and I told her I needed help. She called her husband who had an open newspaper in his hand. He didn't bother hiding how annoyed he was, but still I didn't care. All that mattered was that I was getting him to help whether he liked it or not. I pretended not to hear as he grumbled to himself, and watched him open his closet door and pick out a tan-colored hat with a green feather poking out of it and put it squarely on his head. Then I walked him back to my house where my sister was cooing on the couch and he sat there, smelling of mothballs as he irritably read his newspaper. And so we had protection. After a while my mother came in all worried, explaining about a detour and an ambulance and flares on the roadways, but I wasn't really listening. I surprised myself by not running to her arms in relief. I stayed put. My mother thanked Kimberly's father with some embarrassment, and when he'd gone back to his house she said I'd done the right thing. But I already knew that. Secretly I did an odd thing: I planted a quick kiss on my own shoulder.

A month later my mother was driving us to a doctor's appointment when the car door flew open beside my infant sister in the front seat. This was before there were baby seats or even seat belts, and I jumped up from the backseat and grabbed her and yanked the door shut and my mother said I was a hero. But to me it was easy compared to going next door to the source of meanness. Going next door was something I had to do, and I did it. I'd learned that when you need them to, even mean people have to help. Later, when I read Anne Frank declare that people are basically good, I thought of Kimberly's father putting on his hat to help me even though he didn't want to.

But of course, she wrote that before she got to Bergen-Belsen.

❖   ❖   ❖

We moved to Rowayton. It was better. The yards were lush grass. The walls were smooth instead of scratchy. It had real-life heroes and villains (Art Chace, the beach lifeguard; Mrs. Wilson, the strictest teacher in school), as well as fairy-tale figures—with a store-bought telescope, I could spy on a genuine castle across the street with spooks inside who went by the fantasy name of Heart. I could go bird-watching, getting up at five in the morning and wearing a hooded sweatshirt that was the same red as the cardinals I hoped to spy on. But I had trouble camouflaging myself from a new set of bigkids who seemed to congregate on McKinley Street, named in honor of the assassinated Republican president. Overhung by dark draping hickory trees, it was the street where you had to be most on guard.

One evening I was riding my bike, Tommy, home from Hummiston's drugstore along McKinley Street. It was about five on a darkening December afternoon, and people's Christmas lights were blinking blue and red against the black foliage of trees and shrubbery. On a not-far-away hill I could see my neighbor's giant blue star, which hung from their chimney from November to March. Every now and then a car passed with a costumed classmate of mine being bundled off to some pageant or other. The afternoon smelled from the burning piles of fluffy leaves on the side of the road, smoldering thickets of ash with dozens of sleepy red eyes glinting through. The tar was warm beneath the ashes and I pedaled through the piles in a leisurely fashion, leaving a swerving DNA ribbon of gray-white ash in the heat-softened tar.

Suddenly, I saw two knots of bigkids up ahead, walking toward me on both sides of the street, and I knew I'd have no choice but to ride past them. This was always a dicey proposition. You never knew when they might throw a firecracker at you or push you off your bike. It didn't take more than one time to learn to avoid clumps of bigkids the way a cat learns to avoid a dog.

I could always turn around, of course, and pedal back to Hummiston's, but they'd already spotted me; turning around would incur their scorn. If I showed I was scared, an ordinary impersonal razzing might grow into something specific. They'd know I was vulnerable and would get me worse next time. Already we were within showdown distance. Where could I hide?

Easy as pie, as if I'd been planning it all along, I glided into the driveway of a total stranger whose mailbox read "Lawless," parked my bike, trotted briskly up the porch steps, and rang the bell.

There was a cocktail party going on inside. People in bright clothes were swirling with some hilarity behind the fancy windows. After the sucking sound of a solid door being pulled away from a storm door, a cheery man in a red cashmere sweater faced me with an interested smile.

"Hi," I said. "I just wanted to tell you how nice your Christmas lights are. On your big pine tree out there? And I wondered where you got them."

"Well, isn't this nice," Mr. Lawless said. He put an arm around my shoulder and welcomed me inside, where it smelled good and familiar: rum and wood smoke. More lights twinkled in here, and guests were turning their attention to me even before the man spoke again.

"Isn't this nice," he said, more loudly for the benefit of the guests. "This young fella just stopped in to tell us how nice our Christmas lights are. Isn't that a thoughtful thing to do! Take off your gloves, son, and stay a while!"

"It's a nice big tree out in your yard," I amplified, for the benefit of the others.

The consensus was that this was an even nicer thing to say than the first thing I'd said. Several women were kneeling around me now, stroking my hair and clucking. I felt like Tiny Tim, a waif in from the cold.

"Where'd we get those lights, Jeannie?" Mr. Lawless asked his wife.

"No place special," Jeannie said. She had quilted oven mitts on and was negotiating a pie in a glass dish across the crowded room to a table already laden with food. She flashed me a look that made me worry she was on to me. But then she smiled and said, "Ask him if he'd like a piece of pie, why don't you?"

"Why, how'd that be! C'mon, take your coat off!" Mr. Lawless said, and several women began plucking at my collar. But I shrugged politely out of their grasp, glancing through the panes of the front door to see that both clumps of bigkids had passed by. The coast was clear.

"I have to go now," I blurted, turning to leave. "Thanks again for those nice lights!"

It was the shortest hiding place I ever had, but it worked fine.

❖ ❖ ❖

It seemed like there were a lot of bigkids to hide from in Rowayton but it mostly boiled down to one ringleader, the second of five sons, Manny, who was a bigkid par excellence. Odd that his name was only one letter away from my name, which should have made for neighborliness, yet I was the person he loved to pick on most. He sensed something in me, a tenderness, maybe, that stirred his blood. He was ferocious, wearing flannel shirts with some of the buttonholes ripped wide open from fighting. His front bangs fell down into eyes that glinted with malice. The tongue of his belt always hung down and swung menacingly when he ran. And I was always running away from him. One time I was playing marbles and he emerged from some shrubbery—he always seemed to just leap out from between rhododendrons—and he snatched up my marble and flung it down so hard that it sank several inches into the earth. I've seen many acts of strength in my life since that time, but none that impressed and frightened me more than that.

Another time I went to Manny's house for a birthday party for his younger brother, who was my age, and Manny came to the door, snapping the dirty doormat in my face to shoo me away and singing, "You ain't nothing but a hound dog" until I ran home crying. I knew what a hound dog was.

Manny tormented me in ways that were ingenious in their

cruelty. One time I was playing catch with some friends when he sprang from the shrubbery and said, "Hey, Danny, catch!" and threw a high fly ball. I was flattered that he was playing with me and I got right under it, but when I caught it I discovered it was a rotten orange that splattered my face and stained my beloved baseball mitt, Ted. He started to chase me and I jumped on my bike and blasted off. When I got to the rock ledge above my house I darted inside where I could hear the shameful sound of Manny and his brothers pelting rocks onto the roof of my house. What dishonor, to have the house where I lived with my sisters and parents pelted with rocks. Half an hour later, when it was safe, I skulked out and found an even worse sight: they had tied up my bike, my holy bike Tommy, wound rope through its spokes and weighted it with rocks so that it looked like it'd been tortured. "I'm sorry, Tommy, I'm sorry," I kept crying as I unwound the ropes.

◆ ◆ ◆

Manny must have been a sensitive bully to know my weak spots so well. He was certainly sensitive the day I decided not to run from him anymore. It happened toward the end of my sixth year. I was playing baseball at dusk one November afternoon when he lunged from the shrubbery. My heart lurched. I turned to check my escape route and gauge how many seconds I had to make my getaway. Then something clicked inside me, and suddenly I'd had enough. The hell with it, I decided. I turned back to face him.

Manny recognized it at once. His face lit into a congratulatory smile. "Way to go, Danny," he said, clapping me on the back and putting his flannel arm around my shoulder. "You didn't run."

I'd held my ground. As word spread magically like a signal between wild animals, Manny and the rest of the bigkids suddenly respected me enough to keep their distance. My father came into my bedroom the morning of my seventh birthday and said, "You can hear how much bigger seven is than six. Just listen to the sound: six. Sounds short, doesn't it? Now listen to this: *sevennnn.*"

The world began to shift. One afternoon I spied an amazing thing: two bigkids jumped over our garden running from some cops, and one turned to the other and said, "Watch out for the flowers." In a flash I was racing my bicycle to my mother's art gallery to tell her an amazing discovery, that those rough-and-tumble guys cared about chrysanthemums! Moreover, I had discovered books and was reading like mad, but still not as much (it helped keep things in perspective) as a freckly red-haired kid across the street named McDougal, who was reputed to read after lights out by the flare of the fireflies he captured in glass jars every night. I started to compose stories on a Remington Rand portable typewriter my mother lent me. Even better, I made the best team of the Little League, with blue-and-white pinstriped uniforms resembling the Yankees'. Despite the fact that I was barely a rank above bat boy, I could relate on a more or less equal plane to the bigkids on the team who'd been absorbed into the corporatelike culture of Little League and so had been defanged, as it were, *wanting* to behave. The team photo shows me grave and intense in the front row, the second-smallest kid and the only one wearing a dark long-sleeved shirt under his uniform. This particular shirt had always been good to me—I'd been wearing it the day I'd gone to fetch Kimberly's dad—and I wanted to pay homage by being photographed in it, even if it meant looking different from everyone else. And soon enough in one of my rare forays off the bench I made my first catch, running backward from second base and the fly ball dropping over my head and landing right in my mitt—luck or magic, I wasn't sure which. My teammates, the bigkids, hooted with surprise.

If the beach was the spiritual heart of town—the place where Little League and pickup punchball games were played, where the Test was administered under the tanned gimlet eye of Art Chace, high priest of the beach—the school pond was second in importance. It was like the winter home of the Romanovs, where the royalty of bigkids held court during the frozen months. All decked out with cigarettes and leather jackets, they flowered here in full view of the public, while the rest of us tried to horse around without getting in their way. One Saturday that winter I rode Tommy to the school pond to go skating, and it was so cold that when I got there I decided to carry the bike through the woods to a hidden spot not far from a bonfire the bigkids had constructed. "There you go, Tommy," I said under my breath as I propped my bike against a hemlock tree, "you'll be warm here."

Suddenly I had an inkling we weren't alone. I spun around. A bigkid had overheard me. And not just any bigkid. Manny! Who'd tied up my bike with ropes. Now he knew my secret—that my bike was alive.

We both froze. Then he sent me a look I'd never seen on him, so radiantly generous as to be almost amorous, that said my secret was safe with him.

I saw Manny years later, when I came home from college and he was pumping gas. Same look, only this time he sent it with a nod that meant, *forever.*

Only then, when I was verging on adulthood, did I have the ability to process a strange memory. I recollected that when we were children, Manny's house of five boys had always been hushed. His mother would emerge from her bedroom where the blackish-purple curtains would be drawn even in the middle of a spring afternoon. The room would be suffused with an eerie purple glow that seemed to collect in the furrows of her brow. She had migraines, it was whispered, from trying to keep those boys of hers out of jail, terrible migraines that made her screech and more than once had landed her in Newtown, the state crazy house.

Be gentle with your enemies, I thought. For they are as fragile as we are. . . .

10

DARK N COLD

*J*ump-ahead time. To the most hidden place of my life—as an adult, in my own home.

It was early winter when the boys' mother left. The first snow was on the ground. The moving van came and in one afternoon took all her belongings to her new house. She had to make several treks back and forth to supervise, tracking snow through the breezeway each time. It was a record cold that winter. Her snowy footprints lasted from November to March, twinkling good-bye.

The boys were seven and two. I snowplowed what was left of the garden to its roots and went inside the house and pulled the doors shut behind me. I turned down the heat. I turned down the lights. When Marshall, the baby, would visit me there, he had a name for the newly empty house. Dark n Cold.

It was indeed the darkest and coldest period of my life, a period when, as they say in Greek myths, I "sorrowed grievously." As in a Grimm's story, it was as though a spell had been cast and the love had gone out of my wife's heart for reasons I knew not. I felt I'd made a house of straw and the wolf had blown my family away and now I was sitting there shivering with cold since I hadn't had the foresight to make a house of bricks.

This was a different kind of hiding place from the ones I was used to. It was the kind an animal repairs to after it sustains an injury, the way a dog will crawl beneath the porch after he's been beaten or a wolf will limp off to lick his wounds in private. I understood for the first time why a hurt animal needs to be alone. Feeble in its injured state, the animal needs to heal itself without wasting energy defending itself from, or explaining itself to, outsiders.

I ran from friend and foe alike. Colleagues asked me to dinner and I shook my head no. Neighbors asked me to skating parties and I hid in my house, peering out the curtains. I watched wild ducks fly over my pond but never set down. The world was shrinking from me.

It had simply never occurred to me that I might lose my wife. I took it like a stab wound, as though a knife had been gouged into the red muscle of my heart. I tried to visualize applying a bandage to my heart, which immediately became oozy, like masking tape on a sand castle. By midwinter, the deepest part had somehow closed itself and the wound had transferred to my outer chest wall. It was still black and mean and raw, but it worked as a barrier for keeping infection out and my self in. Gradually it lost its sensitivity, and I could tap it with an index finger to test its give. It was an ordinary healing wound by then; I could run my fingertips over it and feel its gruesome contours.

I had a car that was rusting from the inside because the dimwit dealer had rustproofed it on a rainy day, sealing the moisture in. That's what my heart felt like. Like it was being eaten out with rust.

Corroded by divorce, I was writing but not living—typing stuff I knew from memory, feeding off the old experiences I had amassed, as if I were living off my body fat, a world traveler under house arrest.

The rage, of course, was astonishing. I would rant in protest of all the damage I could feel being done to me, day after day.

Most damaged of all was my capacity to believe I could be loved. Unloved, I made the common mistake of thinking myself unlovable.

I remained cold. Sitting in the office of my sun porch with its fourteen windows facing west, my fingers were frequently too cold to type. I invested in thermal underwear. Inscribed on the plastic wrapper was this inscription: "Be warm, be happy." It struck me as brilliantly true. But the prescription failed me: I cranked the woodstove up till my organs seemed to cook inside me, but the cold could not be vanquished. I had the solitaire's contagion: deep in my bones lurked the clammy fever of loneliness.

I tried to beat my loneliness off, but masturbation only fixed me for the short run. Ultimately I was left with the feeling described in my haiku at the time, entitled "2 A.M."

A tissue of sperm:
weightless in my hand as a
broken robin's egg . . .

I sustained fearsome dreams. Up to that point in my life, I'd paid scant attention to my dreams, but during this period it occurred to me that not paying attention was like getting a pile of letters addressed to yourself every morning and throwing them away unread. *These* I couldn't ignore. I was an Indian fighting for my life, braining other Indians with my stone tomahawk. I was in love with a female matador. Terrorists were forcing me to inject my sons with poison. My childhood home was burning up. My adult home was being flooded. I was trying to call a rescue unit but it wouldn't come; the boys were screaming from windows and I was racing up and down stairs to save them but the stairs led nowhere and I'd wake up clawing at a charley horse in my thigh, with a loud groan in an empty house.

The very sound of the lilac branches tapping on the windows, reminding me to prune them, was enough to keep me on the floor all day. My back was out and there were afternoons I couldn't reach the bed. One Monday morning I was so crazed at the sight of my ex driving off with the boys that I lurched to the bathroom and made unnerving sounds that I tried to smother in the shower curtain so the neighbors wouldn't hear. A few months later an old man two houses down died of throat cancer, and I fantasized that my sounds had driven the disease into him. His garden fell into disrepair after he died, and the rags on his scarecrow withered away to reveal two pieces of wood in the shape of a cross, surrounded by snowy weeds. I felt guilty seeing it, imagining it was the ripple effect of my divorce. I thought of the story of the Jewish mother learning her young son had been abducted into the Russian army and beating her head against the wall of the rabbi's study, so that the rabbi died shortly thereafter.

Each time the boys went back with their mother, I was left alone to ponder why I'd been dumped. She never told me what I'd done to make her leave, except to say what my mother used to say, that I was impossible. I was left powerless to correct my offense. Did it have something to do with our different religions? Only over time did I come to accept the hopeless truth: that most of the reasons were inside her and had little to do with me.

Meanwhile, with all this suffering, I was growing. They call it growing up, but it's really growing out. I was growing compassion toward the outside world. Week by week, month by month, I was noticing that other people had troubles, too—something I never really took in before. Beneath the rage, there was recognition. When I read a newspaper report I was able to understand why a mother had tossed herself and her infant daughter off a bridge, why a man had parked the family station wagon on a railroad track and waited there with his three children for the 4:02 to come screaming in. It was either because of divorce or it wasn't. It didn't matter; we were all having troubles that weren't so dissimilar from each other. I was growing humanity.

I wasn't a man when I entered my divorce. I became a man through my suffering. It's for this reason that I count this as the period of waking up in my life.

And then the suffering stopped. Looking around to see that others suffered, I found pause. The pause after the fury of divorce, in this place called Dark n Cold, was an ascetic experience. So violent had it been that the relief afterward was profound, like after you stop shouting and your ears tingle with the vibrations of silence. My senses were sharpened as after a Zen fast when they say you're sensitive enough to hear the ash fall from an incense stick. I could hear a goat in the neighboring yard pull dead grass up by its roots, grind it sideways to a yellow mash between his back teeth. I could watch a fly rest on a windowpane and empathize with the way it tried to soak up the weak winter sunlight. I could gaze at a dying ficus leaf and sense the instant when it would bestir itself to fall stiff to the floor below.

Eventually, I had a new thought. I was not alone. More than just a solitary being, I was the grandnephew of Yudl and Velvl, the father of Alex and Marshall. Entering my sons' room after they'd gone back to their mother's was like stealing into an abandoned church. Inhaling the air they'd recently breathed, I was reminded that all was not betrayal and falseness and dishonor. There was, for instance, a plastic whistle. Swingline Stapler. Crayons. Open jackknife. Banana slippers, matching pairs. A wedding picture of their parents on its side. I'd collect a face cloth Alex had used that morning, damp in places where it hadn't yet gone crisp. I'd gather a cantaloupe rind from one of Marshall's secret refrigerator raids, the teeth marks still fresh where he'd raked the orange flesh in the middle of the night.

And I marveled at the maps. On the top bunk, beside a snare drum bed lamp, Alex slept two nights a week surrounded by maps of Yellowstone and Grand Teton National Parks, close-ups of Pacific Islands. The major continent groups drifted all around Alex while he worked through his dreams with the concentration of a rocket scientist, lips amutter. On the bottom bunk, beside a bass drum bed lamp, Marshall slept two nights a week in the pale blue-white glow of an illuminated globe that served for night-light. Projected on his soft twitching lids at 2 A.M., the azure shadings of China; the first thing to greet his wide-open eyes each morning was the dream-blue expanse of the Arctic.

◆ ◆ ◆

So I left. Busted out. Took a cue from my sons' maps and split.

By the end of winter her footprints had gone, twinkling one last time and disappearing. But suddenly there was new evidence of my ex-wife all around me: a misplaced bikini top in a drawer of summer things, her inscription in a children's book I hadn't cracked since her departure, April crocuses she'd planted that lay sprinkled across my yard like confetti gone to seed. I blasted my aunt's harpsichord records—we may have been Dark n Cold but we were loud!—and in her triumphant rendition of Scarlatti sought to remind myself who I was. I popped a hole in a wall and put French doors out to a brick patio—suddenly we were flooded with pale light. The gash in my heart was merely a lump on my arm now, raised purply-white and cold.

I fled to Tashkent and Lhasa and Rio. To Helsinki and Santiago and Nome. The farther the better. But still I was cold. I got the Danish Bug in Beijing. The Beijing Cough in Amman. Coming home to check on the boys and heading out again, I was bringing Dark n Cold with me, exporting my desolation flu all over the globe. I sat shivering on the beach of Copacabana. Sneezing in the sun-filled train compartment from Durban to Capetown. I saw a woman slicing a banana into her husband's granola in a ski lodge in the Canadian Rockies and got a migraine on the spot. On a picnic atop Mt. Cook in New Zealand my nose became congested when the man next to me took out a chicken salad sandwich he said had been prepared by his wife. Walnuts! She'd included walnuts in his chicken salad!

Naturally I was cold: I was a father who'd been stripped of his family. My passport billfold was filled with fare-thee-well notes from the boys. "I love you Dad, come back saf." "Don't forget, we love eech other." They hadn't yet learned to fold in half and half again, so the notes were folded like an accordion up from the bottom in twelfths. If I'd had daughters, maybe they would have knitted me pot holders with hearts on them. But I had sons, and these crudely folded notes were as demonstrative as it got. It was plenty demonstrative for me.

Traveling by myself was exhilarating. I liked finding myself in places where baboons throw rocks at trekkers, where spiders build nests strong enough to trap bats. But sometimes, looking out my hotel window at the Chinese husband pulling back a strand of hair from his wife's face as she spoon-fed their baby in a "Yunkees" baseball outfit, I yearned to be home, my boys on either side of me. In a restaurant in London, I spied that look that passed between husband and wife, the private communication that says, "What do you say, dear?" and I'd feel a sting of yearning as if my wallet had been stolen and I'd come across my kids' pictures in the gutter. I was homesick in the most profound sense: for the inhabitants of a home that was no longer there.

Specifically, I was boysick. Every time I saw a father hoist a toddler onto his lap so he could share his croissant in an airport, the grippe threatened. Strolling through a park in Copenhagen while school kids exuberantly posed for their teacher, or listening to a children's choir practice amid falling frangipani flowers in a churchyard in Harare, or seeing an Arabian father rest his hand on his son's head as they passed a bottle of soda pop between them, unaware of anything else in the world . . .

If there's one thing I learned in divorce, it's that missing someone is the purest emotion there is. Infinitely more pure than love.

Things finally came to a head one afternoon at the kabuki in Tokyo. Onstage a father was taking leave of his wife and children. The stage was slowly revolving apart on two separate spheres. The snow was falling like cherry blossoms and he was trudging toward them but getting farther away. The father was calling out and the wife and children were gesturing him to come back but the two spheres of the stage kept cranking apart. The children were weeping and waving and the father was weeping and waving and in my box I was eating my bento lunch of tuna maki with glass noodles and the tears were streaming down my face.

When I called and told them I was coming home that last time, Marshall said he was so excited he was going to bite the phone. And when I parked in front of their mother's house, Alex came running down the driveway and threw himself in my arms. Even as a youngster Alex was never at a loss for words, but this time he was uncharacteristically silent; he just buried his head in my chest and after a minute he pulled back and said: "Sorry I wet your shirt."

The truth was, I needed them for heat. Hitting upon the idea to take them traveling with me was a simple biological reflex. It was the only thing I could do to get warm.

11

A YELLOW LOAFER
FILLED WITH BLOOD

*W*hat clinched it was the evening I erased their childhood on the home video. I had the boys for an overnight and the three of us had just kicked back with the VCR to watch themselves at age five and ten, leaping from the swing set with their hair tousled in the wind. Instead, the screen showed a yellow loafer filled with blood. A bunch of Mafiosi who'd been gambling in the back of a Sicilian butcher shop had been cleavered to death by a rival gang and their bleeding bodies piled in the meat locker.

What had happened was all too apparent: I'd put the wrong tape in the VCR and had recorded over our family history with Prime Time Live.

The boys' hair in the wind, that's what kept coming back to me. But that was all I could remember. What was I forgetting? Something about a baseball game, a lemonade stand. With my stomach in my throat I called the VCR store and asked if there was any way to retrieve the images, to exchange the bodies of two-bit hoodlums bleeding on a tiled floor for their healthy suburban faces selling lemonade at the bottom of a Massachusetts driveway.

"Not unless you find a way to travel back in time," said the VCR shop.

I took inventory, not wanting to overreact. It was just the physical record that was extinct, after all; the memories were still around somewhere. But there was no way I wasn't going to overreact. The divorce was washing over me again, one loss domino-ing the others. Gone! the footage of Marshall being so small he could run under the kitchen table without grazing his scalp. Gone! the footage of Alex grimacing in mock pain with a box of hot pizza on his lap all the way home from the sub shop, and all the others I couldn't remember . . .

"Dad, how could you, you idiot!" screamed Alex. It was the first time he'd ever used a word like that at me. He hadn't permitted himself to really cry since the divorce, but he sat there choking in a kind of tearless suffering, while Marshall stood by saying, "It's OK. We can make some more memories."

Thank God for Marshall. We had to take a trip and make new memories that couldn't be eradicated with the flick of a switch.

That was in December. Alex had just turned twelve. Marshall was already seven. The trick, I acknowledged, is to remember calmly that there *is* urgency.

◆ ◆ ◆

A few days later I was at the IGA, picking through the ice creams to see what new ones Ben & Jerry had come up with. Heath Bar Crunch? Nah—the octane wasn't high enough. Just as I was reaching for the Chocolate Fudge Brownie, I heard a shout across the grocery aisle, from one college student to another:

"Alena, did you get the matzo?"

"*Shhh!*" was my automatic reaction. Clicking into alert mode, I glanced around to see who else might have overheard.

I relaxed, coming to my senses. Christ, I thought, I'm still in hiding. Half a century after the Holocaust, I am still in hiding.

◆ ◆ ◆

I signed us up for temple. I'd been haphazardly looking to repair my center for a long time, doing yoga every morning for years and meditating when the mood hit. I'd tried enlightenment workshops, never going so far as to be what's known in the New Age biz as an "est-hole," but taking abstruse weekend retreats with various other seekers, chanting with the best of them and sleeping with the worst, hoping that some sort of belief system would rub off on me. Like many other disaffected American Jews, I dabbled in Zen and Buddhism: I'd even coined the word "Juddhist" to try to describe what I was. Skeptically but gamely I had from time to time eaten vegetarian to clean my system and swallowed algae to purge it and undergone high colonics to purify it. I'd sat in Quaker meetings and "shared" with those in the here and now; I'd lain in flotation booths and "regressed" with a guru chanting above the water to help me tap into my past lives. I'd subscribed to the cult of wanderlust, too, for travel can serve as a kind of religion; I tried to find faith in the breadth of the globe that substituted for depth. But never in all these years of spiritual mingling did I choose to mine my own back-yard, the old ball and chain Judaism. It was time.

◆ ◆ ◆

Of course, it wasn't as easy as that. Two weeks after recording the yellow loafer, I dropped the boys off at Sunday school and went inside.

Snapshot: B'nai B'rith meeting with two dozen senior citizens, smelling of horseradish. Their hair looked like lint, spray-painted gold. They were constantly nittering, nattering—were these Jewish words?—like children in the back rows. But these fussbudgets and busybodies didn't confine themselves to the back rows. Nor did they, as children would, do it secretly. They chittered loudly from the front row about hemorrhoids and gall bladders and tire treads, leaning stiffly toward each other and rasping, "What'd she say?"—before she finished saying it. The men with their hats on defiantly (making who knew what sort of obstinate point) were snapping their business cards through their beards; straightening out their dollar bills; exhaling mournfully through their lips; slapping crumbs off their laps; rubbing their chins the better to digest the words being spoken: they wanted to hear the speaker!

And the women! Sharing cold knishes with each other; tunneling through their peasant fishnet pocketbooks till they located Dristan to squirt up their nostrils; spilling Nescafe from plastic thermoses on the sneakers of the people in back of them; reserving seats for each other, then canceling the transaction, then horse-trading them back on account of they hadn't expected their dear friends to show up; finally scraping their chairs back so vehemently they left rubber skid marks on the floor: they wanted to see the speaker!

Jews are like people everywhere, it's been said. Only more so.

Snapshot II: Mozart recital at St. Luke's Church in East Greenwich, Rhode Island. A late Sunday afternoon in April, and the five o'clock hour is lit with yellowish spring light. The Episcopalian ladies are craning forward spryly in their church pews to sniff the faint scent of forsythia wafting in from the churchyard beyond. They're wearing pink and blue blazers with white blouses buttoned up to their chins, their delicate hands folded primly atop shiny leather purses in their laps. They wave their fingers *Yoo-hoo!* and then resume tweeting with their neighbors about hip replacements and flower splicings. The men are oh so daring in red and blue bowties, tapping their polished nails with boredom on the mahogany pews, their bifocals reflecting the stained-glass windows as they raise their eyes to the middle distance so they don't have to make conversation with their fellow music lovers. And when the music starts, an instant hush—the men discreetly check their gold wristwatches, decorously cough into cupped hands, then unwrap the business pages so carefully that the operation is noiseless. The dry-skinned ladies incline their heads with patient little smiles to hear the music, as if Mozart is an unruly but talented boy they want to humor, then with no warning let slip a sneeze so restrained you think it must do damage to their tonsils—all that propulsion being discharged internally couldn't help but make you worry about their orgasms, whether they're ever riproaring affairs or merely polite background business like the genial ringing of a servant's bell.

Maybe Episcopalians are like people everywhere, only less so.

The next week, in the hallway before the boys' class, another divorced parent confided that she also found the senior citizens problematic. We decided to play hooky, ending up at her house in a subdivision where, with the curtains closed against the thrumming Sunday morning snow, on her daughter's bunk under stick 'em stars that glowed in the dark, we entertained ourselves while the seniors squirted Dristan without us and our kids studied the Maccabees.

That made me feel like an insider, sure enough, but next Friday I made the mistake of stopping in for Sabbath services. Dutifully I tried praying but was distracted by the dance of light reflecting from people's wedding rings on the walls. When everyone stood and turned to the back to greet the Sabbath it was like my first time in aerobics class. To the left! Now to the right! I went full pivot and the sound of people's watches going off sounded like the penalty buzzer. Fellow Jews stood around muttering the transliterated prayers with such self-conscious zeal, furtive and fidgety, that minus the lofty architecture it reminded me of a men's room in a turnpike restaurant. Who *was* this strange tribe? When they sang, they pounded the floor with their bulky shoes. Someone behind me pummeled my seat. I looked around at all the mouths uttering guttural sounds, at all the skullcaps with nicknames stitched in them, HORACE and ELI, at all the pretty dark-eyed women clapping with the butts of their palms together and thought, I have more kinship with lobstermen!

But none of this was as troubling as a couple of Hasidim on the other side of me. What they were doing at a Reform temple I didn't know—but there they were, the underbelly of Judaism, like bizarre distant relatives you hope won't show up at a family gathering. God help me, but they were white and grublike in their movements, as lacking in grace and radiance as if they'd crawled out from under a rock. If this was how medieval Europe saw Jews, no wonder their poets spoke of "the pallor of the ghetto." They were like those characters who'd sold me a camera lens at 47th Street Photo, their voices girlishly hostile, needling and shy at the same time, as though compensating for a crippling inner tenderness by putting on a gruff front. Even their posture was unhealthy-looking, juggling as it did a cheerful eagerness shot through with prickly defensiveness, their baby-sized teeth offset by their wary grins, their eyes dancing with some kind of angry humor I didn't get. Were they poking fun at me? Did they feel superior? But *how?* With their gimpy gaits and scrubby facial hair, their squeamishness that was directed not just against the modern world but against worldly things in general, extending a feeble damp hand not merely to conclude the transaction but to pull me back to the faith, when I'd never been in the first place. . . .

❖ ❖ ❖

I hated hearing myself sound this way. Intolerance made me scaly, and besides, my posture wasn't so great either. The following Sunday I concluded that this wasn't going to work. I waited in my car for Alex to get over his detention for throwing chalk at the Sunday school teacher. I sat for twenty minutes in the freezing slush staring at a sign that said "Horrors of the Holocaust," and looking at all the Mercedeses and Porsches and Audis and other German cars parked along the curb. Then and there I decided to yank the boys out of temple and teach them Sunday school myself.

It started slowly. We lit candles and huddled around the woodstove reading a children's book about burning bushes and multicolored coats and wrestling angels and golden calves. By January we decided to throw the net wide. Given that Judaism seemed to place a premium on egghead pursuits, we elected to consider almost any intellectual endeavor Jewish. We read Jack London and called that Sunday school (courage in adversity). We read about the Salem witch trials and called that Sunday school (intolerance and persecution). I made the boys a tape of Jewish cantors on side A and Eartha Kitt on side B, bundling them together with the idea that they could take honey with their medicine, and to my amazement they ended up preferring side A. We listened to Neil Diamond in *The Jazz Singer* on a long drive to the Berkshires and debated the son's need to rebel against his rabbi father. We discussed real diamonds, too, the family business—where they came from, what they were composed of, how they got to be so valuable. All through the winter, surrounded by our ritual chicken soup aromatherapy candles, we listened to Carl Sandburg and James Joyce and Dylan Thomas and all the other records I'd stolen decades earlier from the college library and called that Sunday school, too, for no other reason than that it was uplifting and sounded good.

And we loved it. We had Sunday school whenever there was a bowling alley that wasn't too noisy or a Cambodian restaurant that was having a family discount night. Our holiday celebrations didn't always coincide with the exact dates because the boys weren't always with me on the exact dates, so we'd celebrate Shabbos on Monday and Rosh Hashanah a week late. We observed Hanukkah over Szechuan take-out. On New Year's Eve we warmed ourselves with matzo ball soup and on Valentine's Day we cracked open a jar of gefilte fish. We mixed and matched our holidays. Joint custody gave us license to do what we wanted. Freed by divorce from traditional constraints, we were at liberty to make our own traditions. (Oddly, in that manner, we held our holidays the way Jews did in concentration camps. When they had lost track of time they would "declare" the holidays. So we declared according to the custody decree.)

As the days grew warmer, we had one Sunday school in a zoo (Darwinism versus Creationism) and another on the deck of a local battleship tourist attraction (Joshua and his military stratagem). We had one at a drive-in and another at a car junkyard. It was an eye-opener, after a lifetime of viewing only intact cars, for them to see acre after acre of rusting tin; and to extrapolate from that our tin-thin mortality. They got it, and we called that Sunday school, too.

Whenever it conjoined that the mood hit, the boys weren't fighting, and there was a shady tree we felt like stretching out under, that's where we'd light our candles and have Sunday school. We had one about how everything is *not* worse these days (there's more forest in New England than fifty years ago, fewer smokers, cheaper long-distance phone rates). Another about how to read the front page of a newspaper. Another about how strippers are not usually happy to be stripping, about why it was wrong to cheat on tests, about the need to swim parallel to the shore if caught in a rip tide, and to do unto others as you would have them do unto you.

None of it was over their heads because I wasn't talking down to them or up but straight, heart-to-heart. We acted out a skit about how to decline a ride from a drunk classmate at some future teen party. We talked about how artists can succeed only if they help their audience succeed, about how being too rich sequesters you from the world in a bad way, about how if you're unhappy it helps to help others, and how best to conceal a hand buzzer. I taught them what I was learning: that it was right to accept change with the appropriate sadness and not to cover it with fake cheer. I confided in them what I foresaw for them, that they'd grow up strong and gentle and smart, and, lo, they obliged me by growing up exactly that way.

Years later, I gathered that what we were doing had a name in childhood development circles and that name was character education. We simply called it Sunday school, our chance to think about things we were overdue to think about. It was a way of waking up, of paying attention. Of saluting, even, all three of us.

But mostly, of course, it was just an excuse to be a family.

12

A GRAIN OF TRUTH

*F*riday on a train from Brussels to Antwerp. Sunday school's called to order. Issue of the day: deconstructing J. P.'s journal, which is like a small Holocaust scrapbook crammed with everything he found pertinent—sketches of rabbits and fish, bits of colored ribbons, a page of ancient Scotch tape, a cellophane packet of blond curls, a piece of stationery from Hôtel de la Plage. But what *plage?* Where? The pages are out of sequence, and the notations themselves are written in the most rudimentary English.

"Why English?" Alex is asking.

"He was trying to learn it, I suppose. Or he considered it code in case the journal fell into the wrong hands."

"But why not some other language, like Hebrew?"

"For the same reason he changed his name to J. P. Morgan, I imagine," I say. "He hoped to pass for a Yankee."

Alex mulls this over while he roots through our picnic basket. "Do we have any more lime Jell-O mix?" he asks.

"No more lime Jell-O mix."

"Well, pass the butterscotch pudding mix then."

I do so. Alex upends the dry powder into his mouth as he weighs what I've told him. "That J. P. stuff is another thing I don't get. Was he being irony?" he asks.

"You mean 'ironic'?"

"Whatever."

"I think it was just the WASP-iest name he could think of," I say. "But it didn't hurt that the original J. P. happened to be the most powerful and feared man of his day."

Alex looks out past the chicken soup candles we've lit on the windowsill, to the speeding scenery beyond: blackened bricks of squat houses, an old lady in a babushka leaning on her hoe. "Pretty clever," he says. "So where'd he escape to?"

"That's what we don't know. We'll have to feel our way."

"How're we gonna do that, without directions?"

Good question. The journal is the closest thing we have to a guide, and it's *meant* to be indecipherable; enigmatic to protect the innocent. Behind that raw black swastika on the cover, one page is nothing but bicycle receipts. Another is all blacked out. The journal's like history itself, I find myself thinking—full of false starts and stops, random bits and tracings.

"*'Lay zah-nee-moh soh-vahzh veev dawng lah for-reh,'*" Marshall reads from his Berlitz book. "'Wild animals live in the forest.'"

"Yech! What's this?" Alex cries, frantically waving his arms to brush away something that's fallen out of the journal. "Something dead!"

"It's a couple of fly carcasses, Alex. They're not going to hurt you."

Indeed, the carcasses are so old they crumble to dust when we blow them aside.

"Problem is, I have my doubts about the journal," I tell Alex as he composes himself with some peevishness. "Like, why is a whole blank page covered with Scotch tape? That wasn't even invented till after the war, I think."

"Actually, I did a project about inventions for school," Alex says. "Some engineer invented it in nineteen thirty."

"Well anyway," I go on. "What does a bunch of Scotch tape

have to do with World War Two?" I pause to disperse a scattering of beach sand that's fallen into my lap from deep inside the journal. "See why I'm withholding judgment?"

"You take him with a grain of truth?"

"Exactly. That *meshuga'as* about a concentration camp in France, for instance—that had to be his famous poetic license talking. The French may have collaborated, as he said, but I certainly never heard that they allowed camps on their land."

"But maybe there *was* a concentration camp," Marshall puts down his Berlitz to say, "just *maybe maybe maybe . . .*"

"We'll never know," I say. "'Cause think of it: even if there *had* been a concentration camp in France fifty years ago, don't you think the French would have razed it by now to destroy any sign of their shameful past?"

"Or it would be a tourist attraction like Auschwitz," adds Alex with a surfeit of worldweariness, "where they sell snow cones on the street leading in."

Or worse, I think to myself: a friend of mine had reported seeing a gum wrapper in the crematorium of Midonic.

"We need evidence," Marshall says. "Something to show that the journal is true." Then: "*'Lay zah-nee-moh soh-vahzh sohng dawnzhay-ruh zah rawn-kohn-tray.* Wild animals are dangerous to meet.'"

"Marshall, you are such a cheese," Alex observes dispassionately. Spying a (1938) model in the pages of Marshall's Berlitz, he adds: "Wow, look at the jugs on that girl!"

"That's not nice language," Marshall corrects him sternly.

"Thank you," I tell Marshall. "At least one of us has manners around here."

"You're supposed to say 'on that *woman,*'" Marshall concludes.

I've finished writing the name of the hotel where we'll be staying on the back of my business cards, and I pass them to the boys. "This is in case we get separated," I explain.

"Separated?" Alex says with a worried look.

"Look, we won't. But just to be safe."

"What're we supposed to do with it?"

"Put it in your shoe," I reply. It sounds like an insult, but I'm serious. It's the one place they won't lose it.

"I know what it's for," Marshall says. "It's in case we get hijacked."

Alex shakes his head, clicking back into disdain mode. "We can't get hijacked, you camembert," he says. "That's just for planes. On a train we can only get lo-jacked."

"No one's going to get hijacked *or* lo-jacked, guys," I say. But to myself I admit that lo-jacking is an ever-present possibility, if what it means is getting lost or losing each other, if it means all the unnamed scary things that can happen to a family exploring unknown territory, far from home.

Alex wanders up the aisle, trying to lift an ashtray bolted to the floor. Marshall proceeds to make a fort out of the seat cushions while I inspect the Baggie containing two blond ringlets that I assume is the hair of J. P.'s twins. Gingerly I peel open the cellophane and take hold of the curls. And suddenly I feel what can only be described as a hum, like the way a deaf person can sense music by feeling the vibrations. I touch these locks and feel a ringing in my fingertips. A tintinnabulation from the past. I'm reminded of the time as an undergrad I came across a lock of Edgar Allan Poe's hair in Brown's John Hay Library. Simply gazing on it brought back the man in all his alcoholism and anguish. I could almost smell his breath, rank and grapey.

So do these blond curls work their magic on me. Completely unbidden, it comes to me that one of J. P.'s children had a speech impediment. A lisp. No, a stutter. The other was a soccer player, maybe one of the only athletes the Morganstern clan ever produced, looking so fresh in her school uniform, playing goalie . . .

That's all—the hum fades as mysteriously as it arrived. It

doesn't bother me that I'm probably wrong about the details I divined. What matters is that I'm left with a realization I didn't have before, namely that my kids are about the age the twins were when they were traversing this landscape with their father. And all at once a new reason for the trip occurs to me. *It's my task to transmit the legacy to a new generation of people the same age as those killed.*

After all, it's a unique time in our kids' age, J. P.'s and mine. This is the last summer I can still toss mine in the air and catch them without straining my back. The last summer they think it's more cooling if I blow on their soup than if they do, that they still gasp with astonishment each time they find a McDonald's french fry over two inches long, that they're still capable of exclaiming, "Oh thank you, Dad! Thanks a lot!" when I give them something as valuable as a Tootsie Roll.

It's my last chance to be with them as small fry, in other words. Little by little, they've been outgrowing not only their own children's books but also the ones I saved from my youth and passed down to them. Little by little, they've been outgrowing these relics and giving them back to me so I'm being left alone with my childhood, and where is theirs going? To the same place their lost video went?

"Can you find me, Dad?" Marshall calls, burrowed between the cushions. I drop the curls back in the cellophane packet but Alex beats me to the punch. "I can find him!" he calls, yanking off Marshall's Nike and pulling on his toes to crack the knuckles.

"Dad! Ouch! Tell him to stop!"

"Just two more toes, Dad. I'm almost there!"

"Alex! Let go of him!"

But now Alex is done. He sits back satisfied. Marshall wears a grimace of lingering pain as he nurses his toes. "Can you tell about the Regent Diamond?" he whines.

Diamond Sunday school, to take the sting out.

"The Regent," I say, hauling him onto my lap where he can inspect the candle flames up close, "was the biggest diamond in the French crown. Over one hundred forty carats. It was kept in the Louvre, but when World War Two came and the Nazis were marching into Paris, the French hid it in a fireplace."

"Tell about the girl who found a giant diamond in her yard," Alex prompts.

"She found it in her backyard in Louisiana, and it's the tenth largest in the U.S."

"Tell about Brazil!"

"Well, for a while, diamonds were so plentiful in Brazil that the gold miners used 'em for paperweights. One slave found a five carat diamond sticking to a cabbage he'd picked for dinner."

"But how come my Coke tastes orangey?" Alex asks, taking a sip.

"Well, *you* wanted Coke," I say. "Marshall wanted orange juice. So I mixed 'em together."

They blink at each other. *"Awesome!"* they scream. "Tell about the Hope Diamond!"

"The Hope Diamond was found in India over three hundred years ago," I resume, "and sold to the King of France. The King gave it to his son, who was killed by wild dogs."

"Then the King died of little pox," Marshall adds.

"*Small*pox, right," I say. "It was then inherited by Louis the Sixteenth and Marie Antoinette, both of whom were beheaded in the French Revolution."

"I love that part," Marshall says. "Deheaded."

"After which it showed up in England, where it caused even more trouble in a family named Hope."

"*Bob* Hope?" asks Marshall, incredulous.

"Not Bob Hope. What do you think, they name diamonds after comedians?"

I send a signal to Alex but he's engrossed in a new subject,

one eye turning in. "Dad, what do you think is the deadliest animal in the world?"

"Tell me."

"The shrew! If you put a python in its cage and came back
ten minutes later, all gone! And Dad?"

"You have the floor."

"The biggest a shrew can ever get is two inches. Its metabo-
lism is so fast that if he doesn't eat, he'll die in eight hours."

I look over my firstborn with a practiced eye. "Does this
mean you need more food?"

"Sure," he says genially, then steps on his own ankle and says
"Ow!" to himself angrily. I can see he's aching privately. If only
he'd cry once in a while, break this bottleneck of sorrow or
whatever's eating him.

"Yeah, but Dad?" Marshall says, taking another sip of his orange Coke. "The Nazis would always let kids go, wouldn't they?
They wouldn't hurt the children, right?"

I look at Marshall. Now is as good a time as any to get it over
with. "The children were *special* targets of the Nazis," I say,
chipping off the lime Jell-O powder caked on his chin. "They
figured if they could do away with them, they'd wipe out the future of Judaism."

In his unease, Marshall has begun tap-tapping his divorce orphan's Morse code. "But a lot of Germans didn't like Hitler,
didn't they?"

"Put it this way. By nineteen thirty-three, Hitler was more
popular within Germany than any leader in China is today."

Alex has doodled a swastika in the butterscotch powder on
his plate. "It's so ugly," he says, indicating the symbol. "Doesn't
it just *look* ugly?"

"It looks like a spider hit by a shoe," Marshall agrees heatedly. "If I were J. P., I'd throw a Ninja smoke bomb in Hitler's
face."

"Jews weren't really into Ninjitsu in those days," Alex explains patiently. "They were more into origami, stuff like that."

"Oh," says Marshall, the world made clear again by his brother. He nods there in the canned air of the train, processing the imagery as he pulls out a remnant of his breakfast pizza and gums it thoughtfully. At last he says: "Does Mom know about all this?"

"Not that much," I say. "I wasn't so interested in it back when we were all living together. And her clan, of course, isn't Jewish."

"They're Christian?"

"Yup."

"Why didn't they convert when you got married?"

"All of them?" I laugh. "It was more than enough that *she* converted. There was no reason for her whole family to as well."

They think about this. "She smells good," Marshall acknowledges. "Jewels, by Liz Taylor."

"Not Jewels," Alex hisses with a slathering of contempt. "It's Precious Stones, by Jaclyn Smith."

"Liz Taylor, butt nugget!"

"Jaclyn Smith, fart blossom!"

I wave a white napkin. "Can we get back on track here," I suggest, "instead of arguing about which aging movie star your mother's trying to smell like?"

"Whew, *that* was a close one," Marshall says, dunking the pizza in his drink. "I almost spilled the whole glass of—"

SPILL

Sometimes, I think as I lean to mop them up, sometimes I wish I could seal them in amber to preserve them like this forever. As I blot their hair and pull fresh shirts over their heads I feel a bubble burst open in my chest, and think: If anything should happen to them my molecules would dry out. I'd die.

And now is when yet another reason announces itself to me, a reason I didn't even know myself until this moment on a stuffy train. *I was the same age when I was so deep in hiding myself.*

Blowing out the candles and tapping the curls in my pocket, I'm strangely encouraged. Given courage.

Spires ahead: Antwerp.

13

EXERCISES IN HIDING, I

*I*n the early days of Rowayton my hiding places were rudimentary, not much more than holes in the ground. One was a section of our cellar known as the Dirty Part, as opposed to the Clean Part that was my father's domain, where logic and order prevailed, with hammers on hooks and nails in glass jars. The Dirty Part, the unfinished half, was where I hung out. It was dark, half hidden by a cinder block wall four feet high, and so low-ceilinged that even a kid like me had to crouch to make my way through it. It had a wonderfully raw earth floor, soil-scented and musty, with a rock in the middle: the actual slope of the hill our house was built on.

Only a few things were stored in the Dirty Part—old storm doors that had warped out of shape, crates of liquor, an empty steamer trunk from Belgium that exhaled a rich loam of mold—things that took on a magical quality because they spent so much time down there. The Dirty Part was off-limits, which only added to its allure, and was so out-of-the-way that I felt feral when I was in it. McDougal, the redheaded kid who read books at night by firefly light, would join me there in strange brutal battles in which we hurled sand-filled socks at each other in the dark. I even had a corner where I'd urinate, like a wild animal.

One day my father asked me if I knew anything about the odor of urine down there, and after I confessed he just said, "OK, I was wondering if a squirrel had gotten in," and let it go at that. But shortly thereafter he decided the Dirty Part could serve better if we had easier access to it, so he had Mr. Ginther the carpenter put in a door from the garage. Suddenly, fluorescent light from the garage surged into my secret place. I was in awe of my father's power.

This wasn't a bad development, necessarily. It wasn't as special anymore but I had to admit it was more useful. It also meant that I needed other hiding places that would be safe from my father's illumination.

These would come, I felt sure. In the meantime I was stricken with wonder that my father could transform a hidden space with such ease. But he was a doctor, a psychiatrist, and wasn't that what he was supposed to do—infuse those around him with light, even as he vanquished the mystery? He infused me with light at other times, too, and made my life a sunnier place to be. When I had my asthma attacks, he was the only one with the magic ability to talk me down. Just the sound of his soothing voice would make the flaring capillaries in my lungs relax. This was a fearsome power for a father to have, because it meant also that he could suspend it. When he withdrew his affection, which was often, I was lost and dark and small, my whole life cramped into a cinder-block dungeon where spiders roamed.

◆ ◆ ◆

So who was I? I confounded myself, trying to figure it out. I was too smart for my own good, and other times obtuse. I was honorably loyal yet I made fun of relatives behind their backs. I had a ferocious temper, yet was too frightened to take the Test at Bayley Beach that all Rowayton kids had to take, sooner or later. I was squeamish, I was savage, I was solitary, I was gregarious—and always wound too tight, with the curse of unceasing vividness. I was mercurial: calm one minute and wild as a dervish the next. I once stabbed McDougal in the back with a stick I'd whittled expressly for that purpose, and that night angelically sang myself to sleep. I was rapturous but full of bad moods, as capable of crying at the sight of a stranger being affectionate with his son as of pouring boiling water on an anthill for fun. I was by turns lighthearted, grave, rowdy, self-destructive, wide-eyed, girl-crazy . . . and I wasn't yet eight! I couldn't get a handle on who I was, and was so involved trying to that I had barely a thought left over for anyone else. This made me selfish, too. How would I ever get cured of myself?

To get a rest from all this, on Saturday mornings I'd accompany my father on errands in his Morris Minor. I was mostly shy when I was alone with him—shy was another of my colors, to balance the bragging—because I regarded him with such awe. Who was *he?* Sometimes I'd cry with love for this fierce five-foot-seven father whose thinking electrified me in its precision, for the controlled fury with which he'd chop wood or play Beethoven on the piano, for the brusque probity that was manifest in the fact that he liked his breakfast cereal crisp, whereas I liked to wait for mine to get soggy.

For his fallibility, which was the hardest thing of all to grasp. One time I was regaling the dinner table with tales of how McDougal and I'd been shooting bumblebees with a BB gun and he was impressed and said that showed a lot of control. I was proud because shooting bumblebees now seemed a noble thing, but at a deeper level I was sad because I'd made the whole thing up and he hadn't even known. It was tantamount to telling him I'd taken the Test at the beach when I hadn't. It made me feel sorry for him—the worst feeling I could have because it put me above him, a place I had no business being. Shortly after that my sister's green parakeet flapped off into the blue sky and my father came charging out yelling, "Don't worry, we'll get you another one!" and Renee and I shot each other a look because what he'd said was so beside the point. He appeared absurd and even a little tragic, and I cried about that because I didn't want to think of my father as tragic. How gentle his gentleness could be when he chose to hallow me with it! On dark winter week-nights I'd walk up the street to meet him as he puttered home from his office in his Morris Minor so we could share the last block together. He'd sit on my bed and hear me talk and understand me on such a heartfelt level that sometimes I felt sorry for all the other children in the world who didn't have such a fiercely perceptive father. He was conflicted about me, but I considered our relationship holy.

During Saturday morning errands I was content to soak up the wonder of having my father all to myself and to watch how the world treated us. We'd go to the bank, where the pretty Irish tellers would smile at Dr. Rose and offer his son a weekly calendar with the tide charts printed on the back. We'd go down a long driveway to the home of Joe the Sicilian gardener, and Joe would lift a clump of mountain laurel out of the ground, roots and all, and heft it in a burlap bag into our trunk. Then, slapping the peat moss off his powerful chest and belly, Joe would tell my father in broken English about the time outside Palermo when he fell headfirst out of a tree and his head made an indentation in the earth, and maybe that was why he'd been afraid of dogs ever since? Free Saturday morning advice from the head doctor. And we'd go to the gas station where one of the bigkids who'd once thrown a cherry bomb at me on McKinley Street would wash the windshield and blink with awe at "the doc" as if he were from Jupiter.

Finally we'd go to my father's office so he could read his Saturday mail. We'd putter up the driveway of the large Victorian house and park next to his private entrance and climb the steps into his office, where the bamboo shades were always drawn to produce a perpetual hushed twilight. I'd sink into a scooped-out low-slung Danish chair among the African stone figurines and the framed diplomas, and peer into the closet full of Kleenex boxes as I waited for him to finish separating his mail and throwing most of it into the tall teak wastebasket. We had to be quiet because other medical people in the building were practicing their craft on Saturday mornings, filling cavities and conducting eye exams.

One time my father had to speak to the nurse-receptionist in the main part of the building. She had a twinkling aura, bright and eager, and the front of her white uniform had a hard time keeping her bosoms flat. I could see she thought it was something of an occasion for my father to come to the main reception area instead of leaving via his private side door. She seemed to have a crush on him, and demonstrated it by twinkling extra hard at me and trying to make small talk about what kind of winter I'd had.

"And what did Santa bring you for Christmas?" she asked with a smile.

I was so nonplussed that I could think of nothing to say. I blushed. I seemed to lose my breath. My father looked down at me with an encouraging smile and when no words from me were forthcoming he said suavely, "Well, you got a nice sleeping bag not too long ago, didn't you?"

Still I couldn't say anything, which the nurse seemed to think was cute enough to merit a lollipop, and out in the car my father explained it thus: "If you don't want to come right out and say you don't celebrate Christmas, just list what you got for Hanukkah."

◆　◆　◆

So there were all kinds of hiding. All kinds of hiders, too; I was hardly alone in my habit. Jaime Rothschild was a French boy who stayed half the school year in Paris with his father who was an international playboy and half in Los Angeles with his mother who was an heiress. Over the summers and school vacations he stayed with his aunt Olga in Rowayton and he could make up instant hiding places on the spot. Poof! we were in Egypt, racing around the pyramids. Pop! we were among the Aztecs, running from a fertility goddess.

Olga was a European noblewoman married to an art dealer.

They had an attic full of old canvases that he'd collected when he was a student in Paris in the '20s, bartering with starving artists like Braque and Miró and Matisse, and buying more art from a brother-in-law who worked as a French interpreter for Göring. Olga was constantly warning Jaime that he was so lazy he'd amount to nothing more than an international playboy if he didn't apply himself and find his way in life. She embarrassed us both by holding me up as an example of someone who *was* finding his way. I hadn't a clue what she meant by that, and growing up to be an international playboy sounded awfully glamorous to me, but I wasn't about to look a compliment in the mouth.

Jaime was classier than I. I'd never had French dressing until it was served at his house, and I so liked the way it slid down to coat the cherry tomatoes, milky orange over squirt-juicy red, that I asked my mother to get some. A few days later we were taking turns pulling each other in my sled and Jaime was getting tired, so to keep him going I told him he could stay for dinner when we got to my house and we'd have French dressing with our meal. "Yum, French dressing," I kept saying, making him struggle harder in his sled harness. It was better than saying "mush" to a husky. But when we got there, Jaime was crestfallen to see that it was store-bought rather than homemade, and he wordlessly declined the treat.

Jaime was like a junior version of the Billy Zane character in *Titanic*, the urbanely contemptuous fiancé, and I didn't like him much because he was both stuck up and insecure, a deadly combination. My father called him a "poor little rich boy," because although he lived a fancy life commuting around the globe, adults could tell he was unhappy. *I* couldn't tell; he seemed like a perfectly obnoxious know-it-all to me. He'd sit in the kitchen talking to my mother in French for hours when all I wanted to do was go to Heart's Island and play. He also had irritating little quirks that he defended obstinately, like his claim that he remembered what it was like being in his mother's womb. When I pointed out how impossible this was, he defended it against all logic. Maybe it was because he was lonely for a mother he rarely saw that he maintained such a fantasy, but I had no patience for it.

Our friendship never would have prospered had it not been for his passion for the TV show *Zorro*. We both loved the black mask, the black cape, the dashing double life Zorro led, with his hiding place behind the fireplace of his hacienda, and a secret tunnel to the outside. In addition, Jaime loved the swordfighting. He'd taken fencing lessons in Paris and his aunt Olga persuaded my mother to let us take lessons together at the YMCA in downtown Norwalk. Olga explained that we wouldn't grow up to become true gentlemen unless we learned how to fence, and my mother must have been sufficiently impressed that someone could entertain such a notion in the 1950s that she went along with it, which was fine by me. I'd developed a taste for it the winter before. My cousin Mike and I'd found a couple of steel bayonets in my grandfather's garage in Boston and we spent hours lunging at each other. It was a miracle we didn't poke an eye out.

Real fencing was clunky compared to the speed and grace Zorro showed—something like the difference between racecar driving and learning to shift. It seemed to me that we were over-concerned with the positions of our ankles and wrists. Parry one, parry two: it bordered suspiciously on ballet. But I liked my foil Jimmy enough to stick with it and was just getting up some speed when the teacher unexpectedly died. My mother took us to class one Saturday and was told that it had happened so suddenly there'd been no time to contact her and cancel the class. Apparently, the teacher had gotten married a few days before, and when driving away from the church with his bride, they'd crashed into a railroad bridge. My mother was stunned.

Not me: I was thrilled by the idea of someone I knew dying. It seemed to make me privy to a giant secret everyone had always been whispering about. A little kid a couple of years younger than I had drowned, but that hadn't really counted. I'd been in the cellar when my sister's friend Jeannie Booth told us that he'd died and Renee and I stole a glance at each other and tittered at the news. It seemed so bogus. How did that little kid know how to die? I remember feeling jealous that the girls would feel sorry for him instead of me, and if I were to die now it would be anticlimactic because someone had already stolen my thunder. But the death of my fencing teacher didn't make me titter. This was more like it; he could properly pull off grown-up stunts like that. I thought it extremely dashing of him to die, and I was grateful to him for thereby admitting me to an exclusive private club of People Who Knew People Who Had Died. (Knowing a dead *kid* was not grounds for admission.) It inducted me into all kinds of arcane feelings like grief that had been denied me until then.

The fencing teacher had always been nice to me. Just the Saturday before he'd tickled my rib cage against his padded white shirt so we were in a squirmy hug and then he'd hoisted me onto his shoulders and skipped down the smelly YMCA corridor shouting, "You know why I like you? Because you're so full of life! And you know what life is, don't you? It's a weekly magazine!"

In retrospect, it was amazing to me that he'd addressed the very subject that was now at issue. Life. I was dazzled. How can you be full of life, like we were, and then lose it like that? I'd always assumed that death was only for dead people, but here a live person had been familiar enough with the topic to joke about it, yet still he'd let life be taken from him. How vigilant did you have to be to keep it?

There seemed to be no answer. Why had no one discovered a cure for death yet? They spent billions to fight heart disease but not a cent to fight the real enemy lurking behind heart disease: death itself. Disease was merely a symptom for the real issue, and the cure was probably something sitting under our noses, hiding in plain sight. Maybe we'd stay alive if we never cut the umbilical cord and walked around still attached to our mothers? Or if we continued to drink breast milk as adults? Why didn't some company bottle breast milk so we could find out? Was it eating green potato chips? Staring at the moon in daylight? What we needed was someone like Fleming, who'd discovered penicillin from mold on a grapefruit. Was drinking ordinary water what did us in? Something everybody did every day, never knowing it was fatal? Or if people talked on the inhalation instead of the exhalation so they wouldn't always be wasting their breath? Or if we didn't breathe so much? If only we could stop breathing . . .

But his death left Jaime and me with nothing to do on Saturday mornings, so we nosed around trying to find a hiding place in his aunt's house, and in no time he found one in her attic, between the stacks of old canvases. He made a fort out of them, with a roof and four walls. Most were just mildewing canvases in plain wooden frames, but one was a pale watercolor behind glass. A bridge. A river. Anemic gray and blue buildings. It was very static and plain; you could tell the artist wasn't very good. Who was the artist, anyway? We looked closely at the tight scrawl at the bottom. A. Hitler.

This was a bombshell. It meant that Hitler really was. He'd been alive, and he'd killed millions of people. It wasn't a myth. Proof was before me, in my hands, something that had been in his hands also. In a sense, A. Hitler and I were holding hands.

It would be easy to read evil into the picture I held. But the picture wasn't evil. It was more complicated than that. There was care here, no question. He'd lavished something onto this rectangle. It was not a beautiful painting, but what amazed me was that it wasn't monstrous. It was OK. And the painter's impulse to make it beautiful couldn't be denied.

When he had a vision of coming up with a master race, did he have a similar impulse? Was he trying to beautify the world by cleansing it of the fiendish dark Jew? But didn't A. Hitler understand that Jews loved life, as he did? Didn't he know how delicate life was? If he'd had a fencing teacher who'd died when he was a kid, would he have understood that dying was a huge and awesome thing? Was he ever frightened of himself? Did he ever think his dad would be ashamed of how he turned out?

I became dizzy with these thoughts. It was like leaning backward over Pirates Point Bridge and watching the waves come in and out. Jaime and I looked at each other, over the canvas. But I never knew what Jaime was thinking. Maybe he was remembering what it was like to be in his mother's womb. Or about Zorro's nemesis, Sergeant Garcia.

Shortly after that Jaime had to go back to Paris, where he couldn't watch Zorro, so his aunt Olga paid me to watch it for him and write a précis of the shows. Every Saturday morning I'd ride my bike up Highland Avenue and deliver my three paragraphs to Olga and get a quarter in return. It was my first paid writing job.

Later, in our teenage summers after he got his driving license, Jaime came back and demonstrated that in addition to being a champion hider he'd become the best pickup artist I ever knew. I'd tag along to Darien to watch him. He'd find girls to talk to at McDonald's and then when they'd agreed to go for a ride he'd perform the coup de grâce, which was to pull on his brown kid leather driving gloves. They swooned at his sophistication. But Jaime was already a man of the world, well on his way to becoming an international playboy. By that time, his father had stepped out of his Ritz Hotel window one dawn and killed himself, so Jaime was worldly in a great many matters.

14

TRICKS OF THE TRADE

*T*he train from Brussels to Antwerp is only an hour, but it's a hundred years in terms of Jewish life. In Antwerp, a city half the size of Brussels, the Jews form a closed community, unassimilated and easy to target. Just leaving the station the boys and I feel exposed, dragging our luggage cart across the cobblestones under overcast skies. "It's a smudgy day," Alex observes. Indeed, a light drizzle falls from clouds that look as though they've been rubbed out with a fat eraser.

Yet the kids are psyched. "Antwerp is awesome!" says Marshall, passing a line of Pizza Huts and McDonald's and other dregs of American chain culture. It's the first glimpse we've had of the country outside its capital, which is never what a country is about, and I scope it out professionally. If I were to frame an essay about this country, I'd start with two words.

"Poor Belgium." Everyone bad-mouths Belgium. When David Letterman flops onstage, he'd do well to have Belgian jokes as backups. Even Paul Theroux, ordinarily a scrupulous observer, is not above calling it a "hideous . . . dismal . . . clammy little country." The general image, promoted by its xenophobic neighbor to the south, is that Belgium is a suburb of France, its people little more than bridge and tunnel traffic—"Flems," in the incomparable words of Monty Python. The resulting inferiority complex is so severe that the Belgian travel brochures themselves are defensive, mustering only enough enthusiasm to call Belgium "odd, in a nice way." (When we stop in the city's tourist office, the agent is so grateful to see a travel writer that he catches his cashmere sweater on the door handle, scurrying to procure me museum passes.)

But think how a Texan could boast if he were born in Belgium! Seven hundred strong and tasty beers, the world's first saxophone, the world's first skyscraper, birthplace of not only Bruegel and Rubens but Magritte and waffles, too. Maybe France is just jealous that Belgium has more Michelin stars per capita than France, or that Audrey Hepburn, that quintessence of Gallic poise and beauty, is Belgian born. By my lights, Belgian women have the best legs in Europe.

The world's first streetcars, too, and what winsome streetcars they are! With their rubber wheels and horns, they proceed at so leisurely a pace you can run alongside them. Their terminus is beneath a park where bands still play from the gazebos on Sunday, and they're filled with the sort of low-land dreamer who carries his beagle in his tweed pocket, its front legs sticking out.

No matter what Monty Python says, Antwerp remains a city where the G-rated prostitutes and the purple-haired punks will do no more harm than nab one of your pommes frites (invented here, not in France) and will, if asked, give it back. Play punks and play prostitutes to go along with the toy trolleys and a queen whose airbrushed good looks are featured on the covers of all the home-grown tattle sheets—the fact that she never produced an heir is much the gossip. We're charmed: the cheese, the beer, the antiquated crime rate that permits bicycles to stand unlocked upon cobblestoned sidewalks. The drizzle is so fine it's like an aerosol against your skin. Marshall lends me his time goggles and sure enough, hidden behind the noxious fast-food restaurants and the skyline crosshatched with crucifixes and radio antennas, you can imagine the thatched cottage, the poplar and bulrush and glimpse of windmill.

And yet all of this felicity is predicated upon the hard reality of diamonds, which we've come to see at the invitation of J. P.'s younger brother, Schloime. Diamonds make it all run, the punks and the trolley and the queen. Seventy percent of the world's diamonds—25 million carats of diamonds a year—pass through Antwerp, and the Beurs is the diamond center of the world. Its lone security guard wordlessly twirls his mustache *"non"* until I surrender my passport to him and we enter a large vaulted hall with marble columns and a monument: "To remember all the people fallen under the Nazis." Flowers are laid there every year on May 10, the date of the German invasion.

Marshall forgoes the elevator to race up the stairs and is waiting for Alex and me when we emerge on the third floor. "What took you so long?" he says, feigning boredom, but his little chest is heaving. Down the corridor I ring a buzzer and a long-necked youth with a wispy goatee regards us steadily through the double set of glass. "We called from Brussels—"

"Sure, sure," he interrupts pleasantly, and opens the door for us to enter a very jazzy foyer. I couldn't be more surprised: mirrored walls, wide windows, industrial blue carpet, an ultramodern abstract of a diamond in ice-cool blues. Everything my great-uncle's offices in New York are not: electric pencil sharpeners, fax machines, digital scales from Germany . . .

"Why German?" I ask. "Does that mean you forgive the Germans?"

The youth shrugs. "It means they make good scales."

Enter Schloime, three feet wide, from the back office. He looks like the bloated Jew caricature in Nazi anti-Semitic pamphlets—JewNose carrying a fat wad of bills, JewNose smooching up an Aryan girl—yet, as with his older brother, J. P., there's no denying his appeal. He's one of those large-boned men whose frames can't contain all their verve and bluster; overweight in the old-fashioned sense, when overweight was a mark of conviviality. This is *heft:* portliness that's proud of itself. Just the way he comes through the door, plump and comfy with his pants cinched above his stomach with a white belt, makes us feel secure in his presence. We feel at once—it's almost an animal sense—that here is a man who's in the prime of his life and probably always has been.

"Hello, Papa," says the boy.

"Hello," says Schloime, and kisses his son heartily on the cheek. The boys and I instantly like him for this, and he seems to like us. He gathers my hands into his, looks us up and down approvingly, and sweeps us forward in a gesture like a kinetic bear hug to the back door. "In we go," he says, gesturing for us to keep moving into the inner office where his elegant wife, well turned out with strands of gold and turquoise around her neck, sits cutting a mango on a glass plate. (The coffee cups are glass, too—it's the diamond dealer's preference for translucence.)

"Wow," Marshall exclaims, his eyes popping out of his head at the diamonds everywhere. "How much are these worth?!"

"Plenty of millions," Schloime says.

"What do you do with them all?"

"You sell 'em, you buy 'em. You know: it's all for the women."

Schloime sends Alex a manly wink, which Alex sends right back. "Gotcha!"

"Perhaps you would like to learn some tricks of the trade?" he asks. "Here, take a look at this," he says, using a tweezers to pick one up and handing Alex a loupe. "See any black specks?"

"Nope."

"Ha! I took the front lens out. Reduced magnification eighty percent. Now when I put it back in—"

"Wow! Lots of them!"

"And each is a flaw! Stay on your toes, gentlemen! Ever notice how many jewelry stores are blue?"

"No."

"Take my word for it. Because against a blue wall or velvet pad, a stone will appear whiter than it is."

"Why?"

"Blue bleaches out yellow and brownish tinges. Now look at this diamond in a gold setting. Nice, eh? But the gold mounting does the same thing, neutralizes yellow. How you should look at it is this way. . . ." He holds it upside down on white paper.

"Is that why you use fluorescent lights?" Alex asks.

Schloime grins at me and taps his head. *"Yidishkop,"* he says. "Oh, there are many ways you can be tricked. You can illuminate the stone from above, producing a glare that renders flaws invisible; you can zap a black speck with a laser, then fill the hole with acid that whitens the blemish. . . ."

"Enough, stop corrupting the children," says his wife.

But Marshall's into it. "Don't some diamonds shine in the night?" he asks.

Schloime laughs and says it's true that there are some luminescent Brazilian stones, but they shine from a slight bit of manganese in them and not the diamond itself.

"And some are colored, right?"

Again Schloime looks at me with admiration. "You have been teaching them?"

I shrug my shoulders cryptically.

Schloime confirms it. "Some have even been known to change color when heated. There was one that became pink for eight days and then gradually lost its color."

"Magic," Marshall says.

"Maybe yes maybe no," Schloime says. "There are some that if you put under your pillow are supposed to drive away melancholy, others to induce agreeable thoughts, still others to calm palpitations of the heart."

"If you strike them together you're supposed to hear the voice of the one you're going to marry," Alex says.

"And they ward off evil," Marshall adds.

Schloime concurs: "The evil eye shall have no power to harm / Him who shall wear the diamond as a charm."

"What poet said that?" I ask.

"The greatest poet of them all: the PR industry," says

Schloime. "Without which the world of diamonds would collapse. Do you know a diamond depreciates ninety-five percent as soon as you walk out the door? But the PR keeps them rare, eh? There are thousands of tons of diamonds waiting to be mined, so many that the only reason they're not dirt cheap is that DeBeers has run it as a monopoly for years. Rubies and emeralds are infinitely more rare; their mines were exhausted a century ago. It's a fixed market, I'm afraid," Schloime sighs, "based on artificial scarcity. So what else is new?"

"They're still nice, though," Alex says.

"You're hooked!" Schloime laughs, putting the loupe in Marshall's palm and closing his fingers around it: a gift. "And you're right in one regard: They were nice to *us.* In the war they were the difference between life and death. And yet do you know what diamonds are made of? Simple carbon! This most precious thing in the world is composed of the most common material in the world, found in every plant and tree."

"Schloime," warns his wife. "Stop before you get allegorical. Show them what you want to show them."

Schloime erupts from his chair. "Bam bam! We go."

He scoops us up, stuffing mango in our mouths and bumping us forward with his nimble puissance. In the elevator, Schloime plays the role of history guide while Alex and Marshall mug for the closed circuit security camera, pretending to strangle each other. "It is not well known, but our small nation of Belgium was very heroic in the war. When King Leopold fled to England after the German invasion, unlike other rulers he continued to act as leader of his people. He declared the transfer of Jewish businesses illegal and warned that citizens who took part would be prosecuted."

"I've heard that the Belgian queen paid money to corrupt the Gestapo," I say.

"I'm all for corruption," Schloime says, peering at me over his thick glasses. "It's the purists who worry me."

I can see he likes to make playfully outrageous statements to weed out his audience from the start. "I happen to agree with you," I say.

"OK, then we are friends."

The elevator doors open and the boys spill out, arm in arm. Murdering each other seems to have rekindled their affection.

Outside the Beurs on Pelikaanstraat, the street of pelicans, it has begun spritzing again. No one seems to mind. Schoolgirls jump rope with a giant rubber band encircling their legs. Around the corner, an ungainly gaggle of hippies plays soccer with an empty Vittel bottle. Like their younger siblings the punks, the hippies are less seedy in Belgium than their counterparts elsewhere, scrubby instead of squalid. The difference, in Antwerp, is innocence.

"Not only that," Schloime resumes his commentary, "but unlike the Church elsewhere, the Church in Belgium protested Nazi laws against the Jews. The cardinal even contacted the Vatican, which requested Catholic institutions to save Jews—without baptizing them!—and instructed the local populace to help hide them. And the upshot?" he says, walking so briskly that the boys have to run to keep up, "there was a higher proportion of Jews saved in Belgium than in any other country. Almost half the Jews in Belgium survived, as opposed to twenty percent in France and ten percent in Holland."

A cheer goes up when the Vittel bottle slides between two parking signs in front of us. Schloime, oblivious, squashes it beneath his white shoes as he marches on. "Belgium had heart. But what you have to understand is that Belgium was a new nation, put together rather artificially in eighteen thirty, carved from the Netherlands and France, so that everyone was a newcomer. It is a melting pot of immigrants."

"Melting pot?" I say. "I never heard that phrase used except about America."

"We come from all over Europe, with the immigrant's sense of hospitality. But that is only half the story," he says, jaywalking, indifferent to the traffic he's halted on both sides of the street. "It is also not well known that Belgian Jews did more in the war to help their own people than Jews in any other country. We supplied places of hiding, identity papers, food ration tickets, escape routes. We maintained an illegal Jewish press and distributed flyers that said 'To inform against a Jew is to murder him!'"

"Did you use invisible ink?" Marshall asks soberly.

Schloime stops short in the middle of a puddle. *"That's* what we were missing! I've been racking my brains for fifty years wondering what else we needed. . . ."

Marshall smiles gleefully.

"Nevertheless, we had a lot of other tricks up our sleeves. Our Jewish Resistance was the most active in Europe. We made the false papers, we collected the money to send Jews abroad. When the Nazis began deporting Jews, our Resistance broke into the Nazi office and destroyed their lists. Even this: On April nineteenth, nineteen forty-three, we did the unthinkable. We attacked a convoy train on its way to Auschwitz, enabling hundreds of deportees to escape. Unfortunately, as with all acts of defiance, it backfired. In retaliation, the Germans began using cattle cars for the first time."

"You guys were brave."

"In our group alone," Schloime goes on, "there were twenty-two of us meeting every week in one room."

"Can we see the place?"

"Where do you think we're going?" Schloime replies. "But first . . . a long cut," he says, as we make a jog to the right through the entrance to a zoo. "Wonderful zoo," he says. "The oldest zoo in Europe. All the animals were imported from the Congo."

Schloime elbows his way through a busload of biscuit-faced German tourists. We stop before the monkey cages and watch a monkey family play together, the husband and wife picking each other's nits, the Alex monkey swatting his younger brother when he gets out of hand, the Marshall monkey swinging by his tail and making faces at the audience.

"Before the war, my brother used to take his twins here every Sunday," Schloime muses. Then seems to take a breath and summon his energy. "Bam bam?"

"Bam bam!" replies Alex. A crocodile scares him, so at the exit he gives it the finger.

Outside a church a few blocks farther we are accosted by a row of panhandlers dyed lime green and magenta. The good churchgoers, hardened by the sight of too many outstretched hands, ignore them with ease. One of the panhandlers with pierced eyebrows insolently looks at his watch: getting late here. He skips up to us shaking his McDonald's cup in our faces and asks me airily for ten francs for a pizza.

"Marshall, my wallet, please . . ."

Seeing what a soft touch I am he ups it to 12 F for pepperoni. After I accede he turns on his heel and dances off with nary a wave good-bye.

"Sucker," Alex says to me.

"I don't mind," I say.

On the other side of the railroad tracks is the neighborhood where J. P. and Schloime lived, still Jewish, though ringed by Arabs smoking in their cafés while the Jews go to pray. It's Friday afternoon and the faithful are on the move.

"Dad, they're wearing cakes on their heads!"

"Those are Hasids, Marshall," I say, referring to the men in black on black medieval costumes with fur-lined hats, the women in white stockings, their hair washed and braided. Once again it occurs to me that Hitler was not searching out a formidable opponent; they're all clustered together as they were then, sitting ducks; you could practically scoop them up in one hand like jacks.

Schloime seems to read my thoughts. "Rather than the all-powerful threat Hitler said we were, the Jews were the weakest enemy Hitler could have found. We had no land of our own, no government, no central authority, no allies, no political weight. In every sense we were the opposite of a cohesive force."

"*Shabat shalom*," the Hasids say to us, stopping to shake our hands but somehow managing to not really look at us. How can such intense people seem so unconscious?

"*Shabat shalom*," we reply. But I can't help feeling repelled by the children with their milky smiles, their serious unfocused eyes behind oval lenses, their dumpling skin with mean red pimples scratched to rawness on their swanlike necks. One little boy has to run after his father and it's the run of a girl. I'm not only repelled, but angry, too. Why do they have to be such caricatures? Don't they know that makes them irresistible as targets? No wonder they got crushed like ants on a picnic plate!

Again Schloime seems to read my mind. "Their unphysicality is to prove their otherworldliness," he tells me. "Devout Jews do not share the Greek ideal of a perfect mind in a perfect body. To them, the body is just something to transport the mind around. Study, worship, perfect oneself to hasten the coming of the Messiah, this is the goal. Let the body go hang. And the result, as you see . . ."

We're in the heart of the Jewish section now. The streets are deserted enough that Marshall is able to walk down a slippery tram track through the cobblestones. "I feel like the Terminator in these sunglasses," he says.

"Well, you look like a tsetse fly," Alex notes.

But we're all testy: the sight of the Hasids has riled us up in some indefinable way. "'What have I in common with the Jews?'" I murmur to myself, quoting Kafka. "'I have hardly anything in common with myself, and should stand very quietly in the corner, content that I can breathe.'"

"Wow, Dad," said Alex crossly. "Talk about *meshuga'as*. One minute you're teaching us Sunday school, the next you're poking fun at your religion!"

Schloime comes to my rescue. "So he's conflicted," he says. "Guess what, gentlemen? That's what it means to be Jewish." He hitches up the white belt at his midriff and trains his bulky attention on the narrow houses before us, resuming the tour. "All this neighborhood was rounded up," he tells us. "The Germans brought in trucks and blocked the escapes."

"Why didn't the Jews just lock their doors?" Marshall asks.

"They'd take a tank and knock 'em down!" Alex points out.

"Then why didn't they go out to a restaurant?"

"Jesus, Marshall, the war lasted five years, it wasn't just one night!" Alex sputters, offended by the vast gap in his brother's worldview. "Besides, there was no place to go: the restaurants were closed to the Jews, the schools, the movie theaters . . ."

"Well, why didn't they hide somewhere dark and crowded, like a video arcade?"

"Marshall, they didn't *have* video arcades in those days!" huffs Alex, at the end of his rope at last. "All they had was pinball!"

We've arrived at the doorstep of a synagogue built on the site of the one burned by the Nazis. "Dad, look!" says Marshall. He's pointing to a red swastika spray-painted on the stone base. "I can just imagine the Nazis doing that a long time ago!"

"It wasn't a long time ago," Alex points out. "Look at the cameras everywhere."

Sure enough, the perimeter of the synagogue is dotted with closed-circuit cameras and klieg lights. Unobtrusively, a small police car sits in front of the synagogue for protection, two of its wheels on the sidewalk. Inside sits a smoking policeman, his pockmarked face lit by the orange glow.

Marshall is stunned. "You mean there are *still* Nazis!? You said they were long gone!"

"*Most* of them are long gone. . . ." I waffle.

"Great, Dad," Alex volunteers. "That's like telling a kid there aren't *many* monsters in his closet."

We go to the door of the synagogue and knock, but are brushed aside by a man who rushes up behind us and heaves open the door to let himself in, brusque and sweating.

"Can we enter?"

"Yes-of-course!" A one-word aspiration, including a suspicious glance at my notepad and a shoulder admonishment not to take notes, it's Sabbath.

Inside, the place is vacant, the brusque man nowhere to be seen. In the empty lobby there's a plaque with the names of those killed in the war, also in rather a more prominent place a plaque with names in gold of *bienfaiteurs* and the sums of their benefaction. There's a pile of flyers advertising a local Israeli restaurant.

I can summon up little piety. We peek into the sanctuary but it's dark and empty. Perhaps if I borrowed Marshall's time goggles I could discern J. P. sitting here reading *Mein Kampf* from inside a brown paper bag, trying to figure out whether Hitler really intended to do the things he said he would.

Suddenly I hear the singsong of prayers from somewhere above. Climbing the stairs to the second floor I open a door to find a chapel full of Jews: men sitting in their pews clucking to each other while they sway and pray, little boys in bow ties and green sneakers rolling in the aisles and playing a sort of subdued tag around the pulpit. The entire congregation is facing front, toward me, and they gesture: *In! In!* I turn away.

Outside once again, the neighborhood is quiet as a country village. What little traffic there was has disappeared. The cop is gone, too. Following us out to the sidewalk is one of the rambunctious green-sneakered little boys, being scolded by his father as he rubs his eyes and is hustled home.

Sunk in our individual thoughts, the four of us walk a bit more in the drizzle. We'd almost forgotten where we were heading until Schloime says, "Here we are." It's a little alleyway—44 Carnotstraat—between a café and a bakery playing Madonna, at the end of which is a corner apartment under a simple yellow roof. "This was where we met, our group."

This is where the Resistance met? It's so ordinary a location, we can't help but be disappointed. What's so great about it? Busy people rush by with pink and blue faces under their candy-colored umbrellas, not giving it a second glance. A woman steps out of the shop with a box of jelly tarts that Marshall eyes greedily—she too is unaware. But that's the point of hiding places: they're special only in the sense that they don't stand out. Like spies, it's their unobtrusiveness that makes it possible for them to be what they are.

Still, we're let down. Sensing our disappointment, Schloime probes: "Come, what is your question?"

"Why did you choose this place? Why here?"

By way of answer, Schloime places his finger to the side of his nose and inhales ceremoniously. "Breathe deep," Schloime says.

Puzzled, Alex and Marshall do what he says.

"Not with your mouth, gentlemen! With your nose!"

They snuffle in deeply through their noses. And choke on the smell of elephant.

"The Gestapo were very dainty," Schloime illuminates. "They did not care to loiter at the hind end of a zoo."

So that's what it is. In our walk we have described a circle and stand now behind the famous Antwerp zoo where the scent of animal excrement is vented.

"Tell me, was this a good trick of the trade?"

Holding their noses, Alex and Marshall nod vociferously.

"Right in this spot we plotted to blow up the convoy train."

We manage to feel a little of the romance of conspiracy. A sense of stealth attaches itself to the fact that we can't even make out the apartment window from the street, just a corner of a yellow roof. Even fifty years later it feels clandestine; we can envision coded signals, hidden panels, secret passageways, maybe even invisible ink. . . .

"I can just see J. P. here," Marshall says.

"My brother?" Schloime chuckles, sticking out his tongue derisively. "Oh no, Jacov was not here. He and his family fled Antwerp at once, he was far away."

We look at each other, dumbfounded. "Away where?"

"God knows. All he ever told me was the coast. . . ."

15

ERA OF GOOD FEELINGS

So, Dad, were you a chickenshit like J. P.?"

"What makes you say *that*, Alex!?"

"Well, J. P. split for the coast. And you were always hiding and worrying about being called a hound dog. So were you like chickenshit or what?"

Good question. What *was* I afraid of? Let's put this into context. The two decades after World War II are considered by most social historians to be the golden age of American Jewry. From the end of World War II, when the horrors of the Holocaust first became known, until the '67 war, when Israel began to be perceived by many as too mighty for its own good, there was an unprecedented wave of Jewish acceptance in the United States as official and unofficial barriers began to fall. Advertising agencies as well as Ivy League universities dropped their restrictions and welcomed names ending with "berg." *Gentleman's Agreement* became such a hot film that it pricked people's consciences, much the same way *Uncle Tom's Cabin* had a century earlier. The whole period reminded me of what my American history books called the Era of Good Feelings, a period in the early 1800s when everyone apparently got along.

I was the beneficiary of all this. Whatever anti-Semitism still existed among my fellow Baby Boomers was in the nature of a trickle-down anti-Semitism: kids heard it from their parents at the dinner table and it trickled down into their consciousness, but it wasn't as if they disliked Jews themselves. And even that mild variety was more than offset by a kind of reverse anti-Semitism, a philo- or pro-Semitism that the world had never seen before. My generation invented perhaps the planet's first positive stereotypes about Jews: that the men made good husbands and the women passionate lovers. (Jews had often been seen before as mysterious and carnal and magnetic and sensitive, but up till now those qualities had been viewed in the pejorative to make Jews untrustworthy.) In addition, a large number of our up-and-coming heroes were Jews: not only the hippies and student radicals like Abbie Hoffman and Jerry Rubin but established cultural rebels like Lenny Bruce and J. D. Salinger and Bob Dylan, preparing the world for such movie stars as Dustin Hoffman and Winona Ryder. Of course, Jewish stars had often changed their names: Betty Joan Perske had become Lauren Bacall, Issur Danielovitch became Kirk Douglas. TV shows had always been written by Jews but now they were also about to be written *for* Jews like Jerry Seinfeld and Paul Reiser and Michael J. Fox. Woody Allen even did the unthinkable: made schleppiness sexy. Sort of.

Jews, in short, had become white. For the first time in millennia, we were so far off the defensive that some Jews took the offense. Alan Dershowitz came up with a new term to replace "anti-Semite." He recommended the term "Judeopath" to put the onus on the perp instead of the victim, though perhaps "Judeophobe" would be better, borrowing as it does some of the glory of "homophobe" and other politically correct words. Jews were in the vanguard, and the result was a kind of Judeo-tropism. In its heyday, many Rowayton and Darien debs were among those who caught the fever. Fresh off the sand of Wee Burn Country Club, they counted the Holocaust among their favorite causes, right up there with migrant workers and Latin American guerrilla fighters. They thought Jews were cool. At beach parties, after a couple of drinks, a lot of white-lipsticked mouths would playfully bite you on the nose and say, "I just love your Jewish looks!"

I tracked our progress on a personal index scale personified by one of the WASP-iest of all, Lynn Williams, a girl who was not only the loveliest in school and who lived in the Beach Association, a neighborhood with a slightly more explicit no-Jews policy than the rest of town, but was also in Renee's class, a year ahead of me. This made her unapproachable on several fronts. But approach her I did. "I like you," I said, one morning outside the library where I was memorizing the poem "If" to recite at closing assembly. Lynn waited expectantly, as if by age nine this fox already knew that such declarations usually had strings attached. But strings there were none. It was simply a fact of life I couldn't stand her being unaware of any longer. Plus, I was almost scientifically curious to see her reaction.

"Thank you. I like you, too," she replied politely. And thereafter seemed to attend to my assembly recitation ("If you can keep your head when all about you / Are losing theirs and blaming it on you") with fractionally less boredom than had I not declared myself.

This, however, was inconclusive. The greatest evidence that we were living in a Judeotropic age came four years later when Lynn Williams's neighbor divorced his wife and married a Jewish woman. Of course, an event of this magnitude didn't go down without commentary. It was rumored around the Association, less by way of explanation than of giving context, that the neighbor's father had once had a Jewish mistress during the Depression. As if there were a propensity for that sort of thing in the family, a weakness in the genes that disposed them toward Semitic women. "Twink" was the new wife's name, being that she was of the country club set, but even so . . .

To be sure, even during this new Era of Good Feelings, the people of *Gentleman's Agreement* were still living their exclusionary lives across the river in Darien, still as pasty-faced in their party dresses as white Rhodesians after their country had changed to Zimbabwe. But it was no longer considered good taste to let their biases show. By the '50s, the anti-Semitism that had bedeviled earlier generations of American Jews did not, as a rule, occur. It wasn't like it was for my father growing up in Boston during the Depression, when he was chased by a couple of thugs for being Jewish, and later, as a day student at Harvard, when he was eating his paper bag lunch with another Jewish day student and a snit from Adams House referred to their pairing off as "a synagogue." (According to the memoirs of Nat Hentoff, Boston in those days was considered the most anti-Semitic city in the country, and Jew boys habitually had their heads beaten by "Irishers.") And even that was nothing compared to what went down in *his* father's day, when they performed forced baptisms on Jews, or what had been going on for millennia in other countries. In France in 1888, for instance, newspaper editorials were not above calling for Jews "to be stewed in oil or pierced to death with needles. They should be circumcised up to the neck. A new gun should be tried out on the 100,000 Jews in the country." In our own century, even so gifted a soul as Céline had declared that "Jews have caused all the European wars since 843," and demanded their massacre.

French anti-Semitism, in fact, had traditionally been so toxic that some historians hold to the view that Nazism could have germinated in France as easily as in Germany. But of course it was in Germany where they elected Hitler chancellor after he spewed such ravings as this: "The cleanliness of this people, moral and otherwise, I must say, is a point in itself. By their very exterior you could tell that these were no lovers of water, and, to your distress, you often knew it with your eyes closed. . . . If you cut even cautiously into [the general decay], you found, like a maggot in a rotting body, often dazzled by the sudden light—a kike!"

(On the other hand, by his own admission Hitler imbibed much of his anti-Semitism from that home-grown American

Henry Ford, who in the '20s distributed his venomous flyer "The International Jew" throughout his Ford dealerships in the United States as well as Germany, helping to inflame the mind of young Hitler.)

Compared to such goings-on, what was I complaining about? Next to pogroms and box cars, Spanish inquisitions and Soviet oppression, the sort of stuff I encountered, or not even encountered so much as *anticipated* encountering, was bush league. The worst I ever heard it got for American Jews in my generation was yeshiva boys getting the lids of Hoodsies ice cream cartons slapped on their backs by local toughs. "How ya doin'?" *Thwack!*

Then what, in such an historically friendly period, made me hide? Even more to the point, why did I need to hide and other Jews didn't? In second grade Jaime Rothschild spent the fall semester in Rowayton and jokingly announced to one and all that it was his ambition to grow up to become the first Jewish pope. Even the teachers laughed fondly at the image. Was I chicken-shit because I deduced from my mother's stories that admitting Jewishness meant putting my life in jeopardy? Yet Renee, who also heard the stories, would matter-of-factly reply, "Jewish, why?" when someone asked her what she was.

"Oh! Sorry!" they'd say.

"Nothing to apologize about," she'd reply.

"But wow, I never met a Jew before!" they might go on. "And I mean, I haven't only lived in Rowayton. I lived in New Canaan before that, and I mean . . . Do you mind if I touch your hair?"

"Knock yourself out," she'd say.

Such straightforwardness was beyond me, as ballsy as the chants being contemporaneously sung by the Jewish Defense League against a battery of club-swinging cops on the streets of Borough Park: "We are Jews, we couldn't be prouder, and if you can't hear us we'll shout a little louder!" It was as incomprehensible as the courage of a fisherman of my acquaintance who grew up in Florida with a Russian Jewish father and an Irish

Catholic mother and who had a foolproof way of dealing with grade school anti-Semites. "I flattened 'em," he says simply. "But then, that was just my way." Why was *my* way to pedal furiously down the hill in front of Lynn Williams's house blindfolded?

I once asked Rothschild if it was difficult to do his Jewish pope thing in front of Lynn Williams.

"Nah," he said airily. "It's no big deal."

"That takes a lot of guts," I stammered.

"Oh, I wear my Judaism lightly," he said.

◆ ◆ ◆

In fairness to myself, I suppose the fisherman had his own issues, as Renee had hers. A man in a car had once wanted to show Renee something he was hiding in his lap beneath his newspaper, and she was bashful with boys for a time afterward. It was also true that she was frequently concerned about not being popular enough, while I took my popularity for granted. I wore my popularity lightly.

No one's all brave. I once spent a week in the Andes with a man who'd summited Everest four times and he freely admitted that he was afraid of swimming. Choose your poison. A rule of thumb might be: the braver the bullfighter, the brighter his night-light.

◆ ◆ ◆

Nevertheless, I wasn't so taken with my own separateness that I was unable to see that some kids were hurting more than I, in ways that had nothing to do with Jewishness. One Halloween night I stomped up a neighbor's porch in my devil's horns and the kid came to the door looking like a cricket hiding in a crack with its legs folded under itself—only he wasn't in costume, that's just what his *behavior* looked like. He began to apologize in a whispery voice that his family didn't give out candy and I couldn't understand what he was talking about until he was elbowed aside by his hawk-voiced mother, who bellowed that they were Jehovah's Witnesses and didn't celebrate Halloween.

Another time there was a girl in school who smelled so bad the teacher sent her home to take a bath but she came back with damp hair after lunch and still smelled. It wasn't her fault, it was just her body giving off the stink of vulnerability, and the way she dealt with it was to be defiant and run up to kids in the playground and make them run away holding their noses. She'd laugh at the power it gave her, but it was such a lonesome power to have.

All this reminded me of the ad campaign that was ubiquitous during this Era of Good Feelings, wherein a Japanese monk or a Native American chief in head feathers was shown happily munching a slice of rye bread, above the caption: "You don't have to be Jewish to like Levy's Real Jewish Rye." Nor did you have to be Jewish to feel a sense of alienation. Lots of people were minorities in their own minds.

Case in point: our next door neighbor could have been the poster girl for Miss Rowayton Tomboy, 1958. Jeannie Booth was an outdoorsy girl who upheld the time-honored local standard of treating the mallards at the school pond as though they were sacred, becoming so outraged when a little kid once threw a rock and accidentally killed a duckling that she chased him all the way home and knocked him down on his driveway. She had a big brother who was one of the original bigkids and so mighty that I once saw him jump into a moving car. Her dad gave me envelopes from around the world for my stamp collection and one night on his brick patio, the ice clinking musically in his gin glass, he pointed out a white diamond inching between the stars—it was *Sputnik* and the skies were opening—and he flattered me by calling me Dan'l, as in Dan'l Boone. They were a totally Rowayton family and I envied Jeannie for what appeared to be her effortless sense of fitting in. With the Booths next door, I was connected to the world through stamps and satellites and even a string telephone that stretched between Renee's and Jeannie's bedrooms, across the chrysanthemums.

Years later, Jeannie called me out of the blue from her grown-up home in Virginia to say that she'd envied our family. We seemed more a part of things than she was.

I could almost hear the crickets from those summer nights. "What in the world are you talking about, Jeannie Booth?"

"Well, you just said it. *Booth!* As in *John Wilkes Booth!* You didn't notice that I was absent every Lincoln's birthday!?"

It helped me realize that I was lucky, being Jewish in a non-Jewish town. Others were more challenged to find reasons for the aloneness they felt as a natural condition of childhood. One kid felt it because he was born on April Fool's Day and he always got booby prizes for birthday presents. Another because he had a harelip, though I thought it was called that because it gave him the cute mouth of a cottontail rabbit. Some kids chose to blame it on their good fortune, that their grandmother was too rich or their father happened to be on TV every night delivering the news.

It wasn't just Rowayton, of course. Years later I found myself chatting with the curator of a well-known museum who was raised in the Five Towns section of Long Island, across the water from Rowayton. Hers was the reverse of my situation—she was one of the few Christians in a Jewish community. But what made her spend two and three hours nightly sobbing in her bathroom was not her religion, but something else: this cultured teenager, already writing precocious papers on Manet and Degas, believed no one would ever marry her because she had hair on her toes.

Maybe the truth is that no one ever feels entirely accepted— not even Lynn Williams *before* Twink. Maybe Jeannie Booth chose to be embarrassed about John Wilkes Booth, instead of being proud about William Booth, who founded the Salvation Army the same year Lincoln was assassinated, because it was the closest thing she could find upon which to hang her native sense of estrangement. Maybe the kid Jeannie knocked down for killing the baby mallard is writing a book about how he always felt an outsider because of that incident. Maybe Hitler did what he did because, with his big ears and black hair, he never felt like a true Aryan—that it isn't so much being a Levy or a Booth but being human that makes people feel out of place.

◆ ◆ ◆

None of which changes one thing that J. P. is certifiably right about. It's amazing how often the number six million comes up. I'd noticed it myself, throughout the Era of Good Feelings. Once you're attuned, you hear the number in some way or another all the time. Six million residential burglaries occur in the U.S. every year. Six million Internet users claim to have fallen victim to credit-card fraud. Social Security computers process six million applications for benefits each year. Television's Bionic Man costs six million dollars. Six million is the number of farms still working in the U.S., of American students with disabilities, of Filipinos living outside the Philippines, of worldwide followers of the Dalai Lama. The number of Jews in both the United States and Israel is not five million or seven million but—guess how much? Right.

It's like a magic numeral through time, where the digits are trying to tell us something about ourselves. The question is: *What?*

16

400 REVELATIONS

I'm in the plow position, toes over head. The boys are mountain climbers traversing my body. Marshall's talking through a toilet paper tube to my feet ("Come in, team leader, can you hear me?"), while Alex makes a discovery that astonishes him. "Dad, you've got a hair growing out of your ear—*a white one!*"

I lower my toes and come to rest, sitting lotus for a moment while I collect my thoughts in the overheated Antwerp hotel suite. As a travel essayist, I'm used to traversing the globe in two giant steps. But with these kids, I'm doing it in a million baby steps. Moments like these—when I realize I haven't been more than twenty yards from them in a week—are when I'm being nibbled by guppies or pecked to death by ducklings. With a full breath I come to a decision. "I'm going out for a jog."

"We'll come! We're not sleepy! Two against one!"

"Overruled," I say. "I need R-and-R."

Alex seizes his main chance. "Do we get three stars for today, Dad?"

"We'll see. So far you're only up to one."

"*One!?*" they mouth to each other with astonishment in a manner that tells me they know one is fit and proper.

"Marshall, you OK with my going out for half an hour?"

Marshall burps back a hiccup. "But what if you get lost?"

"Dad never gets lost," Alex says. He says it almost wistfully.

The issue settled, Alex puts on his Walkman. Marshall's in a sudden state of hilarity as he bunny-hops around the room with his pj's around his ankles. "I hope the Nazis don't get you!" he titters, exiting the room.

But a minute later I follow him to his room and find him weepy. His moods are tropical: blue skies one minute, thunderstorm the next. I haul him onto my lap before the tears have a chance to fall. "What's the matter?" I ask.

Marshall shrugs. "I don't know," he says honestly. His lip's out, his shoulders turned in. Bedtime sleepiness frequently makes him tearful, the tiny rips and tears of the day stinging all over again.

"Is it missing your rabbit?"

That's good for starters. "She doesn't have anyone to talk to all month, and she gets lonely in there by herself."

"Was it also the zoo today? Those monkeys being such a family?" I ask. Because it's always a good guess that at the bottom of his bedtime mournfulness is divorce. The fact that his mother and father don't live or eat or travel together, that we continually shred the fabric of togetherness, this he's used to. But that we don't put him to bed together at the end of a long day? That he can never get through his head.

With half a tear under his eye he says simply, "It looked fun."

To such a plaintive statement, I have only one rejoinder. "Want to wrestle?"

"Sure."

We wrestle for a minute, I making growl noises and he making growl noises an octave higher. Marshall's noises are not proportionate to his effort. He has no idea we're supposed to pin each other. He thinks the noises are to ornament the wrestle just as grimaces are supposed to accompany wishbone breaking—neither has a point beyond the pleasure of grappling with a slippery project together.

We stop. The wrestling's helped a limited amount, but his shoulders are still eloquent of distress. Deciding it's time to pull a J. P., I perform a quiet trick of my own.

"Hey, look what I found," I say. Flashing my palm to show there's nothing in my hand, nothing up my sleeve, I reach around into the breast pocket of Marshall's pajamas and pull out a jelly tart from this afternoon's walk, neatly wrapped in a white napkin.

"Oh!" he breathes. "How'd that get here?"

"Beats me." I shrug. And as I bring the tart to his lips I ask, "Are you also sad because it's hard to have a big brother who picks on you?"

Craning his neck to take a small bite, he nods. "*Jacyln Smith!*" he says, as if this is the single most profoundly stupid thing he's heard in his life.

"You're pretty nice to him," I say, "considering how much you hate him."

He sniffles. "I try."

"So are you also sad," I ask gently, "because there still seem to be some Nazis in the world?"

He bursts into tears suddenly. "I'm just so sorry all the little kids got lo-jacked!"

"Is that what you think?"

"Maybe the Nazis offered them candy, and then they dropped their bodies in a Dumpster somewhere. I want to be as old as Alex so if they want to lo-jack me I could jump out of a cattle car . . ."

He's crying silently now as he chews. And so I rock him, gently there on the bed, surprised as always at how heavy his tears are, as though made of mercury. "Well, hey, you can't cry *and* keep eating your tart," I tell him. So he stops chewing and I hold him awhile. Then I ask if he wants to go to sleep and he says no, he doesn't like to sleep when his cheeks are still wet.

"Is that what's making you sad?" I probe, gently. "That nothing seems safe anymore?"

Marshall nods. "And about J. P., too," he says. "He must have been lonely, hiding everywhere to keep from getting concentrated—"

"Here, I know what you need," I say to quell his sad ranting. "You need some of my strength." The ritual. Marshall turns to face me as I open my arms to let him hug me hard. He breathes a small sigh then, half filling his lungs with encouragement. But the rest of his lungs are still troubled. "I can't sleep with that picture," he confesses, indicating a picture on the wall.

"What's wrong with it?"

"It looks like a girl's dick."

Sure enough, the grays and whites resemble a hermaphroditic groin. Could the hotel be conscious of what they've hung here, like a clitoral hard-on? What a pity, I think, not for the first time, that the bold and noble adventure of abstract expressionism has at the close of the twentieth century been relegated to bad art in mid-level hotel rooms.

"What do you do with something that scares you?" I ask.

"Make friends with it."

"Can you make friends with that picture?"

"But I hate it and I'm scared of it."

"Can you make friends with it anyway?"

Marshall considers. He closes his eyes and concentrates. I always love getting the chance to see his face, rapt and composed, when he labors to make peace with something, a process I admire without fully comprehending. "Did it," he says, coming out of his fear and ready to roll again. "So Dad, was Hitler a vegetarian?"

"I never heard that. Why?"

"Well, maybe that's why he was so mean, because he never got to eat meat so he had to kill people. . . ."

"Actually, vegetarians tend to be gentle people, if anything."

"That's interesting. But can I change the subject for a minute?"

"Of course."

"When I grow up? I'm going to visit you and Mom every weekend. Because I love my relatives."

"Gee, Marshall, we thank you for that."

"First, I'll visit Mom, because she's my mother. But then I'll visit you. Because you're my relative, too."

"I'm sure I speak for all your relatives when I say we're honored."

"Or maybe sometimes, I won't have time to visit both places, so I'll visit you both at the same place. You can stay at Mom's with us, or she can stay with *us*-us."

The diplomat. Always trying to get us together.

"And if *I* ever get divorced," he goes on, "I'm going to stay friends with my wife, like you and Mom."

"A fine idea," I say.

"You still love each other a little, don't you? Not *in* love but you love each other as friends."

"That sounds about right," I say.

"Yeah, but Dad? Do we really have to die?"

I'm caught off guard. He uses the same tone of voice as if he were asking if he could stay up late tonight. "Isn't there some way we can keep from falling off? If we get a good grip? I'm going to hold on to a big rock."

"I'll be holding on with you."

"I'm going to hold on to something better. *You!*"

As I snuggle the blanket around his ears, Marshall lets out his chuckle of coziness. "Give my regards to Dreamland," I say.

"Tell 'em I'll be there in two hours."

Marshall takes my face in his hands and rubs my cheeks so my three-day-old beard scratches his palms. "Sparks!" he says.

"Boy, you really love life, don't you?" I say.

"I love life," Marshall sings, "because it keeps us company!"

And falls asleep just like that, his hands interlocked under his chin like a dictionary illustration of a sleeping child. I turn my attention to Alex in the other room. Our favorite game when they were small was something we called "up-down"—as fast as I could get one to lie down on the carpet, the other would pop up—an allegory for all the mental up and down that is so much a part of early child rearing. I still feel I've just tamped down a fire in one boy when it flares in the other.

"I just can't stand having him near me all the time," Alex says, seriously exasperated in the living room where he sits drinking coffee and studying J. P.'s journal, rearranging pages like a jigsaw puzzle. *"Jewels!"* he says. "As if Mom would possibly wear a perfume from Elizabeth Taylor!"

"It must be pretty awful."

"You don't understand, Dad, I've got to *live* with that stuff. Every minute of the day there he is, following me everywhere I go! And don't say it's because he admires me!"

"Never!"

"Oh sure he does. Then how come he won't even do what I tell him to?"

"Maybe because he looks up to you *too* much. He's got to prove he's not your clone."

Alex thinks. "Yeah but still: *ughgugh!* If I've got to have someone next to me every day, I don't want it to be such a little Roquefort!"

"OK, it's settled. Marshall gets shot at dawn."

This seems to settle him down inordinately. He reaches for a box of croutons on the end table and scores a handful. "But Dad?" he asks conspiratorially. "I asked Becky."

"Who's Becky?"

"Becky, the girl I told you about two hundred times."

"Oh, Becky. Your main squeeze."

"Not 'main squeeze,' Dad! 'Girlfriend'! Kids don't use stupid words anymore."

"Sorry," I say, contrite. "So what'd you ask her?"

"Out."

"Yikes," I say. "When did this momentous event take place?"

"At the school assembly, last Thursday. And Dad, guess what?" he says, pointing to his lips. "I got to first base!"

"Gee," I allow. "You don't think you're rushing things a bit?"

Alex gives me the benefit of thinking about this for a moment. "Would you rather be a goodie-goodie or an asshole?" he asks, passing me the box of croutons. "If you had to be one or the other?"

"Are you afraid of being a goodie-goodie?"

"I just don't want kids to not like me."

"Hmm. Was getting to first base with Becky your idea, or the other kids'?"

Alex decides to answer this one sideways. "I don't know why everyone thinks first base feels so good. I thought it was . . . just regular. Maybe not even regular. I mean, she's not that old. She only weighs eighty-six pounds."

"That's not that old," I agree.

"Yeah." We sit there nodding our heads in male sympathy for a minute. "But you know," I offer, cautiously. "You don't have to do anything you don't want to do. I'm certainly not going to consider you a goodie-goodie. And I doubt Becky will, either."

Alex looks the tiniest bit relieved. We nod together a moment more, the box of croutons passing back and forth. "Marshall's not *that* bad," he volunteers.

"You don't think?"

"When he's asleep and everything."

We listen to the snoring boy, picturing the tiny bubbles blowing in and out.

"Yeah, but Dad? How could the Nazis kill little kids like that? They weigh only forty-five pounds!"

Up till now I've been feeling my way along behind my son, but now it's given me to dart ahead, measuring how much reality to let into the conversation. "They weren't exactly nice to kids your age, either, you know," I say.

"I know. But kids my age, we've been on the soccer team, we've gone to first base, we've *lived*. But someone like Marshall . . . I get all these thoughts in my brain all the time. Like how could people *do* that? And what if someone murdered you or Mom? I just get these thoughts in my brain and they stay there and I get all glued up. . . ."

Alex is staring at me so hard his nostrils are flaring.

"There are a lot of those thoughts going around," I say. "The trick is to let them float on through."

"You mean, they go through everybody?"

"Especially these days. But if you let them float through, they'll pass right by. It'll be like watching a parade."

"Do you think those German tourists at the zoo today have those thoughts?"

"I daresay they do."

"That beggar with the McDonald's cup?"

"Sure. From time to time."

Alex looks at me and blinks. "I'm glad we gave him twelve francs, for whatever sucker reason we did . . ."

"Yeah," I say. "Me too . . ."

We share a small smile then, and release it at the same time. He passes me another crouton.

"Do you think the Nazis had those thoughts?" he asks.

"Yes," I say finally. "I believe they had an extra lot of them, and that's why they did the things they did."

This makes sense to Alex. He blinks again, and I can almost hear the *click!* and whirring of gears as he switches to a related subject.

"I'm so spoiled," he says then. "Do you think I'm spoiled? I've got food and everything, and two houses . . . one for you and one for Mom . . . when all those people had to hide for their lives. . . ."

"At least you're aware of how fortunate you are," I say. "That's a good thing."

"Well, I don't want to be mean to everybody. Insultous to Marshall all the time."

"Those times you *are* insulting?—are because you're beginning to put the world together, and his childishness upsets the order you're trying to create."

"Yeah. I'm such a jerk all the time."

"Well, listen. It's hard being a jerk all the time. Most of us are only jerks off and on."

Alex misses the humor in this, so hard is he concentrating.

"I *am* trying, you know, Dad."

"I know you are," I say, reaching over to touch his arm in a way that should confer conclusion. But Alex has pulled back an inch to come up with a new angle on the subject.

"How do you think a person gets better?" he asks. "By being mad at himself for the things he does wrong? Or by being nice to himself for the things he does right?"

"The latter. Try complimenting yourself more. Be kind to yourself."

What I love. How Alex will rest his head on my shoulder. When I least expect it, how he'll wind his arm through mine. "Oh, I get it!" He's marveling silently, with a little internal gasp of wonder. "You need to encourage yourself, just like you do with other people!" It's as deepening a discovery as when he learned to read the night globe I'd given him back in second grade. Stars *do* have an order and design. Life *is* a matter of lightening up as well as bearing down.

In her lifetime, they say a woman has only 400 eggs destined for possible fertilization. So, too, I sometimes think, all of us are allotted 400 Revelations. This is one of them, and it's as wondrous to him as when he was crying as a baby, and I leaned down in his crib and said, "What you're doing is called *crying*," and Alex suddenly looked stunned, to understand that what he was engaged in was a bona fide activity that had characteristics and a name, it wasn't just a torrent of wet inchoate sensations. . . .

A great sigh comes out of Alex from somewhere deep within. "Thanks, Dad." He punches me in the arm. "You're not that bad a guy. For a Yankees fan."

And that's that. I help him into bed, where he sits with the blankets up to his waist. But now he has one last thing to get off his chest.

"Do you believe in God, I don't mean *God,* like a man with a beard, but God as in godly, you know? Godliness?"

"I believe in a power that's good," I say, "that's responsible for the beauty in the world. And I believe we honor that godliness by making beauty ourselves."

"But what about all the bad things in the world?"

"I'm still working on that one," I confess.

"You know what I'd like to ask an old man of eighty?" he says. "I'd like to ask him if a long time ago seems like a long time ago, or is it just like a minute ago. Like does your life go by in a second or what? I'd like to ask an eighty-year-old that."

"Well," I say, "I'm not eighty but sometimes I look at you and I see the way you were as a baby and it's like it was yesterday. That's why when Marshall says he remembers being a sperm, it doesn't matter whether it's literally true or not. The main thing is he's feeling his life: the sadness, and the wonder. Isn't that better than not?"

Alex sits there feeling his life: the plainness of it, and the richness. It all adds up to a feeling of miraculousness—one of those moments, breathing in and out, when we're both able to glimpse the possibility of living in a state of grace. Not because we're so deserving but simply because we're alive and thus humbly entitled to the rewards of God's earth.

"Thanks. But Dad? Betcha still don't want to give us three stars for today, right?"

"Right. I don't."

"OK." A wink, very fetching. "So Dad," he says cheerily, planting a kiss upon my lips and slamming his head into the pillow, "do you think *I* should believe in God?"

I put my hand on Alex's hair. I rub it for company. I rub it for luck. And get a whiff of my ex's perfume. Shalimar. By no movie star at all.

"I think it's important to have Someone to thank. . . ."

17

GRASSHOPPER SPIT

I always wanted to believe in God. Despite the fact that I wore a transistor radio earphone to High Holiday services, I wanted to give God my devotion; partly because I felt a little sorry for Him. What a Klutz, to let such a big war slip through His fingers! He couldn't have been a very capable God to let one like that get by Him, and this made me pity Him a bit, when He so obviously wanted everyone to revere Him. I felt toward Him the way I felt toward 7-Up and its somewhat pathetic ad slogan of the 1950s ("You like it; it likes you"), which led me to drink 7-Up despite the fact that I really didn't enjoy its taste. It set up a corollary I couldn't disappoint. If He liked me, I wanted to like Him, too. The big Lug.

I'd have conversations with Him, sometimes, when I was calm in bed at night, waiting for sleep, and they'd flood me with joy for no reason that I knew. The world seemed good, with each star in place like thumbtacks arranged perfectly. In my happiness, I'd murmur "thank you" and lie there feeling blessed and sorrowful both, and not understanding why I felt either one. But even more satisfying was worshiping an idol I found not far from my house amid a formal garden on the granite estate of the Remington Rand corporate headquarters. I'd sneak in the back way, through a dead-end road that culminated in a field of chest-high grass. The stalks were topped with grasshopper spit, a foamy concoction of insect bubbles that horrified me—I'd heard once that you could drink it if you were dying of thirst—but also exalted and sanctified me, because it was all part of the ordeal of getting to the idol. It was what you had to do to cleanse yourself before you could properly worship.

Having emerged chastened and purified from my thicket of grasshopper spit I'd sneak through the garden to my idol, a black stone statue of a goat-boy, and I'd use dead leaves to wipe the spiderwebs off. After a few minutes of tending to it, I'd sit there and be in a kind of communion in this hidden place, feeling calm and present and thankful. Then I'd leave.

It was idolatry, pure and simple, but it was deeply satisfying to wade through the spit—I later learned that Bible scholars think the manna Moses found in the Sinai was really white edible insect secretions—and then to stroke the statue with leaves and clear off the spider gunk. There was something about the conjunction of smooth human fingertips and rough stone that felt right. I was touching the divine to aid it, and God was pleased with my efforts. He liked it just as He liked it when I invited Him to rest in my bed, if He was tired, when I was falling asleep at night. I liked Him; He liked me.

I also worshiped the clothes hook in the family bathroom. It was the simple double prong that was screwed into the back of every hollow bathroom door in every mass-produced subdivision house of the '50s, but to me it was God. I would silently salute it whenever I was taking my clothes off before a shower. It was one of the few things in the world to gaze upon my nakedness, and I felt no shame before its witness, only a kind of supple joy that I was alive; and the hook also was Someone I could wordlessly thank.

I told no one about the clothes hook, but one time I did entrust McDougal with a visit to my idol. He liked it, too, and so we decided to spend that night in its presence. We drew a map to satisfy ourselves that we knew the way and we put it inside the brown plastic seat of my mother's sewing machine that she, being a lapsed sewer, never used. Not that we needed a map, of course, but we felt that no runaway plan was ever hatched without one, and so being good little suburban runaways we had ours.

Evening arrived. My mother said good night to me. I set my orange-faced alarm clock for midnight and tucked in to wait. However, a few minutes later my father came in the room and sat down solidly on my bed. He told me that he'd just received a phone call from McDougal's mother across the street and the jig was up. It turned out that at the same time my mother was innocently saying good night to me, McDougal's mother was innocently saying good night to him, and he'd asked her to kiss him good night when she went to sleep.

"Why?" she'd asked him.

"Because I've got to make sure I wake up at midnight," he'd blurted out. After this ignominious admission, it took Mrs. McDougal but a moment before she'd coaxed the entire scheme out of him. I was secretly relieved that we didn't have to make our way through the grasshopper spit by the dubious cold light of the moon. But for the rest of our childhood I never let McDougal know I was relieved.

◆　◆　◆

(Years later, I learned the history of this granite estate that I so blithely appropriated for my hiding place. It had been the home, complete with eight full-time servants, of the president of the U. S. Steel Corporation, at the time the world's largest industrial enterprise—and formed, incidentally, by J. P. Morgan, *the other*—before being purchased by James Rand of Darien, who used the place for the headquarters of his corporation, Remington Rand. By coincidence, not only was Remington Rand the builder of the typewriter I was beginning to type stories on, but during the '50s it was one of the earliest companies to devote its attentions to the computer and was developing the Univac, one of the world's first, under top secret security right there on the premises. It was in that sense *their* hiding place, too. While I was lost to the world in my own hiding place outside, they were hard at work inside theirs, creating something that would change the world forever.)

◆ ◆ ◆

But the same time that I was feeling all this divine benevolence, I was also alarmed at finding myself capable of the greatest rage. . . .

My brain would feel zapped. Recollecting my mother's stories, I'd feel woozy with hate, becoming aware of my breathing, shallow yet labored. I'd grow conscious of the smell of my fingertips, which I'd notice I was holding over my mouth . . . *drop babies on bayonets?* . . . and then suddenly I'd have to take a deep breath, as if there weren't enough air around, or I'd stopped breathing for a minute. Asthma happened.

I felt something a young boy ought not to: an anger so vast I didn't know what to do. It was an anger that made me trip up the stairs, that made me stumble into screen doors, that caught in my throat and made me gag with words as yet unformed. It made me want to crush crushable things with my fingers: cardboard egg cartons I'd been saving for a science experiment, toy gliders made of balsa wood, little forts for my army soldiers that would splinter into razor-sharp plastic shards. My rage was all-consuming; I could feel my brain burning up like the old vinyl film that would get stuck on a frame and catch fire, and you could see the film bubble and dissolve right on the screen. My tears felt like they were acid, capable of scorching anything they fell on.

After these bouts, I was like a wire that had been burned by a blowtorch till it glowed red and crackled, then been left to cool gray and brittle, its energy burned away to nothingness. My eyes felt colorless. I'd continue breathing but my respiration was filled with the creaking noises of my lungs because there was no fresh air anywhere on earth. I was inhaling air made stale by others of my species who were evil.

It felt like I was reared on rage. As an infant I drank it in with my mother's milk, or instead of my mother's milk, since I wasn't breast-fed. Sometimes I thought my mother wanted me to inherit a rage she didn't fully allow herself to feel. In *Children of the Holocaust,* Helen Epstein theorizes that "survivor parents . . . might unconsciously encourage aggressive behavior in their children, aggression they themselves could not permit themselves to express toward their own dead families. . . . [They] took a secret delight in their child's aggressiveness because during the war, whether the parents were in concentration camps or in hiding, they could not allow themselves to express the aggression they felt toward their oppressors. To do so would be to invite death."

Did my mother, in other words, neglect me and rail at me because she was compelled to inflict on the next generation the trauma she'd experienced? As a refugee, was she inflicting her wound on her firstborn son in order to have me act out a rage she was at a loss to express? Was she bequeathing me her rage because for her to feel it would have incinerated her?

It worked, for whatever reason. I felt like a house with the furnace chugging heat right out the open windows. In 1977 an Israeli psychiatrist working at Stanford noted, "The effects of systematic dehumanization [of the Holocaust] are being transmitted from one generation to the next through severe disturbances in the parent-child relationship." The result, in one of those neat reversals of modern life, was that I was like a Palestinian baby, weaned on tales of bitterness. In fact I've often thought I could have grown up to become a terrorist, and was spared such an existence only because of a bewilderingly contradictory sense of joy.

❖   ❖   ❖

Or maybe it was Grimm's that saved me. Bruno Bettelheim says fairy tales fulfill the need for magic in a world that seems to lack it. And certainly any parenting guide will tell you that fairy tales aren't bad for a kid. The violence and malice teach valuable lessons: right triumphs over wrong, evil is punished. Revenge is exacted, as foretold in the Book of Psalms: "He will execute judgement upon the nations and fill the world with corpses. He will shatter the enemy's head over the wide earth." Grimm's helped make up for the real-life stories where mothers clutched their tortured infants while SS men got off scot-free, living happily ever after on Argentinian haciendas.

◆ ◆ ◆

At Passover at my great-uncles' apartments we used to sing "Dayenu," the traditional song that means "enough, we are content." Yet for all my horsing around at these seders, it occurred to me that a better song would be the opposite: it is *not* enough. We will *never* be content.

> Had He taken us out of Germany,
> but also executed judgments on them,
> *Not dayenu!*

> Had He executed judgments on them,
> but also upon their gods,
> *Not dayenu!*

> Had He executed judgments on their gods,
> but also slain their firstborn,
> *Not dayenu!*

But wait a minute. *Drop babies on bayonets?* Apparently it's an image that enjoys considerable currency among victimized groups. An Irish friend told me that his grandmother said Oliver Cromwell did the same to Irish babies back in 1651. The English accused the kaiser's forces of spearing babies in World War I, American propagandists said Iraqis unplugged Kuwaiti infants from their incubators during the Gulf War, Palestinians have been known to resurrect the tale that Israelis use goyish baby blood to make matzo. . . .

It doesn't mean that victims are consciously lying. It only means there's enough hurt to go around.

Item: Of course, it should be noted that in Grimm's, which made the Not-sees palatable for me, the anti-Semitism is taken for granted. A staple of these Germanic folk tales is the haggard and grasping Jew who is the butt of gratuitously cruel jokes perpetrated by otherwise good-hearted peasants. The Jew "with his long goat's-beard," a creature both cunning and feckless, stubborn and ingratiating, gets his comeuppance for always fleecing people and is usually left screaming, jumping up and down in frustration, hoist by his own petard for being too clever by half.

Contrast this with the folklore being produced in America during this time. While the Grimm Brothers were collecting their dark folk tales in Germany, across the ocean America's first great comic writer, Washington Irving, was creating soufflés of gentle satire about Rip Van Winkle and Ichabod Crane. Nothing else so starkly shows the difference between my dark European past and the bright American one all around me.

Nevertheless, growing up I took limited comfort in the fact that others felt rage, too. When a wormy little man named Eichmann was smuggled to Israel and put on trial, I was heartened to learn that the reason he was placed in a glass case (always referred to, inexplicably, as a "cage" as if made of steel) was for his own protection—that the public would have "torn him limb from limb." Now there was a concept. My party-girl mother would tear him limb from limb? "With my bare hands," she told me. My studious father? "Gladly." Normally calm people were enraged at the thin-lipped monster whose twisted smirk was the face behind the concentration camps. (To this day, people who lived through the Eichmann trial have only to see a license plate with a certain combination of random letters to get a hot chill: ECHM.)

But mostly I felt isolated in my rages. I'd flee or be banished to my room downstairs, away from the rest of the family, where I'd rage so fiercely hot that I was freezing cold. No one could hear me down there to comfort me. Howling in my arctic isolation, I'd cry with anger to cover my shame and with shame to cover my anger, and all of it was mixed in with yearning for something I couldn't begin to understand.

I didn't even know what I was raging about. I raged for every spider that had its legs torn off by sadistic children, for every lobster that swam around in a restaurant tank with its claws bound by a thick rubber band, for every maple tree surging with protoplasm sawed down to a stump—for everything muzzled, constrained, or gagged with its life curtailed or its tongue cut out. I raged for the victims everywhere, great and small, and most bitterly for those who were downtrodden by my own hand: for Miss Hunnibell, the dancing school instructor, upon whose porch we'd place firecracker-laced eggs, and for the people I played prank calls on, especially a drunk black man named John Silver in Bridgeport to whom we pretended we were drunk, too. How shameful, that we spoiled Rowayton boys would torment a foundry worker on his day off. I raged for all these things and never ever about the Holocaust per se. Never at the Austrians for cheering Hitler's troops marching into Vienna, the Poles for turning in stray children, the French for deporting more Jews than the Germans asked for, the Americans for not lifting quotas, and especially never at the Jews for allowing themselves to be so abjectly victimized in the first place, so that all their great and cantankerous individualism boiled down to this, that they should allow themselves to be herded off to their deaths like sheep.

Which proved my rage was really about these things all along.

◆ ◆ ◆

I say no one came to comfort me but that's not quite true. I was sent to a psychiatrist for a few weeks for an "evaluation," was pronounced normal, and stopped seeing him. But during those sessions Dr. Blaine looked at me with such kindliness that I forgot myself. Simple, saltwater tears welled up, neutralized by the grace and clemency in which he bathed me. It frightened me, almost, how his presence consoled me. We never even talked about my rages but he soothed me just by his attention, bestowing compassion on me like a salve. Dr. Blaine regarded me with so much sympathy—his eyes dancing over me while his lips remained fixed in a languid smile—that I found myself yearning to confess things I didn't even know were in my heart.

Back in my room my rages continued unabated, but thereafter I felt I had company—I was being watched with great mute sympathy by my desk and my short-wave radio and my model airplanes and also by my dog Nick. When I was crying only lightly, Nick would jump up on me and lick my face. She thought she could kiss me out of it, and she tried to lick my neck and lips and as much of me as I'd let her. When I was crying heavily, it was a different story. She'd regard me with a confused expression, then come over and try to hump my leg. She wanted to bring us both comfort against these scary sounds coming out of me.

My rages scared me, too. I'd take a Spanish dagger I kept on my desk and stab holes in my T-shirt. Of course, the dagger was only a letter opener, and since I had no letters to open (except from stamp companies who couldn't seem to bear the rejection of my having stopped collecting), I used it as a paperweight to hold down my growing pile of firecracker labels. But still I'd imagine that the dagger was a terrible instrument of destruction and I longed for it to cause regret among those people who'd ever wronged me: my parents first and foremost for being all the things I loved and hated, and Miss Hunnibell for very likely not being a horrible person and spoiling the raison d'être for my firecrackers, and Lynn Williams for never really returning my attentions. Wouldn't they be sad! I rejoiced at this newfound grief-causing power of mine. "I wish I were dead," I hissed, invoking my magic power, then rationalized my continued aliveness by imagining that every time I said it I moved into a new dimension of living while leaving behind a dead Danny in the previous world whom everyone would feel sorry for. I'd say it eight, ten, thirteen times!—gloating at the destruction I was leaving behind each time. By the end I'd be sated; I'd caused thirteen sets of parents to mourn for me, thirteen Lynn Williamses, and that was enough for one night's work, and I could play with my army tanks in peace.

◆ ◆ ◆

Eight out of nine Jewish children in western Europe were killed.

◆ ◆ ◆

In French, the word for rage is the same as the word for having rabies. To be rabid is to have *la rage.* My rage infused my everyday activities. As a boy raking leaves from the garage, I imagined I was rounding up Nazis. A couple of *kommandants* were trying to get away by hiding behind an old tire: "Not on your life, Gustav! Into the fire!" Pruning branches, I was a Nazi and the various branches were imploring me to spare their baby twigs. "We're alive just as you are!" cried the branches as I lopped them one by one. Consolidating two bottles of shampoo, I was force-feeding Breck the way Nazis forced a rabbi's mouth open and poured beer down his throat until he exploded.

Growing up, there remained a black hole in me that was too easily accessed. When as a young adult I heard of a six-month-old raped by her mother's boyfriend, I dove into a tailspin of fury, my lungs starting to wheeze as I tried to come up with a word to express my rabidity. At times like those I knew I never really got over my asthma. The doctors said it cleared up over the years. But I understood that something else happened to it. It moved into another realm where it remained for years: an asthma of the soul.

From the You Get What You Resist Dept.

Of course the anger stuck to me as I grew older. As a young man it followed me like a shadow, attracting more anger. I'm thinking of a time I passed a few hours in the bed of an older woman who tended bar at a college pub, only to learn at the end of the evening that she had a husband. He was a carpenter; his red Ranger truck was parked at the curb across the street while he was away for the weekend. I was young enough that the concept of marriage was daunting by itself without the added peril of having been the instrument of adultery. I hadn't even known till then how an act of love could be used in the adult world as an act of war. In my haste to back out of the woman's driveway at 2 A.M., I hit the Ranger and knocked one of the letters off, leaving me to stare at the message in bold block characters: **ANGER.**

I thought of it this way. In some unknown corner of World War II an anonymous Jewish Resistance fighter was led to the gallows with a tallis stuffed down his throat so he couldn't scream out, and somehow years later an eight-year-old boy in Connecticut had inherited a piece of that man's rage. My biggest fear was being kept from shouting, from expressing! I had riches in my mind I needed to share with people, but no way to get them across. My task was to somehow convey myself safely till my forties when I might accumulate the wherewithal to say it.

The bottom line was that I became used to anger and frequently preferred it to peace or contentment or whatever was supposed to be its opposite. It reminded me of the folktale where Brer Rabbit says, "Oh please, don't toss me in the briar patch, anything but the briar patch"; then when Brer Fox *does* he laughs that he was "bred en bawn in a briar patch, Brer Fox—bred en bawn!"

Anger was my briar patch. I had the secret knowledge that's

known only to those who truly rage: that rage kept me strong. I was reluctant to surrender my hate because I knew hate kept me fit, in case anyone tried to brand a number on my arm. Rage was my insulation: it warmed me in winter and cooled me in summer. Somewhere inside I hung to this dank bit of knowledge: that when they've stolen your clothes and your rings and your hair and you're naked before your tormentors, rage is the only thing they can't take from you because at bottom what it really is is grief.

◆ ◆ ◆

A question. Why had my mother not better protected her babies from stories of the Nazis? For years I was angry at her, wanting her to be as gay with me as she was with the rest of the world at her cocktail parties. I wanted her to be rid of her pain and guilt, just have it vacuum-whisked away, the way an airplane toilet works—*flooooop!*—and it's gone, so she'd be left with only happy memories and tell me only carefree American stories about people pulling themselves up by their bootstraps and running away down the Mississippi on rafts. Or if they had to be European stories, then stories of little Dutch boys valiantly saving their villages by putting their fingers in dike holes, not the tale of starving children unable to retrieve a grapefruit through a crack in a cattle car.

For a long time I was bitter that my mother filled my head with this. But years later I had a friend who dated a Vietnamese woman who'd lived through the Tet Offensive. She seemed, he said, very sunny and well adjusted. But she'd box his ears in bed. They'd be making love, and suddenly she'd haul off and box his ears. He never knew what to expect when they went to bed, he said; it was like sleeping with a tiger.

One time they were lying around and she said, "Shake my hand." When he asked why she said, "No ask question, you shake my hand." So he shook her hand. Before he knew what was happening this 105-pound woman had him in a choke hold. Another time she got up for a drink of water in the middle of the night, and when she came back to bed with a bandaged hand, he asked her what happened. "Nothing," she said. But when he got up in the morning he saw that she'd smashed every mirror in the apartment with her bare hand.

"Her sister had warned me about her," my friend said. "She used to say: 'Clazy, clazy, clazy.' I thought her sister was just jealous because she was so beautiful. But it was true: Vietnam had made her crazy. Bad things do that to you. It's not just you lose an eye or an arm, you know, or you have a bad memory. There are all kinds of ways of becoming wounded. What do you think, war comes to your door and you're not going to get twisted?"

❖ ❖ ❖

"Of course," my friend added, "war can sometimes make you a *better* person. But that's a whole 'nother story."

18

FAMILY ENOUGH

So there's a receipt for bike rentals dated May tenth, nineteen forty—same day the Germans invaded Belgium. My guess is the cabs were all hogged, so J. P. took his family and escaped on bicycles. But why to the coast, I wonder?"

Alex is giving us his interpretation of the journal he's been piecing together as we ride rented bicycles down the Belgian coast. The boardwalk is a ribbon of butternut-colored tiles running along the beach that's caked hard as cement, an expanse of beige running to the sea.

"It was the best way to get down to France," I suggest. "Also, this is where the Belgian royal family escaped during the First World War."

"So can you picture it, Dad? These fat cats in their suits and gowns riding bikes while the Germans were strafing them from airplanes?"

A baby-sized beach trolley comes rattling by, kicking up the sand. We continue following the trolley tracks that gird these seaside towns where grandmothers in throat-high bathing attire don't so much swim as "take the waters." However, it's clear that this antiquated toes-in-the-sand charm will soon be gone. The shoreline is lousy with bulldozers. Presently the little hotels with orange tiled roofs will be swallowed whole by unimaginative apartment buildings with names like Palm Beach and Dune Vista, great monoliths of concrete with fake brick facades and undersized wrought iron balconies.

But not yet. As we continue to bike through, heading south toward France, a beach ball borne by the sea breeze blows onto the main drag and stops the line of traffic as it bounces with slow-motion insouciance on top of car hoods. And all of this with running bardic commentary from Marshall, behind me in the child's seat:

> If we could color the air blue
> Would the rain wash it out?
> I love butterflies. They're like God
> Waving his fingers at us.
> But how come every time something falls
> On the floor and you pick it up
> It has a hair on it?

A few miles farther the dunes on the other side of the road are topped with barbed wire and seem to cover a long low fortification. Something I'd better check out.

"I'll come, too!" Marshall cries.

"What about you, Alex?"

"I'll just draw," he says, his eye floating.

Marshall and I walk fifty yards along the barbed wire. The sea wind whips fine cementlike particles of sand into our faces. Finding a low spot in the wire, Marshall scoots up from my cupped hand and I clamber after. The sounds of beach life are smothered out the moment we slither down the other side of the dune.

"Are you happy?" Marshall asks me.

Just like that? Out of the blue? He asks me so simply, it reminds me of the way guides use the term on safari in Africa, to describe the animals when in a state of nature, undisturbed by man: "Shhh, they don't see us, they're happy." Happy was the default, when the animals were doing what they were meant to be doing.

"Yes," I say, "being here with you guys makes me happy. Stay here," I add, for we've come across the opening to a man-made tunnel. "Your brother has to see this."

I scramble back up the dune, leap over the barbed wire, and trot down the road to the bikes, where Alex is drawing a schematic of a Luger 9mm semiautomatic pistol. But by the time we return, Marshall's in the custody of a baggy-eyed care-taker with a menacing pair of oversized garden clippers, who softens to our protestations that we're blissfully ignorant Americans, and volunteers to be our guide to the tunnels. "If my supervisor comes, I am kicking you out," he says with a heavy-lidded wink.

Down we go into a warren of tunnels used by the Germans to defend the coast, complete with bunkers for sleeping. This was the famous Atlantic Wall, the caretaker tells us: the great defensive line the Germans threw up against an invasion that eventually took place not far south of here on a beach called Omaha. It was an enormous construction project—a line of fortifications extending from the Netherlands to the Spanish border—but today some of the batteries grow mushrooms while others are used as seaside vacation villas.

"Watch your head," he warns. "Bats."

We duck as the bats swoosh by our ears with a sound like tiny leather baseball mitts flapping through the air for invisible fly balls.

As he talks, the caretaker snips the wild poppies and strawberry vines that grow against the brick, leading the way through the tunnels at a good clip. Some bunkers are so dark we need to snap Alex's camera flash. In this spooky strobe lighting we can see the rusted coils of a cot and clumps of wires hanging out of the wall like spinal nerves after a beheading. It's kind of thrilling: what if we were to develop one of Alex's flashes and find a skeleton of some old Nazi lurking in the corner? Or an old Nazi himself, who'd been hiding here for a half century the way old Japanese warriors are said to still hide out on remote South Pacific islands, unable to comprehend that World War II is over?

"You like beer?" he asks, ushering us down to where he keeps his stash cool in a cement vault. "Good Belgian beer, stronger than American," he says, handing me a frothy brew the color of resin.

I make the leap. "Stronger than German beers?"

"Phuff!" he says, his face a mask of contempt.

The transition is done. "You don't like German beers?"

"Phuff! I don't like *Germany.*"

Marshall is sniffling because he didn't get any beer, wiping the dirt-stained tears on his cheeks with his camera strap. I give him a sip from my bottle and his mood shifts to burping laughter. Trying to ignore him, Alex asks the caretaker if he's Jewish.

"No! I am Belgian." Unaware that his cigarette is singeing the split ends of his thin hair as he runs his fingers through, he says, "For the Jews, it was absolute bad."

"Did you see what happened to the Jews?"

"Everyone saw! First they wear yellow stars, then they're forced to build this *Chemin des Juifs.*"

"*Chemin des*—?"

"It means 'the path of the Jews.' Because much of this Atlantic Wall was built by Jews used like slaves during the war." He watches our faces as we mull this over. "History, hey?" he says. "But I don't think it's coming back, dis shit."

"It's nice to meet an optimistic man."

"I think the next war will be coming from Asia," he clarifies, sticking his cigarette above his head so the wind takes the ash.

◆ ◆ ◆

As we continue biking south toward the French border, we're looking for an open field where the journal seems to indicate J. P. and his family slept *"sous les belles étoiles,"* waiting for the border to open. But with morning's light they discovered it was a bull pasture, or so we surmise from the comic picture of a large bovine with horns leering from the wizened page.

"He was able to joke about it?"

"I guess at this point he didn't know how bad things were going to get."

It's still an open field, we're pleased to discover, and a good-smelling one at that. We get off our bikes to breathe the air and puzzle what magic crops are growing to scent the air so well. Rhubarb? Raspberries? Such fragrance! And then we realize it's not the smell of crops but of refrigeration, for on the far side of the field is a giant supermarket air-conditioning its produce to the world. Lacing the smell of refrigerated food is the scent of truck exhaust from a queue of diesel transports.

"Where to, Alex?" I ask.

"I don't know. There's mention of a French town named Andres and a farm family named LeClerc. But we're never going to find it."

The boys are excited for their first border crossing. Tucking in their chins, they brace themselves for this all-important rite of passage. But the two bored guards take one look at Marshall's overeager face and, with a miserable chuckle, wave us through. The kids are crestfallen. "They didn't even look at our passports!"

Nonetheless, suddenly it's French. No matter how disappointing the transit, the atmosphere's changed perceptibly. A heron flies with *a great French wingspan* alongside the canal. A father in a beret stands beside his daughter fishing with a *long curving French rod*. Others *font le pique-nique,* eating secretively with the elegant furtive manner of raccoons. People in roadside cafés pout and shrug with a peculiar Gallic eloquence. Immediately, not a soul speaks English.

Heading inland, the golden wheat fields begin. Wooden shoes are lined up outside doors. The road winds through meadows of wheat with fretted white tops that must have reminded the homesick Jews of Belgian lace.

> You know how to get through barbed wire?
> Just grab it in the middle!
> That's how to never get trapped!

With Marshall's optimism fueling us, we follow a swath of tar until we come to a small village. Hills of wheat sway lazily in all directions, nearly swallowing the few wooden houses; from a far distance, farm machinery hums with agitation.

"Pardon, savez-vous la direction de la ferme de Monsieur Le-Clerc?"

An old farmer with broken blood vessels in his nose points his bony finger like a staff. *"Oui, oui, c'est là. . . ."*

We pedal on a heavily rutted dirt road past a ramshackle barn amid petrified cow patties and soon come to a dead end. We ask a little girl who stands with a white horse, sipping from a spring where freezing cold water churns forth in slick tawny clay colors.

"Oui, il y a la ferme de sa mère," she says with a twinkle, pointing us back the other direction. She thinks we're funny, the sight of us.

"The water, it is good for swimming?" I ask.

"Oh non, monsieur. Très dangereux, le sinkhole."

"What's a sinkhole?" Alex asks.

"It's a hole connecting with a subterranean passage," I explain.

"Cool!" says Marshall. He throws a pebble into its liquid roiling clay. But Alex takes a step back and resumes looking internal.

Again we find ourselves passing the ramshackle barn that looks swollen by decades of sun, beside an old white farmhouse with sagging cobwebs spun across its front door. This couldn't be the place, could it? But our bikes follow the ruts in as if they have a mind of their own, like horses who know their way home.

"Something tells me . . ." Marshall says.

Barn swallows dart through the air heavily perfumed with hay. There's the lavish sound of bees buzzing the punk-headed clover, purple and white. I rap on the wooden door of the farmhouse and watch a daddy longlegs pick his way across the jamb. Of course no one comes. The place has been deserted for years.

Behind us, Marshall has his head inside the barn and is pointing upward. "Dad, look! A secret loft!"

Sure enough, above the empty cow stalls, there's a false ceiling with the decrepit remains of a ladder. As we clamber up, a pigeon flies out through a square vent hole. We inspect a crumbling space. The walls are chalky, as if whitewashed a lifetime ago. Half a century has passed, yet the clues are intact.

"Dad, we found it! I can't believe we found it!"

In his exuberance, Alex tries to lift me up, turning red with the futility of his effort. "It's not a goose chase after all!"

"*Bonjour?*" Down below, a stout farmer with orange cheeks seems bashful about finding us on his property. "What do you want?" he says in a gentle voice.

We climb down and tell him. Yes, he confirms with a blush, it's true that his father let some Jews stay in the barn during the war. But this was very long ago, before he was born. His name's Gabriel and he's reluctant to talk about the war. In addition, he's self-conscious about his role as owner and embarrassed for us in our role as trespassers. As so often happens with stilted people, he soon makes me stilted. He seems anxious to get out of the barn and he invites us to the spanking new house, which we now see for the first time, a stone's throw on the other side of the barn.

In psychic terms, it is more than a stone's throw. It's a suburban ranch with plastic potted geraniums at the end of a driveway of synthetic crushed pink pebbles. Everything inside looks as if it were just off a truck from Wal-Mart. Our shoes leave white dust prints on the gleaming Congoleum-tiled floor. On the mantelpiece, pewter mugs serve as bookends to a Naugahyde set of classical books glued together. Silk azaleas adorn the entertainment console. Portraits done up in the overdeveloped syrupy colors favored by grade school photographers grace the walnut paneling of the opposite wall: a son aged ten, a daughter aged twelve.

Gabriel chases a chicken out the kitchen door and is back with two beers and Cokes for the boys.

"I'll take a Stella Artois," Marshall volunteers. "It has a nice peanut flavor, not as sweet as Dekonick."

Blushing, Gabriel half rises to comply before I assure him he needn't bother.

"One time I knew this kid," Marshall says conversationally, "who crushed a Milky Way in his apple juice and then tried to suck it up his nose with his straw—"

"Marshall," I interrupt, "is this going to get disgusting?"

"Never mind, I'm not going to finish," Marshall says, wounded to the core. Then, brightly: "Dad, was it kind of like Jews were herbivores and Nazis were carnivores?"

Gabriel shoots me a helpless gaze. I take a sip of beer, signaling that we should both ignore whatever we like. But so uncomfortable is our poor host that he takes small sips of his beer only when I lead. Marshall proceeds to climb on the furniture and produce periodic hollow *boomph*s when he falls on his head. Alex is hard at work in his drawing pad. Shifting in his chair, crossing and uncrossing his arms awkwardly, Gabriel tells me that his father was mayor when a strange convoy of Jews biked into his village seeking refuge. His father put them up. His father died in the '50s; Gabriel, a part-time farmer who's on holiday from his regular job as a realtor in Calais, is the product of his second marriage.

"And your stepmother?" I ask. I cast a glance behind me at Marshall who, loupe in hand, is examining the silk azalea for evidence.

"She also is not with us," Gabriel says.

"I'm sorry," I say.

"No, she is at the beauty parlor in Calais."

By now I've adopted the English of someone who barely speaks the language. "Your father, this thing he did, to hide my family. It was most generous."

"It was nothing, really. For a few nights only."

"He was offered money for it?"

"Perhaps, but he would refuse. To take would make what he did not good."

Gabriel goes on, suddenly animated. "But I will tell you something. In our barn also was a man whose wife was hiding in a Paris church with a Jew who is now cardinal of Paris."

"A Jew is cardinal of Paris?" I ask.

"*C'est vrai.*"

Marshall is on my lap now, amusing himself by scrunching my various facial parts as I try to pursue the subject. "I'm interested to know what motivated your father. Surely it was dangerous for him?"

Gabriel makes a steeple of his squarish farm hands and examines a purple-black bruise under his thumbnail. "Yes? You know more than I do, I think."

"But the war, was it very difficult here?" I ask, my nose squashed down to my mouth.

"I am only thirty-eight, I do not know."

"I also am thirty-eight, but I want to learn."

"I am on holiday," he says conclusively, mopping his brow. So this is how far my host will go.

The boys' watches go off simultaneously. "Time to motor, Dad," Marshall says, sliding off my lap.

"Where you travel from here?"

"I'll have to consult my navigator. Alex? Any clue what comes next?"

Alex references the journal. Part of a chipped page falls to the shiny Congoleum. "What's this?" he asks. "'Claudette two times up top. Mimi. Babba. Rochelle—'"

"Lemme see that," I say, grabbing the paper and putting it in my pocket. "What else does the journal have to say?"

"Belgium surrendered May twenty-eighth, nineteen forty, then France was taken over also." He turns the journal upside down and shakes it to see what else might fall out. The chicken pecks at the kitchen door to come in. "My bet is they went back to someplace in Belgium."

❖ ❖ ❖

We drop our rental bikes at the train station for the return trip, and now, out the train window the corn leaves are shining in the late afternoon sun. Perhaps because the beer in me is still operative, Marshall's hair and the shining corn silk seem related, each lustrous thread alive with history—every living thing related in a wondrously loose-jointed way. "What we just did was historic, guys! We found one of J. P.'s hiding places!"

No sooner are these words out of my mouth, than a voice comes from a seat three rows ahead of us: "I also was not catched."

I'd thought we were alone in the train car, but up rises a rumpled figure out of a Belgian fairy tale, long and reed-thin and as knock-kneed as Dorothy's Straw Man, with an extraordinary collection of keys hanging off his leather belt on a brass bull's ring.

"Pardon?"

"You talk of Jacov Morganstern? Who hid in Ghent?"

No, this is impossible. But I quickly recover from my surprise. "Ghent? I don't think so. I mean, his journal doesn't mention Ghent. . . ."

"He was in diamonds?" the figure says, shoving back a wedge of lank gray hair, only to have it fall in his eyes immediately. He mumbles something about *"schmeering."*

"*'Schmeering,'* what is?" I ask in my broken English.

Very animated now—dear God, another self-exciter—he clears his throat with a shriek and makes the universal gesture of rubbing his fingertips together to indicate money. "It means to grease the wheel. If you give something, you can get something. Sure, it's a small world! We were all hiding at the same time! I can put you in touch with my cousin who knew him in Ghent."

Suddenly he seems to reconsider his words, violently wiggling a long-knuckled finger in his ear. "Better than Ghent," he decides. "Go to Ardennes, where he stayed in a hunting pavilion, what is in English—?"

"A lodge?"

"Yes, but also with horses . . ."

"Like a horse farm?"

His laughter is ungoverned. He's a little bit crazy, I think, or ecstatic.

"Now it is a horse farm. For well-to-do French and English. A castle with horses, you understand? But then . . . a retreat for the Gestapo, a *maison de passe!"*

"What's a *maison de passe?"* Marshall asks.

"A house of passage," says Alex.

"Bright lad," says our friend, brushing back more gray locks. "And do you know what a house of passage is?" he says, leering into our faces. "A house of passage is where you bring your girlfriend," he says, "and your wife is none the wiser!"

"You mean, like a Japanese love hotel?" Alex asks.

"Precisely, where you bring your own companionship!" he says, and winks in such a way that we all feel included in his crafty male goodwill. Even the seven-year-old is twinkling with innocent male conspiracy. "Your own companionship!" he says, with no idea what he's referring to. He just likes the sound of it.

"Jacov spent there three months alone in the wine cellar of this Gestapo love nest, among Jew-haters who never caught on that downstairs was a Jew, right under their nose! Sure, under the nose was the safest place! The Germans were so far-sighted, building a thousand-year Reich, they never thought to look so close!" He jiggles his keys, peering at me sideways. "This journal you speak of, it mentions none of this, yes? I am not surprised. He does not mention Pelican, either? Most of the stories, they are not spoken."

"Pelican, I've heard the name. . . ."

"A saint who sacrificed herself for his children. Pelican was not her real name, of course; a *nom de guerre* only. As mine was Mistral, for the wind that you can never tell where it's coming from. But better than Leopold, eh?"

Mistral? Leopold? Both unlikely handles for this scarecrow figure. But Marshall has insight into one of them. "Were you named Leopold for the Belgian king?"

"So! The big boy is bright but the little boy is wise," he says.

"A snare drum and a bass drum," I confirm.

"Why doesn't the journal just come out and *tell* us this stuff?" asks an exasperated Alex. "The pages just get worse as time goes on."

"In what sense worse? Spottier? Perhaps that is because Jacov was less and less inclined to divulge information."

"More pictures and *junk* instead of words. . . ."

"As he saw what was going on, he may have not had the words to describe . . ."

We think about this. Outside the train, we see a battalion of lambs lying tenderly in a dewy meadow.

"What about J. P.'s wife and children?" asks Marshall.

Leopold raises both hands. "His wife, already she was *kaput*. She was drinking coffee twenty-four hours a day to simulate a heart condition, hoping the Germans would take pity on her. And then she suffered a heart attack for real! They had to leave her body in the bathroom of a train station. And his children, off in a nunnery twenty miles away. It was unsafe for them to stay with him. You know who you should contact?" he goes on before we have a chance to react to this data. "My niece Elodie. She is French but in the Ardennes to teach ballet at the summer camp! Take the train to Namur! Elodie will show you!"

"But we—"

"Maybe you can even find Pelican, hah? *There* is the mystery of goodness, which is always greater than the mystery of evil. To perform sins, this is easy, anyone can do. Ah, but to do good, this is a mystery. . . ."

I demur; it's all happening too fast.

"Come, we have no time, my stop is here. I will call her!" He digs out a cell phone from his pocket and begins punching numbers. "She will be expecting you!"

"But—"

"But yes?" He smiles into my face.

Haste makes me blunt. "But we are not family!"

He blinks at me. "You are Jewish?"

I blink at *him*. "Yes . . ."

"Phhh . . ." He smiles, indicating that the phone is starting to ring, and leaps from the train in a surprising grand jeté. The train hardly slows. Already he is ten yards away and getting smaller. "Family enough . . ."

19

EXERCISES IN HIDING, II

I was becoming aware of life beyond my family. My mother's homeland, Belgium, was giving up the Congo, and Europeans were fleeing widespread violence. The first TV news I ever paid attention to showed a piece of white paper being pushed into a black man's face—Premier Lumumba was literally being forced to eat his words by President Kasavubu. The names were as wondrous as the images. When the last UN troops left the Congo a few years later, the new president was someone named Moise Tshombe, a splendid combination of Belgian and African.

Closer to home, I was learning about our place in the world. Long before it was a lobster town, Rowayton had been the largest producer of roses in the world. In school I devoured a book called *Tory Hole* about a shallow cave across the river in Darien where colonialists loyal to the king hid during the Revolutionary War—a genuine hiding place just a few miles from my house. My favorite period was reading: usually I made a beeline to the class bookshelf to snag the book of fairy tales first, only gradually noticing as my greed and haste declined that no one else had any intention of selecting such a book. But the most enthralling one was a true story about four French boys who in 1940—*while my relatives were hiding not far away*—followed a dog down a small hole, only to discover the caves of Lascaux with their breathtaking array of prehistoric paintings.

At the same time I was more seriously trying to take stock of myself, daring myself to leap from a cliffside rope swing into the water during lightning storms and to "skitch" rides during snowstorms, a practice that frequently entailed leaving most of my chin on the tar when the car towing me hit a dry patch. In Little League I was promoted to the infield, despite my habit of making the magic plays and bobbling the easy ones. At school I learned that there was a whole profession devoted to the art of hiding, and I so ardently wished to be a detective when I grew up that I fired off a note to J. Edgar Hoover, less a fan letter than a memo between colleagues, advising him of my undercover skills and inviting him, if he were so inclined, to be my pen pal.

Continuing to take inventory, my temper was bad enough that I was driven to put my fist through not one but two storm doors when my sister locked me out of the house, yet I still hadn't mustered the guts to take the Test. Figuring perhaps that I hadn't done a good enough job being the boy in the family, my mother had another boy, but even though he was put in a nursery next to her room, I took it on faith that she was just trying him out and would soon come to her senses. From my bedroom downstairs, two flights away from everyone else, I felt both special and exiled. Which was I? The evidence was indisputable that I was becoming the black sheep of the household, the lightning rod through which the family channeled any bad energy that visited us. When my mother criticized me, I'd feel demolished. "You're impossible!" she'd scream. "You're hopeless!" In every argument, my soul was at stake.

With her words ringing in my ears, I developed a coat of armor. She could rant and I'd be locked away inside. She'd kick me out of the house and I'd repair to the places where she couldn't find me. I never had a tree house, but I sat in the branches of a wild cherry tree in the backyard where a squirrel would give me a fierce sideways look, full of cockeyed disaffection, as if to tell me this was his hiding place, not mine. Eventually the squirrel would tire of me and leave. Soon a robin with straw in its beak might light on a branch nearby, glower, look away, then look back as if to say, "What, *you* again?" And as the parade continued, my anger would dissipate.

A nine-year-old boy could walk around a lobster town at night by himself in those days. When everyone was asleep or getting ready for bed, I'd sit on the cold rocks on the shoreline and wait for the last of the house lights to go out. On summer nights I'd walk to a small wooden bridge and find minnow traps made from glass milk bottles with bread crusts in them, hanging in the water from string. Once in a while I'd take a sip from their muddy necks, a kind of sacrament that made me appreciate the adventure of being warm. On winter nights I'd decamp across town to Pirates Point, a rundown beach and bait shack owned by a larynxless ex-lobsterman named Jupe. Dozens of rowboats were upturned for the season, one hull on top of the other, and I'd wedge myself underneath and lie there, breathing the smell of old paint and the rubber boots of fishermen. I could hear the wind rocking across the dock and I'd let the armor click open so I could feel things again. This calm was something precious, to keep coming back for. Afterward, I'd smell like rowboat.

Sometimes I shared my hiding places. My friend Kip and I found a throne in the cliff rocks along the shore near my sister's private school; one person could sit in the throne to survey the Sound and be absolutely deaf to the rest of the world. We'd take turns, and afterward Kip would confide that he was embarrassed about being left-handed, though I assured him I admired the otherness it seemed to confer on him. He divulged that he worried his left-handedness would injure his chance of becoming an airplane pilot, and later gave me black-and-white glossies of single-engine planes to tape to my closet door. Years later, Kip died in a bar fight. He'd knocked his opponent down, but then felt sorry for him, and was extending a hand to help him up when the fellow kicked him in the nuts. He died a few weeks later. I always wondered—was it his left hand he extended?

With my pal McDougal I frequented an empty lot that was covered with cattails twelve feet tall. From across the street, we'd get up speed on our bikes and charge into the cattails, crunching through until they clogged our spokes. Deep inside the cattails, three hiding places were marked: Homely Home 1, 2, and 3.

I respected McDougal because he seemed troubled. He never spoke of his troubles, but I knew he was Catholic, so something of an outsider himself, and he'd watched his grand-mother die with his own eyes ("with his own eyes" made it so heroic, as if he'd taken an active part). His divorced mother was a teacher in Rowayton School—which caused him all kinds of woe—and his little brother was a puckish mischief maker called Hurricane. I was aware that McDougal had his cache of private grief. The one time we took sleeping bags to Homely Home, in-tending to spend the night, we spooked each other badly enough to pack it in. But in the daytime our hideaway was truly a home away from home and we were able to broach subjects it never seemed right to broach elsewhere.

It was here McDougal tried to convert me. "Everyone *saw* Je-sus rise!" he cried in frustration. "It wasn't just a few people, but lots of them! Why don't you believe us?"

I was touched by his concern for my eternal soul, but I wasn't buying. In the ensuing discussion I happened to mention the word *Judaism*. He thought this was the funniest word ever.

"Jud-Y-ism? As in, the worship of Judy!?" He'd always thought it was pronounced "Jud-ism."

When we were in high school, Homely Home was bulldozed to make room for three ugly suburban ranches, and McDougal eventually became a realtor who favored bulldozing cattails to put in new homes. "Huh!" he said, laughing at himself good-naturedly at one of our high school reunions. "I've become everything I always hated!"

But I would never forget the drag of cattails slowing our bikes down, and aiming the quills at each other in cattail fights, and lying on the carpet of the stalks that made the world smell like popcorn, crunched by the fat rubber tires of our bikes. And once McDougal taught me how to do the twist, both of us triumphing over the self-consciousness of grade school by learning our moves in the privacy of our reed hideaway. When I think of my childhood in Rowayton, it's cattails I remember first, even before the saltwater and seaweed. Here we were happy.

◆ ◆ ◆

Not all my hiding places panned out. One that didn't was the dryer. I closed the lid one night when my parents were gone and accidentally locked myself inside. Tottering down from her room upstairs, "our Juliette" was tipsy and found it hysterical. She wouldn't release me until she'd roused Renee from bed to show her. (This was to get back at me for my habit of lying in wait for her on the counter top and leaping onto her shoulders when she ambled into the kitchen.)

A more successful one was Juliette's room itself. Juliette and I could touch upon things here that we didn't dare bring up elsewhere, including the taboo topic of race relations. We'd watch Yankees games on her precolor RCA in the afternoons while she ironed tablecloths, I betting on the colored players and she on the white.

"Look at that," I'd say, "Hank Aaron's going to belt a homer!"

"No sir! Harvey Haddix gon' strike that boy *outathere!*" she'd riposte, simultaneously crunching ice cubes between her back teeth and smoking Kools.

For all our off-and-on closeness, however, the one subject we never broached was Jew versus Christian. She must have been conscious of it, because years after she'd left our employ Juliette paid an unexpected call on us, weaving up the driveway—she must have been *very* drunk to weave uphill—hollering, "House o' David!" But on those afterschool afternoons in her room, mid the hiss and sizzle of her scorching water drops on the collar of my father's white shirts, we'd also bet on "Queen for a Day" to see which lady told the most heartrending story. I was always amazed that although Juliette's life must have had its share of heartrending material (the only detail to which I was privy was that she'd left two baby boys in Alabama to find work as a "domestic" up North), it didn't harden her to others. On the contrary, it seemed to make her extra compassionate, and she clucked with sympathy for all the ladies with troubles greater than her own. When a woman came on the show to tell the story of her family perishing in Birkenau, Juliette shook her head and said, "Lordy lordy!" in a way that warmed my heart toward her forever.

Near dinnertime one winter night the family realized no one had seen Juliette for several hours and we searched through the house and finally my father found her in a hideaway of her own—on the toilet of my bathroom downstairs, drunk and incoherent with a bottle of Four Roses between her feet. After that I couldn't help wondering if the Four Roses represented the four Rose children, my siblings and me, whom she'd left her own children down South to take care of.

❖ ❖ ❖

In a hiding place, you were emboldened to experiment with things you might not elsewhere. It was in a hiding place that Jaime Rothschild once told me how good it felt to pump your fist into your crotch, and one on Heart's Island was the site of my only quasi-homosexual experience.

Heart's Island was a refuge adjacent to Heart's Castle that was half swamp and half thorn-infested hillock, where several generations of Rowayton kids had cut trails. My memory of the act became murky the second it happened. Hotdog and I were wrestling there one afternoon and somehow I got the feeling he found me cute. He seemed to find me pleasing in a girlish way—in a Jewish way, almost. He was the strapping Dutch Christian and I was the smaller and more sensitive Jew and as we wrestled his gaze softened with something akin to fondness, it seemed to me. I'd never felt girlish before, or Jewish in this way, but seeing how it pleased him, it pleased me, too. He enjoyed the fact that although I was smaller, I was able to turn the tables and pin him beneath me: that gave the contest more suspense. The afternoon was waning, we were overdue to part company, but still we wrestled and then suddenly I was up, flicking the grass from my shirt front. Something had happened. I forgot what it was immediately. Hotdog's reaction was to chuckle indulgently. Years later, I reworked the memory and deduced that I'd been groped.

If it happened, it was both shocking and not shocking, natural and unnatural. It came and went in an instant, as though a hand had risen from the murk to squeeze me. But if it happened, it distinctly happened from a Christian to a Jew, and from the only person I ever heard say an anti-Semitic remark at the bus stop.

◆ ◆ ◆

By this time I had befriended a classmate named Lawless, whose Christmas-lighted house had been the one I'd taken refuge in a few years before. His name expressed my ideal, not to be fine-grained and tame in the Jewish manner, but to be the way Mark Twain described Huck Finn: "idle, and lawless, and vulgar, and bad." And the best thing was that Lawless managed to be these things despite the fact that he wore a dazzling display of orthodontia and resided in that fancy house of his, which featured a pet monkey and a central vacuum system that seemed to keep the house miraculously free of the complexity my house was subject to (intellectual relativism, quibbling ambivalence, riddles within riddles). The gamy odor from the monkey blended with antique wood polish so the house smelled like a luxury safari lodge, and I wasn't supposed to know that hearty Mr. Lawless, who'd retired early from Wall Street because he'd inherited a lot of money and who called his nightly cocktail "Loudmouth Soup," kept photos of Mrs. Lawless's naked butt on their bedroom wall.

Lawless was also the best swimmer of our grade, the first to pass the Test, and the perennial winner of the annual Bayley Beach race in which I was perennially thirteenth. I was a little ashamed at how graceless I was in the water, slapping the seaweed that Lawless seemed to slice through, but I didn't think it bothered me until one afternoon when he was showing off his swimming medals, one first-place star for each of the previous four years. His mother called from the kitchen. "Quick," I told McDougal when Lawless left to see what she wanted, "let's take 'em." McDougal obeyed this spur-of-the-moment impulse without question. We each pocketed one medal. We continued to play the rest of the afternoon and I thought no more about it until the next day when McDougal confessed. There was nothing I could say to Lawless to protest my innocence, for the simple reason that I was guilty as charged. He eventually forgave me in the most gracious way he could, by stealing a 1943 zinc penny (there'd been a shortage of copper during the war) from my penny collection. So we understood each other.

One winter day Lawless and I noticed that a large puddle on the deserted parking lot of the town beach had frozen over. We promptly commandeered a bedsheet, knotted it around our fists, and went ice-sailing, standing up in our shoes and letting the sheet tug us around the parking lot. It turned out to be one of those recreations that sounded better in theory, and after ten minutes we allowed a cat to spark our interest—something about the purposeful way it ran with tiny mincing steps across the ice—and we decided to follow it. Soon it slipped through the fence onto the property of the adjoining off-limits beach club. We followed it onto the grounds of the estate, boarded up now for winter, and up to the main staircase, where it suddenly dropped from sight down a little rip in the earth.

This was just like what those French boys had done, following an animal down a crack in the earth to discover the cave paintings of Lascaux. Widening the rip so we could squeeze through, we discovered a passageway beneath the mansion.

Daylight slipped through cracks in the foundation, and at intervals we bumped into wooden beams. It was just what we wanted, a no-man's-land of darkness and danger that spread out for thirty feet on all sides, like the Dirty Part of my cellar magnified by a hundred. Deeper and deeper we explored until we came to a dead end against two giant boulders with only a narrow space that we couldn't possibly get through. That's the space we slithered through to get to our Cavern.

The mansion and grounds above us were once a famous amusement park where during World War I they'd had casino games like Kick the Kaiser, but we didn't know that then. To us it was just an abandoned beach mansion like others that littered the shoreline. We soon had the Cavern decked out with candles and incense, and in this place that was impervious to light and sound we swapped information. He told me it was his secret ambition in life to catch an atom bomb falling from the sky. How heroic that would be, to make a final futile gesture! Never having been involved in divorce proceedings, I said I wanted to be sucked into a tornado and live to tell about it. It was here, too, that we developed a soul handshake routine that became the envy of the third grade. But the *pièce de résistance* was the comedy skits we put on for each other, playing out personae we didn't dare attempt elsewhere. Pulling his lips over his teeth, Lawless played a toothless drunken cowboy, which may have been prophetic, given the fact that in high school he yanked the braces off his teeth with a pair of pliers and ran away to spend a summer on a dude ranch. I did a black Jew. "Get your tuchass over here, mufucka. You be giving me so much tsuris, you don't know what omgublozum is, you meshugah!" It had Lawless screaming with laughter.

Most of the skits and persons died right there where they were born, but a certain character was too good to lose. Mr. Pinanski was created the day I discovered I had the ability to access a lower register in my voice, a technique that felt like playing fiddle on raw vocal cords. When I got home for dinner that night, Mr. Pinanski burst full-blown upon the scene. A seventy-six-year-old geezer with gruff ways and a good soul, he was a garbageman by profession but a poet at heart, a rude charmer who quickly became as integral a part of the family as Nick the dog. In the weeks to follow, he was able to intercede on my behalf with my parents and give them useful counsel. Frequently after Danny had been banished to his room for some transgression, Mr. Pinanski would give them a gravelly-voiced talking-to that was sympathetic to all sides of the dispute, explaining to them in his maturity (he was older than both of them put together) that what Danny was exhibiting was nothing more than growing pains, and that with all due respect for their *own* growing pains, they weren't helping matters by overreacting.

Interestingly, Mr. Pinanski was not Jewish. He was a Polish redneck, related to those folks who stood by while their Jewish neighbors were being shipped to Auschwitz, and who appropriated the Jews' houses once they were out of the picture. Maybe having him be Polish was my way of integrating the enemy and thus coming to terms with my own capacity for good and evil. My aunt the harpsichordist had another theory for it. She thought I was going schizo. She became alarmed when she spent a night on the Castro convertible in my room and heard me talking in my sleep. Or rather, Mr. Pinanski talking in my sleep. My father assured her I wasn't going round the bend. I spied on them when he theorized to her that it was merely a passing prepubescent phenomenon, that if there was any psychological significance to Mr. Pinanski at all it was a witty if unconscious transformation of Mr. Penis. That it was, metaphorically speaking, the voice of my penis on the brink of maturity.

Wow, that's what I loved about Freudianism: it always made everything sound better than it was. If my father's reading was correct, that was pretty damn clever of me. I'd created a Polish redneck penis that was the hit of the dinner table night after night. Whether this was a valid interpretation or not, I hadn't the faintest idea. All I knew was that marching out of my room in my Mr. Pinanski voice was a whole heap better than poking holes in my shirts with a Spanish dagger.

◆ ◆ ◆

The best part of my relationship with Lawless was my friendship with his grandmother, a real-life contemporary of Mr. Pinanski. Not only was Mrs. Snyder our baby-sitter, living with us for weeks when my parents went traveling in the winter, but the rest of the year she was the last stop on my paper route and I'd periodically seek her out as a refuge from my various moods, spending part of an afternoon at her house, and no one from the outside world would know where I was.

No monkeys or central vac for Mrs. Snyder: She had the only rental apartment I knew of in Rowayton. It was in the attic of a private house, so I had to press the raspy upstairs bell. After she'd holler down for me to come in, I'd push the door, making the glass shake delicately, then climb the stairs, inhaling the sweet scent of old people's talc, and feel my blood settle down.

Mrs. Snyder was doughy, with a paper napkin wedged between her large bosoms to collect the sweat that resulted from living in an attic. She had a goiter, soft and jiggly, that she got from not eating enough iodine as a kid. Iodine comes from fish, and she was from the landlocked Midwest. Mrs. Snyder was a person who made sense. She and her husband lived in this airless walk-up with a fan going night and day and they were the whitest-skinned people I'd ever met, as white as the Wonder Bread they seemed to live on. (Wonder Bread's slogan in those days was "Helps Build Strong Bodies Twelve Ways," and watching her gum those spongy slices above her quivering goiter was enough to make me finish my flounder.) She was who she was: kind, sweet-smelling, and deeply slothful in a way that was sure to please an eleven-year-old boy, calmly sucking down her Raleighs and stubbing them in a little glass ashtray they gave away free at the dry cleaners.

When I'd arrive, Mr. Snyder was usually about to walk to

Hummiston's to get a loaf of Wonder Bread. I felt it was cordial of him to leave us alone together, Mrs. Snyder in her flip-flops and me in my baseball cleats, because with him gone we could get down to the business of stories. She had the best stories of early Americana I'd ever heard: yarns of an insulated, rural farm culture without a care in the world. I'd sit at her kitchen table under the bare bulb and hear the melody of her flat voice tell me tales that were wholesome and harmonious and which always ended happily—quintessential Midwest stories about cows getting their heads stuck in fences till they were rescued, and kids tricking their teachers by wearing cowbells to school, and getting the blind man to walk out into the cornfield and step in a field muffin.

"You don't know what a field muffin is?" She'd laugh, the wattle wagging on her throat. "Gracious, child, what have you been doing with your life? It's a clod of cow dung! But of course we all helped the blind man wash it off his boots afterward."

I needed to hear these stories because they were the antidote to my mother's gothic European Not-see tales. They put out the fire of Hitleresque fairy tales with which I often lulled myself to sleep. Having lived a life that wasn't affected in the least by the Third Reich, Mrs. Snyder was a Christian grandmother to me, one who instead of hiding for her life in a pig sty had played hide-and-seek in a hayloft till she sneezed, lordy how she sneezed!

But it came to pass that Mrs. Snyder had to stop eating her beloved Wonder Bread when her doctor put them both on a yeast-free diet. I was present the day the two of them debated the ramifications of this thunderclap.

"What're we going to eat?"

"Crackers, I guess. Those little cracker packets with the cheese already in the pockets?"

"Too salty!" Mrs. Snyder decided, blotting the sweat on her brow and sticking the napkin back between her breasts. That was that. Stalemate.

I had an idea. "You like crackers?" I asked.

"'Deed we do."

"You could try something we've got over at my house," I suggested. And a few days later I had a most appreciative duo on my hands in their kitchen.

"Mm, good, what do you call this here stuff again? Ma-zuh?"

"*Tsuh. Tsuh,*" I said, proudly biting my nails. "We eat it for Pesa*chchchch.*"

Lawless's grandmother, my very own personal convert. She was particularly partial to it with sliced cucumber on top, as I recall.

20

COMMERCING IN KINDNESS

Our friend on the Belgian train never dropped this detail: his niece Elodie is beautiful. Waiting wild-haired for us on the platform in Namur, she's a breath of fresh air: a French Sarah Jessica Parker in gold ballet slippers, with queenly eyebrows, a black beauty mark on her neck, chipped nails, and the most enticing soupçon of what used to be called BO. Clearly, she's one of those women who doesn't pay attention to the fine points of her own life because she's taking charge of everyone around her.

"I take you to the cathle with the wine thellar," she says with the adorable reverse lisp one sometimes hears with the French. "But first in honor of our American guests I take you to Bathtogne."

"Bastogne?"

"Battle of the Bulge, Dad!" mutters Alex. "The Nazis' last offensive, with the aim of recapturing Antwerp!"

We drive through the Ardennes region, which seems more like Vermont than the flat, industrial Belgium we've seen so far. Queen Anne's lace filigrees the lush green forests. Black-eared sheep trot bashfully between the wildflowers. Brown and white cows look somnolent, posing by rivers. The landscape is dotted with brick castles and stone monasteries where many of Belgium's thirty cheeses are made. It smells like mushroom country, the climate moist and warm.

At the war memorial in Bastogne, America is clearly the hero, every state chiseled in granite beneath fifty American flags. In the round exhibition room are displays of uniforms and weaponry; gritty black-and-white footage conveys the complicated maneuvers between Allied and Axis powers.

"Alex, look at that bazooka!"

"It's not a bazooka, Marshall, it's a grenade launcher."

"Speak thlowly, please, my English is only tho-tho," Elodie reminds us. "*Who* is the grenade?"

Perhaps to exorcise its wartime legacy, the town of Bastogne is all candy shops and patisseries now. When we stop at a café for crepes, everyone is of a certain age. Suddenly I realize they're veterans from opposite sides of the battle: the aging German with his roly-poly grandchildren, the aging American from Indiana with his long-suffering wife, still using military jargon, saying, "Soon's you finish eating that strudely thing there, we ought to beat a retreat." Behind identical large pale Calvin Klein eyeglass frames, the vets' rheumy eyes can't meet each other's; the candy-shop souvenir maps they're holding in their leather-lean hands are trembling a bit and bending just a little into the whipped cream.

In the late-afternoon sunlight streaming through the sparkling plate glass window, Alex lines up his butter patties to smear them one by one onto his brioche as Marshall doodles extra testicles on the peasants dancing on the Bruegel place mat.

"What's wrong with this picture?" he quizzes Elodie.

"Nothing is wrong," she replies innocently. "That's how Flemish painting is, filled with life, with gaiety—"

"I'll give you a hint," Marshall says. "They have extra—"

"Don't start," I warn him.

So Marshall adroitly gets a new angle on the subject. "Dad," he posits, "do you think Hitler was so mean because he had only one ball?"

"Oh, right, Marshall," says Alex. "*I have only one ball. Kill the Jews!*"

I signal the waitress. "Check?"

◆ ◆ ◆

If the café was Bruegel, the hunting pavilion where we'll stay the night is pure Rubens: a pink brick chateau with crenellated turrets and moss growing on the slate roofs. It's a castle straight off a chess board, fit for noblemen, with a formal garden and corpulent servants so waxy-white they could've been painted by Rubens himself. The only note of earthiness comes from the flies: the place is abuzz with them from the forty horses boarded in stables just behind.

"Don't worry about the airs they put on," Elodie reassures us when we meet for dinner. "The owner is German, but the kitchen," she says with a wink, "is French."

The boys have accommodated themselves to the surroundings. Alex has mastered his cologne. Marshall is resplendent except that his fly is wide open. The four of us silently wind through narrow castle hallways toward the dining room and then, all at once: alabaster and rosewood! Beveled mirrors and stained glass! A hubbub of waiters dance in attendance as we're led through acres of pink roses to our table under an oil painting of cows reposing with all the splendor of garden nymphs. The tuxedoed sommelier has the girlish brown eyes and doleful style of a fellow who's both at home and homesick anywhere.

A fellow teacher from Elodie's dance camp awaits us. Monique has kinky hair and the most delicate shade of skin and is from Senegal. "*Très exotique,*" I say; she blushes olive.

"Your J. P. had expensive taste," Elodie remarks, bringing a sculpted flute of Calvados to her lips. "According to my uncle, in the war this place was frequented by no less a figure than Göring."

"Can we see the wine cellar?" I ask.

"I am sure the owner will not let you," Elodie says. "We shall ask in due time, but I believe this is as close as we get."

We're in a world of our own tonight, which is emphasized by the fact that "the winds" have knocked communication out. I look around the dining room that's supposed to be one of the finest in the Ardennes. At another table a regal horseman with velvet pants and dirty nails sits with a man who could only be a baron, barking out his gutturals in a way that makes me wince. Everyone has the bearing of titled noblemen and wears an expression of superiority. Yet somehow the superiority is layered with softness. The French guests pout with disdain that nevertheless entertains room for doubt. The English sneer in a way that isn't fully contemptuous; they somehow manage to be game at the same time. A British dowager, tipsy and confiding as only a British dowager can be, leans into our table with a twinkle. "I'm on an errand for caviar," she stage-whispers.

I have my eyes on a trim fiftyish man courting a lovely young snip, the exemplar of Parisian hautocracy. If he worked any harder he'd be chewing her food for her. For her part, she does nothing but measure his charm and gauge his labor. But in her low-key way, she *has* deigned to fall under his spell, and what compels her is his dark allure, his martyred romance. It dawns on me: he's a Jew. There it is, that sleepy longing about the eyes, that graceful mournfulness, reeking of history. He's an outsider, with all the outsider's grave appeal. Just as I'm formulating the thought that it's a melancholy mistaken for mystery, the Jew raises his eyes, recognizing something in me. . . .

It's odd to be eating well at a place where J. P. festered, but I have no time to dwell on the contrast because the boys are cutting up. With his time goggles distorting his depth perception, Marshall manages to get his chin stuck in a glass of seltzer. Alex pounds the table to kill a fly that turns out to be a pansy petal. The poor sommelier is beginning to look more homesick than ever.

"'*Lay zawn-fawng ohng puhr duh lohb-skew-ree-tay,*'" Marshall recites. "Children are afraid of the dark."

"No problem, don't worry about it," the sommelier reassures him, incongruously.

Alex mashes escargots in his strawberries as he informs the waiter, "Do you know a baby shrew is the deadliest animal, doubling its body weight every four hours?"

"Plus, your bow tie looks like a swastika," Marshall points out, blowing bubbles inside his lemon wedge through his straw.

Elodie's chortling so hard she wipes tears from her eyes. "Oh this is rich, this is really very rich." From their various corners, the Jew winks sleepily, the British dowager sends me a thumbs-up.

The waiter's been reduced to a state of extreme flappability. And so after another appetizer of *lapin*, whatever that is, I excuse the boys to run outside while the ladies and I proceed to the second course.

The kitchen specializes in exotic varieties of meat. I try the blood pudding, but another dish I must spit into my napkin. My lovely companions are fond of me when I do this; I must appear about four years old.

"Qu'est-ce que c'est?" I ask.

"C'est la cervelle."

"Cer—quoi?"

Elodie leans over the table to take my pen and write in big block letters: C E R V E L L E. "The brain of lamb."

I mug for their benefit, and put a big X through her word. Giggles! Peals of laughter! With the boys gone, they've adopted me as the child in the group. All through the remainder of dinner I'm doted on in this fashion. It's wrong, I realize, to think that the French are so proprietary about their language that they are cross with anyone who molests it. On the contrary, these women love it when I try—their fondness in direct proportion to how linguistically feeble I reveal myself to be. *"Cer—quoi?"* they repeat to themselves, and the glances they shoot at me as they giggle behind their napkins are pure mother love.

There's nothing the French like better than someone who knows he's inferior but is valiant anyway.

"You are married?" they query with an abundance of nonchalance.

"*Oui.*"

"Ah," they say. Studiously they avoid looking at me for a moment.

"To them," I say, nodding out the leaded bay window beyond our table where Alex and Marshall are parading back and forth with little Belgian flags.

This, of course, is irresistible. Two more courses, three more; each platter brings new levels of forgiveness and flattery, nor does their mother love abate with the addition of wine. I order more *lapin en moutarde aux champignons.*

"*Oui!*" They clap their hands with motherly pride. "You are very glutinous with it," says Elodie, sucking her fingertips. "How you say? 'Greedy.'"

By now our little orgy reeks of womanly BO, very bracing and nice. Finally their love overflows onto the American language, itself, and all manner of things American.

"I like very much the Wrigley's chewing gum!" confides Elodie.

"And the Pepsi Lite!" admits Monique.

"*Oo-la-la!* Football is great!"

"Especially the Lakers! Such buns!"

"Americans are the hunks of the world!" offers Elodie thoughtfully.

"But not the Rambo!" cautions Monique.

"*Non non non,*" agrees Elodie. "He is too thtupid to be a hunk. A dumbo!"

"An idyot!"

"*C'est vrai!*" they both cry. For several minutes we deplore Rambo and the sort of America he stands for. My hostesses gaze upon me with a mother's soft pity. "I like very much the Bill Cosby!" they offer.

"I like very much the blueberry charlotte of France!" I say, taking another bite of the delicious dessert. They giggle in assent, putting their hands in front of their teeth that are turning blue with the blueberries.

We've been at dinner three hours, I suspect. I look around for the time but that's the thing about eating in a castle. Every round thing your eye looks to isn't a clock but a hanging plate.

The boys are back, goose-stepping to our table with German flags. I'm afraid to ask where they got them.

"Just in time for éclairs," I say.

"No way, I'm filled to the top," says Marshall.

"Me too," says Alex. "My ears are ringing with escargots."

The boys have the only take-out in the history of the chateau. Never having prepared a doggie bag before, the waiters disappear to engage the engineering skills of everyone in the kitchen. They emerge fifteen minutes later with a splendid tinfoil contraption three times the size of the éclairs.

Clapping twice, the waiters toe up to a receiving line to say good-bye.

The last summer the boys would be young enough to leave a restaurant doing karate kicks out the door . . .

◆ ◆ ◆

Monique departs. The boys go upstairs to our room. Elodie and I sit on the white gravel of the driveway, waving away flies and listening to the crying of baby birds in the eaves. A strawberry lands near us, tossed by the boys from their turreted third-floor window where they're keeping an eye on us. "I must tuck them in," I say.

"No no, it's only ten-thirty," Elodie says, showing her watch. We're both drunk but it's a magic drunk, the kind where you knock over your goblet and the wine stays inside, garnet against the white pebbles. Everything is slowed down, self-contained and lugubrious. It's a ruby drunk, with my skin temperature registering hot and cold and my senses both dulled and sharpened. Elodie rests her head on my shoulder, her hair so wild beach plums should be growing in it. Her scalp has a dense, blowsy scent and, from the forest beyond, I smell the enticing aroma of rotting pine needles. I see fireflies, dozens of them, like a necklace of pale green neon blinking and beckoning, and then a shy dog puts its nose through the hedge across the road and gingerly sniffs the air.

"Chien! Chien!" I call softly, but immediately it retreats to the meadow, and something about the way it slinks answers the question only half formed in the back of my smart and stupid brain: it's a wild dog.

Elodie raises her head and together we watch it emerge again under the moonlight at the distant edge of the meadow, a white unhappy shadow. It engages our pity but the pity's tinged with respect for the way it sneaks off with a sideways movement, the furtive dodge of something beyond the fringe of society, brooding and cagey, as if habitually prepared to have sticks thrown at it. When I close my eyes the dog takes on the face of J. P., for he too must have been skulking around these parts; hunted, despised, beyond the pale of human companionship.

Another strawberry lands near us. "I must go," I whisper into Elodie's hair.

"No, no, it's only ten-thirty," she says, showing her watch again. And in the moonlight I see her watch has stuck.

Elodie turns so swiftly that the hair I was nuzzling is now mouth. She is murmuring into my lips. "Thleep with me," she lisps, a sibilance that makes my tongue vibrate.

❖ ❖ ❖

"What do you think of her?" I ask the boys a few minutes later, in the bedroom we share under a ceiling painted with clouds.

Alex thinks. "Great bod, Dad," he allows. "I even like her beauty mark, which on anyone else I'd call a wart."

"Your chivalry is gratefully acknowledged. And you, Marsh? Marsh? Oh dear, is someone here?" I ask, taking hold of a lump in the flannel sheet. "Is someone *here?*" I ask, squeezing a different lump. I rip the sheet off to expose chewable shoulders and a head dense with joy. But there's sadness here at bedtime, too. Marshall beseeches me with half a tear.

"I like her," he says hesitantly. "But what happens when you break up? Will I have to go between your house, Mom's house, *and* Elodie's house?"

"Never," I promise. "There won't be any more houses you'll have to go between."

Alex can resist no longer. He lands in between us to bring more shoulders to the mix, more hips and elbows. All three of us are conked out at the end of a long day and curl around each other amid the faint estimable smells of grass and old urine. This is the time to count our blessings, and to these souls I pledge my devout and abiding faithfulness.

"Thank you," I say aloud.

"Who you saying thank you to?" they ask.

"Damned if I know," I say, slapping their butts. "Get in your pj's."

❖ ❖ ❖

In bed a minute later Marshall wants to know the facts of life. I start to tell him.

"I know *that,* Dad."

"What do you know?"

A patient sigh. "The sperm cells travel from the testes to the vas deferens and out the urethra."

I trust my astonishment does not show. "And then?"

"Up the vagina to the servants."

"Cervix."

"Whatever."

"So you know everything. What do you want from me?"

"*Dad.* You know."

"No, I really don't. You seem to have gotten into your brother's manuals. What more do you need to know?"

"What does it *mean?*"

"Oh. Well, when the sperm leaves the urethra?"

"Yeah, that's the guy-part."

"And when it enters the vagina?"

"That's the part I don't get. What does he do—go to the bathroom in her?"

I put two and two together for him. At the critical juncture the clouds on the ceiling seem to part and his eyes are wide and shining. "Oh." He pushes an internal pause button while he considers this. *"Oh!"* he says again, the oh getting bigger in his brain for one of *his* 400 Revelations. "Now I know the facts of life!"

"So don't take any wooden nickels."

"I won't. But Dad? What's sexy?"

"Kind of like it makes you want to go up to a girl and hug her. Why?"

"Sometimes I think Anne Frank was sexy. Is that bad to think?"

"It's fine to think," I tell him. "But is it like you admire her or you think she's a babe?"

"Babe."

I put out my hand. "Welcome to the club," I say. "I hope your crushes bring you only good things and never bad."

Then in Alex's room, it's the postgraduate course. Tonight's topic: puberty.

"So," he says, "am I going to get wicked hairy balls like you?"

"That's the game plan, yes. Is that OK with you?"

Alex falls off his bed suddenly. I give him a hand up. "Yeah, but Dad?" he says. "Does it hurt to have puberty? Not to *have* it, but to have it *happen?*"

"You mean to have an orgasm?"

"Whatever. Yeah."

I'm exhausted. But the garnet wine has lent me clarity. "Remember when we went on that water slide and we finally came out in the open, splashing like crazy? Pretty cool, wasn't it?"

"It was awesome."

"If you liked that, you'll love this."

This registers pleasure, but Alex is still divided. In the context of this place and time, no pleasure is unalloyed. He takes a grape from the nightstand and swishes it around with a sip of coffee. "So if the guy comes before the woman, what're our options?" he speculates.

"Next topic," I say.

He sighs. Back to war: love and war, the two poles of adolescence. "Dad, I hope you know the ancient Chinese were just as bad as the Nazis. They used to plunk their enemies in cauldrons of boiling water and make the relatives drink the soup."

Right, I think. And Red Guards made parents pull the triggers on their children in Tibet. Americans fired their rifles into the vaginas of Vietnamese at My Lai. Rwandans were killed at a daily rate higher than Nazis killed Jews. Russian seal hunters would line up Eskimos to see how many bodies their musket balls could pass through. Even our beloved Belgians slaughtered countless numbers of Congolese. But I say no such thing aloud.

"Life is short," I say. "How about we finish with our Holocaust, and then we'll deal with the others, OK?"

But Alex is looking inward. I don't mean to be glib. "I know what you mean, though," I say, wanting to rescue him from getting lost amid his eternal fears and fantasies. "There's no shortage of heartbreak in the world. We don't have to hog any holocausts for ourselves. Even today, Burmese are being tortured, Armenians are still mourning their losses at the hands of the Turks, gays are being oppressed. . . ."

But the word *gay* seems to bring a flush to Alex's cheek. He takes a deep breath that catches beneath his rib cage. "Dad, I've thought about it a lot and, well, this is hard for me to say . . ."

"Take your time."

"I just don't think I'm attracted to men of my own sex."

"Oh! Well . . ."

"You know, I've tried to keep an open mind, because I don't

want to think of myself as prejudiced or anything, and sometimes I've tried to convince myself maybe I could be, I mean
I've really tried but . . ."

"No go, huh?"

"I'm afraid I'm just not cut out to be a homosexual, Dad."

"Well, we're just going to have to try to live with it, son."

He pops three grapes in his mouth by way of closure. "My
record is fourteen."

"You can eat more than that, can't you? Growing boy like
you?"

"No, I mean, in my mouth at one time."

◆ ◆ ◆

A little later, the boys are sleeping and I'm almost asleep, meld-
ing myself into the sound of baby birds crying in the eaves,
when there's a soft knock.

"Are you awake?" comes Elodie's whisper through the door.

I could still do it, take one of those giant steps instead of
these billion baby ones. But I stick with my choice.

"Non?" she asks again.

I think of the mouthy pleasures promised by her lisp. But
again I don't answer.

"All right, you prefer to stay married to your boys. I understand. It's better. What?"

She listens carefully, giving me one last chance.

"Bonsoir," I whisper.

"Bonne nuit," she whispers back.

She tiptoes away.

◆ ◆ ◆

Next morning I'm wakened by someone shouting at a servant
downstairs in a voice that makes me quake in my bedcovers. It
reminds me that I have no idea how I'm going to get into the
wine cellar without incurring the owner's wrath.

The boys are already up and out. The tinfoil dessert looks like
wild raccoons have gotten into it. Coming down to the lobby, I

see Elodie before she sees me, sitting on a padded leather bench, studying her freshly painted nails with a troubled expression. I'm touched. She must have done her nails last night to make herself feel better about the business between us. She brightens as she turns her attention to the boys: Chocolate-lipped Marshall's walking through the lobby with his eyes closed and an éclair extended before him like a blind man's cane.

Elodie has arranged for us to sit down with the owner, who turns out to be the horseman from last night with velvet pants and dirty fingernails, a stout German with a swaggering manner and cranberry-colored cheeks. He and his wench of a wife have such lung capacity they sound like they've had mikes implanted in their throats. The interview takes place in the dining room, which is empty but for a monkish couple from Switzerland; the flies have us all to themselves.

"Please tell him he has a very lovely place," I begin.

Elodie translates his response. "He says he knows all the compliments already, to get on with your questions."

So that's the way he wants it. We'll cut the flattery and get right to his boasting. Impatiently smacking the dust from his stiff thigh-high leather boots, he yaps on about how he arranges to have VIPs chauffeured in from the airport, how his morels are considered four times better than those of any other place on the globe. But his proudest claim, also printed in the four-color advertising brochure he waves in his hand, is that he has 25,000 bottles in his wine cellar, among the finest selection in Europe. He's immune to compliments because he supplies them all himself. After three or four minutes of this, when he hasn't looked at me once, I decide to make my move. Swatting away the flies, I say to Elodie: "Tell him I'd like to see his wine cellar now."

"That's like asking to see the inside of a man's wallet," he sputters angrily.

"Here's mine," I say, holding it out.

There's froth on his lip as he looks at me for the first time. "It is like asking to see a man's cock, if it's long or short!"

The boys don't notice or care. Marshall's still wandering around the room with his eyes closed and éclair extended, placing random custard marks on various doorknobs and chair rails. Sitting at a nearby table, Alex is drawing a picture of Hitler with yarmulke and *payis*. "Except that you advertise the precise number of millimeters," I say, tapping the brochure in his hand.

Elodie's eyes are dancing. His bluff's been called. He rears back in his seat imperiously, summoning his arrogance.

Which will be his undoing. Rising with a harrumph in his horse boots, he continues sputtering to Elodie as we follow him, picking up the boys and the loud-mouthed wife as well. I'm sure he's telling Elodie how he has an extensive clientele among the crowned heads of Europe, how he was born into a well-to-do family of Prussian war heroes and now has to prove himself to this upstart American and his ragamuffin kids. Harrumph!

The wine cellar is indeed magnificent, but it's the ghost of J. P. that intrigues me, lurking in this dungeon for three months while his babies were at a nunnery twenty miles away. The dust! The flies! Worst of all, the darkness! Funny that the journal has no mention of it. Unless . . .

"Dad! Dad! The blacked-out page!"

"And the dead fly carcasses. They must be referring to this place!"

Just what I was thinking. "Kind sir," I ask the owner, "could I ask a favor?"

"What is?"

Elodie asks him to hit the lights for a minute. Baffled, he complies.

We're pitched into blackness so deep our ears twitch. The floorboards above us creak as the kitchen help prepares lunch.

"What in the world—"

"Shh, please."

It's so Jewish of me, so pushy, to hush the owner in his own wine cellar! But greedily I imagine so many things. How did J. P. mark time, in his isolation? Who brought him food? How did he mourn his wife down here, and yearn for his twins? Was he huddled? Did he cry? Whom did he know to show him his way here in the first place? Was he boinking any of the women upstairs? Parting from his children, did he put the twins' hands in each other's and say, *"You must be each other's parents now,"* or something like that? So many mysteries, lost in time. I imagine conjuring up the twins from their hair the way the scientists do in *Jurassic Park:* reconstructing an entire prehistoric creature from a few cells.

Elodie clears her throat in the blackness. "My uncle says J. P. was able to hear the BBC broadcasts on the radio upstairs. The Germans were listening to it for laughs."

And suddenly, I imagine the Germans above us. Surprisingly, it isn't the usual Nazi caricature of braying and gloating. It's a pleasant sound. They chuckle happily with good fellowship, believing they are doing good for the world.

Another real-life hiding place! But this brothel was also a hiding place for Germans to go with Belgian girlfriends, so for J. P. it was a hiding place *within* a hiding place. Yet another subset.

"Tell him it's a most impressive cellar," I say in conclusion. But he has the last laugh. On the way up the narrow stairs I crack my head on the low threshold. For the next half hour they minister to me, Herr and Frau gently holding an iced washcloth on my temple and saying, "Good lad, good lad." They wave to us from the doorway as we take our leave.

Or perhaps they just don't want me to sue. We're not only pushy; we're also a litigious people, don't you know.

◆　◆　◆

It's time to find the nunnery where J. P.'s children were hidden. Elodie is fired up like a freedom fighter now. The passion we didn't allow ourselves last night has found an outlet. "I will take you anywhere you want to go," she says, pressing her gold ballet slipper to the accelerator. We roar down the highway.

An hour later, in the city of Liège, we come across the quintessential convent, with dozens of tiny finches twittering at a feeder inside the gray stucco walls. We zoom in, frightening the birds and a little Franciscan nun tending them. She's so otherworldly in a brown tunic and brown sandals that we're embarrassed at our urgency, but she picks up our mood at once and tells us: Wrong one! The one with the German nuns was moved to the opposite end of the city!

"The nuns were German!?" I ask Elodie, when we roll our windows back up.

"Sure. Did you think all Germans were bad?"

Elodie kicks off her slippers and, alternately gunning it and braking past construction pits and barricades, she cuts through a line of traffic, honking back at them when they honk at her. Stopped by a cop for speeding past a truck in a school zone, she tells him off. Nothing can stop her. But when we turn into the courtyard of what looks like a Midwest junior college dormitory, she and I both agree this couldn't be it.

"Yes it could, Dad," Alex says. "I saw a movie once with nuns. They're all supermodern now."

And how. It's like a not very well-endowed Corn Belt teaching college, with glazed bricks and skylights that don't open. If the other nunnery was an ancient abbey with the peaceful dust of the centuries, this one has a temp-controlled security system. Inside we tell them our mission and are ushered over the industrial carpeting—the perfect flooring for the quiet shuffle of a nun's gait—into a kitchen with a giant microwave oven. One of the nuns has her sleeves pushed up to program in some Pop-Tarts. Her arms, like the necks and brows of her sisters, have the prickly-mush quality of strawberries that haven't been eaten in time and are mottled with angry fuzz.

Except for one. After a minute in struts the hatchet-thin mother superior who, despite her eighty years, has creamy white skin and appears so fit she could hurl a crucifix over the roof if she wanted to. Kindness is her commerce; she doesn't squander it unnecessarily. After listening to our request in a businesslike manner, she lifts her gray-tinted eyeglasses to tap a phone with arthritic fingers: *Zéro, zéro, neuf . . .*

"She is calling for the records," Elodie tells me.

Presently an old janitor shuffles in with a large ledger. Unceremoniously the nun hoists it from him, and licks a fingertip to summon the page she wants. "Ah-ha!" she says brusquely.

"Well? Did you hide two Jewish children?"

She shakes her bladelike face vigorously.

"She says absolutely not. She saved only two children, and they were Spanish."

"Is she trying to protect them still?"

"Maybe. Or maybe she really thought they were Spanish. . . ."

"Ask her if they were twins," Alex prompts.

Obligingly, the old nun's crooked white finger traces a row of ledgers. The answer comes back: "Yes. Spanish twins."

We're being stonewalled. She sees the boys exchange looks and tightens her lips irritably.

"How did she manage to hide them?"

"They were ordinary children," comes the translation. "They played. They studied. One time there was a close call. The soldiers came here; she hid them in a laundry hamper. They loved dried fruits."

"Apricots," the janitor says. It is his only word.

The nun casts him a look I can't read, then unleashes a torrent of German words, the meaning of which causes Elodie's face to darken with embarrassment.

"She says she had no special love for the Jews, for the Spanish, for anyone. She just didn't want to do what the Nazis told her to do."

The old nun smiles, satisfied. And I get it, I think. There was nothing mawkish about her deed. She did it out of defiance, to show her contempt for the Nazi thugs who'd taken over her

beloved Germany. Hers was an act of heroism that was unsenti-
mental to its core.

Intimidated at last by this creature, we're brought up short. I
don't know what to do next. Until I get an idea. I reach into my
pocket for a plastic Baggie. "So she's sure they were Spanish?
Blond Spanish?" I ask, displaying the curls.

A transformation takes place. "Ohhh!" groans the janitor
standing behind her, and a similar sound escapes the nun. Her
eyes mist over for a second as she reaches to touch, the shine on
her pale eyeballs magnified behind her gray-tinted lenses.

But hers is a kindness made of steel. When her beeper goes
off, the one she carries next to her rosary beads, she scurries off
down the carpet. Her farewell handshake is a no-nonsense
good-bye bordering on a push out the door.

"Be on your way," she says in broken English. "Off to Paris
with you."

"Why Paris?"

"That's where the father took them, after retrieving them,"
she says in halting English. "To the synagogue where he served
as lookout. You did not know that?"

We're excited now. "Then they *were* Jewish!" I say. "And there
was a synagogue in Paris that stayed open during the German
takeover? How's that possible? A *shul* in the middle of the Third
Reich?"

But the nun has her hands around her ears, and she's lost her
English again.

"This is merely what she heard," Elodie translates. "Perhaps
it is apocryphal."

Nevertheless, off to Paris we go. . . .

21

HIDING IN PLAIN SIGHT

*W*e may have lacked nuns and Not-sees in Rowayton, but that didn't mean we couldn't hide under the nose of other terrifying creatures. It's a classic strategy, such conspicuous hiding—as familiar to players of hide-and-seek (who looks *under the table?*) as to manufacturers of domestic hidey-hole storage bins ("Hide It in Plain Sight!" say the advertisements for cans of lookalike Heinz beans with space for your valuables inside). In "The Purloined Letter," Edgar Allan Poe noted that one can "escape observation by dint of being excessively obvious," and that's what I tried to do in Rowayton, hiding in full view of my two scariest enemies.

Pirates Point, the bait shop at the other end of town, was loaded with wooden crates of mud-darkened crabs. The store sold ice cream and sand worms, fishing hooks and Hershey bars. Signs ringing the ceiling sported messages of a humor I took to be salty. ("Listen, and you may hear Long Island sound.") A child's dream store, you might think, but the larynx-less Jupe Darling, who ran Pirates Point, was a bristly thick-necked old German who'd changed his name from Doebbels (the sound rose deep in your gorge like *Dachau*) and who hosed down the crabs while muttering all sorts of things under his ginny breath about the clientele, many of them the day-trippers from New York who were paying his bills.

He hated me. He didn't do me the courtesy of hating me specifically; it was something *about* me that he hated. I could feel it in his chewing tobacco and in his rheumy glare, in the way he licked his bottom teeth when I entered his store. I could easily imagine him donning a brown shirt and storming into my house, smashing our paintings, tossing our books into a pile and igniting them. Every now and then Jupe was replaced by a woman named Honey whom I couldn't get a bead on. Sometimes she seemed to like me all right, telling me shaggy dog stories that I tolerated out of tact, but other times she'd fly off the handle and threaten to call the cops if I skidded my bike onto the gravel of the parking lot one more time. One day I confided to her what a crook and a scoundrel Jupe was, but I noticed her turning veiny and asked, "Uh, is he any relation to you?"

"He's my father," she sputtered.

Honey herself was short and wide and wore dungaree skirts that made her look even dumpier. She had her father's ungenerous eyes, wadded in gristle. So explosive were her rages that years later it came to me that perhaps she wasn't anti-Semitic so much as sexually frustrated. In any case, both she and her father tended to look at me as though I had horns and to credit me with more malice than I was capable of. In a way, since they had no power over my life, it was kind of flattering.

It was on this property, of all places, under a sun-bleached dock crusted with mussel shells and goateed with seaweed, that I established the not-very-secret hiding place "Stein-Frank." McDougal and I went there because it was shaded and smelled of seagulls. Yet for all its peacefulness Stein-Frank was a place of surpassing violence, for it was there we told ourselves Nazi torture stories of siccing German shepherds on the genitals of prisoners or pushing spiked dildos up their butts. It shocked us both, the detail with which we could invest these things, but we couldn't help ourselves.

Maybe that's why we called it Stein-Frank—saying Franken-stein backward was taking something scary and turning it around so it'd be safe. I was reversing the curse Pirates Point held for me. In any event, the images we concocted were bad enough to cause a physical reaction in us. We'd open our mouths wide to release the pressure. The more heinous the tor-ture, the wider our mouths would go. Imagining a man's balls crushed, we'd hug ourselves in misery, rocking back and forth as we groaned. With the tide calmly sliding in and out, we'd make up the most savage stories we could think of, and always the kicker was our knowledge that they weren't as bad as things the Nazis actually did.

◆ ◆ ◆

Or the Japanese at Nanking. Or the Cavalry at Wounded Knee. Or the Stalinists in Russia. I say again: Hog not the Holocaust.

◆ ◆ ◆

When I was ten Renee wanted to muscle in on the hiding biz. She offered me a deal: we could form a sister-and-brother team. She even had a name picked out for her half: Sleeney.

"Sleeney? What does Sleeney mean?"

"It's like a Slinky," she explained. Renee was proficient in the use of the Slinky, and figured she could use it to avenge our en-emies in the duo she proposed we become.

"But why Sleeney?" I asked. "Why not Slinky? Where's the letter *k*?"

"*K*'s too tough," she explained.

Sounded reasonable to me. Now *I* needed to come up with a name. That night in the shower I hit upon Tornado. It had punch, drama, verve, pathos. It was what I confessed to Lawless in the Cavern I wanted to be sucked up into. It was like Hurri-cane, the name of McDougal's little brother, but more focused. Thus were born Tornado and Sleeney, the Jewish superheroes of Rowayton, hiders supreme. To perfect our plans we spent hours in the crawl space above the kitchen, a wonderfully claus-trophobic place filled with dented lampshades and the yellow cotton candy of fiberglass insulation. We wrote chalk messages to each other on two-by-fours, and plotted missions of revenge against anyone who'd ever wronged us in any way, beginning with Pirates Point.

We cased the Point from top to bottom, amassing evidence. We deduced that the reason the benches in the bathhouses were spaced six inches out from the walls was that Jupe and his daughter hoped babies would fall through and break their skulls. They charged three cents for a Tootsie Pop when every other place in the world charged two. We were going to avenge these injustices by getting Jupe to chase me up the wooden stairs of the boathouse behind the store, then down the dark corridor to the door-sized window at the end. Then, just as it looked as though he were going to get me, I'd swing out to freedom on a rope, and Sleeney, waiting on the rafters overhead, would konk him on the head with a frying pan.

But then shouldn't Sleeney's name be Frying Pan, since *that* was her weapon? Renee wouldn't hear of it. In the end we spent so much time debating the point that we never got around to undertaking our plan. Typical Jewish superheroes: talking instead of doing. That, and we wanted our parents' blessing. We found it maddening that they thought our plans totally plausible and weren't skeptical in the least. "We can tell you don't believe us," we charged.

"But we do!" they protested. "It sounds like a good plan, especially the frying pan part, and we have every faith you'll pull it off."

"See, just the way you're saying it, we can tell you're thinking, 'They're just kids, they'll never do it.'"

We spent so much energy trying to convince our parents that we had none left for the mission itself. Pirates Point remained unpunished, not because we lacked resolve but because we spent so much time *insisting* on our resolve.

◆ ◆ ◆

However, the real reason our superhero syndicate broke up was because my sister never had the nerve to go after the true bad guys. Which meant I had to go alone to infiltrate the Hearts' property.

I'd flirted with their estate before—Heart's Island was the site of my being groped. But the residence was the real thing, a fortress that not even bigkids dared explore. Heart's Castle, directly across the street from my house, was occupied by the most mysterious people of my childhood. Mr. and Mrs. Heart were "private people," is how the adults put it, as if that explained something, but we kids saw them shake their heads after they said it, because they had no better handle on them than we did. The Hearts "kept to themselves." They knew no one and no one knew them, not even on a waving basis. They were generally assumed to be aristocrats from somewhere down South but no one knew for sure because no one ever talked to them. They had a big old-fashioned dusty-blue car in which they crunched down the long shadowy driveway and through the two stone pillars, and no one seemed to know where they went or what they did once they got back inside the Castle. From afar Mr. Heart seemed guarded, with long overhanging eyebrows and a clammy, hidden violence coiled inside him. Mrs. Heart was always attractively made-up and there was something eerily sexy about her, something pitiless and erotic; with her knife-thin nose and icy lips, she had a gift for witchiness. The main thing I remember was that behind their genteel exterior, their eyes were hard. They lived with their nearly grown-up son Teddy who never seemed to leave the Castle. On one of the few times I saw him we were swinging on a neighbor's rope swing and he emanated from out of nowhere, a wan figure with his hair perfectly combed and blue jeans perfectly creased, gave us one gigantic push that sent us higher than ever, then disappeared again.

Incomprehensibly, I once went to a birthday party of Teddy's. It was kind of pathetic that someone who was nearly a grown-up needed to invite McDougal and me along with a few of his contemporaries, who were equally pale and spectral. I was beside myself with curiosity to see what was inside the Castle but the whole party took place out on the driveway. It was the most unfestive party I'd ever been to. Solemnly, we lined up and shot baskets on the driveway and when I finally made one, Mr. Heart handed me a silver dollar. Though I was glad to get it, silver dollars always seemed suspect to me after that, freighted with gloom. We had vanilla cake out on the driveway, too, as if the Hearts were intent on not letting us inside the house. But then, amazingly, Mr. Heart asked if we wanted to see a special room in a special wing. Everyone said yes except McDougal, who was so freaked by the entire scene he could barely talk. He stayed outside, entertained by red-fingernailed Mrs. Heart, which did little to lift his mood, while the rest of us filed behind Mr. Heart to a turret on the side of the Castle where, he said, a room had been closed off and left untouched since it'd been hit by lightning in the '30s. Mr. Heart used a skeleton key to open the door. I was granted only one brief glimpse, but it stayed with me the rest of my youth: an empty formal room with peeling walls, and in the center, alone midst the paint chips, a bone-white piano.

If all the Rowayton kids knew about Heart's Island, no one knew anything about Heart's Castle. It wasn't merely off-limits, it was unthinkable to consider exploring. Mr. Heart was rumored to shoot at trespassers, for one thing, including the only group of trick-or-treaters who ever dared start up their driveway. But I worried that my kind was especially unwelcome there, which is why I had to go. Hadn't Mrs. Heart once asked me if I was circumcised, or was that just one of the dreams I was always having about them?

It happened shortly after the birthday party. Seeing as how I was the closest thing the Hearts had to a neighbor, and since I was kind of on a roll after the silver dollar, I feigned a neighborly familiarity one spring day and sauntered up the driveway under the guise of a school collection drive. I rapped the heavy iron knocker on the front door. I didn't think the flat sound would carry far into the recesses of the Castle, but soon Mr. Heart appeared, home in the middle of a Thursday afternoon, and for some reason not startled to see me. I told him I was collecting old baseball mitts that were going to be sent to some disaster area in the South that had been ravaged by floods—a pretty resourceful way to get a better look around, I thought, and one that had absolutely no basis in reality.

"Old baseball mitts, eh?" Closing the door firmly behind him so I couldn't peek inside, he led me across the driveway to a separate stone structure that housed his dusty-blue car. This, I was given to understand, was the garage. It was the size of an average house, and had a staircase that wound up to a second-floor room filled with tiny gnats. Alone with Mr. Heart for the first time in my life, I could see that he was spryly loose-limbed, with surprisingly fine hands and shiny nails, and that his eyebrows were even longer than I thought, giving him an expression of quizzical authority. I could smell dill on his breath. We poked around a bit behind some abandoned bedsprings and then Mr. Heart said: "No baseball mitts here."

He led me outside, facing the slope of lawn that stretched down to Heart's Island. I was trembling with excitement for I was under the very windows I had my telescope trained to night and day. I could see that a favorite theory of mine was incorrect: what looked, from my bedroom across the street, like a perpetually scowling face in the window was actually some kind of house plant. I also saw with a shock that my house wasn't the most pleasant thing to look at from this angle. For the first time, I imagined that the Hearts saw *us* as mysterious intruders, in our nouveau cardboard palace overlooking their ancient redoubt. But just as I was thinking this, Mr. Heart fiddled at a latch beneath the stone foundation and opened a door.

Never would I have imagined it: a genuine trapdoor. Stooping, Mr. Heart beckoned me to follow, and we entered an inside-outside place that wound beneath a spacious porch looking out over an inlet. This part of the property had always been the dark side of the moon to me, a place I had no access to from my telescope. The lawn sloped down to the water and a blond tangle of cattails. To see those cattails on the far side of the Castle was no less invigorating than if I'd been given a glimpse of Mrs. Heart's bleached pubic hair.

Inside was even better. Part of the interior was the stone ledge upon which the Castle was built, and the rest of it was filled with an odd assortment of stuff: antique rusting bicycles; some sort of giant wooden snow shovel; an antique wicker rocking chair; bales of chicken wire; oars hoary with disuse; paintbrushes stiffened with time. And unbelievably: a wooden spinning wheel, of the sort princesses prick their fingers on to fall into a hundred years of sleep. This now was the belly of the beast: the rampaging engine of the Other. I'd made it as far as I was ever likely to go into these frightening depths, and when Mr. Heart wasn't looking, I twisted my head around to give my shoulder a quick kiss.

I don't remember leaving. I don't remember feigning disappointment that Mr. Heart could rummage up no baseball mitts. I remember only being calmly ecstatic at my find. I sneaked over to revisit this place at regular intervals, carrying a skeleton key that I was amazed to discover was sold at the hardware store for $1.29. I always went alone and maintained perfect silence, content just to breathe the secrecy, though one time I took my little sister when I was feeling close to her. After blindfolding and twirling her a half dozen times, then stomping on some yolk-colored jellyfish and telling her that was how you got orange juice, I led her wordlessly through the latched door. The first thing she saw when I removed the blindfold was the spinning wheel.

For years Heart's Castle flowered in my unconscious as the hiding place supreme, an image that was not destroyed even when, in my college years, it burned to the ground. On the front page of the *Darien News,* I saw I'd had their name wrong all these years. The name I had understood, with what Anatole Broyard has called "the odd literalness of young boys," to be Heart had been simply Hart. Turned out that Mr. Hart was an ordinary insurance salesman with an office in Stamford, and in one of those gothic twists I would have expected of him, he lacked adequate fire insurance. "Private People Turn to Neighbors for Solace" was what the subheading said, going on to say all about how the Harts had no idea their fellow townsfolk were so friendly. The Harts were blanketed and fed and cared for. There were even tears of gratitude.

But I dream about Heart's Castle still, faithful to my original vision. In my dreams I'm carrying a skeleton key or I've suddenly, tragically, lost it. I can fly there, sometimes, but my wings are too big to fit through places that seem to have grown small over time. I have a sense of accomplishment or I'm bereft, with no ability to navigate. I'm sneaking up their driveway, but I discover the Hearts have had their telescopic sights trained on *me* all along. Sometimes I'm being shot at by Mr. Heart, my pulse pounding through my chest as I lunge from rock to rock. Other times, many other times, I'm being seduced by Mrs. Heart. She's terrifying, but it's worth it.

22

GESTAPO SOUP

*T*he train from Liège in the drizzle is a homesick ride. Looking through the train window, the three of us are a little blue. When J. P. picked up his children from the nunnery to take them into an uncertain future, did they put their hands in his, saying *"Can you be our father again?"* The truth is I'm missing Elodie a little bit. On our deathbeds, will we remember the missed opportunities of life more than the ones we seized . . . ?

Arriving in Paris after such a lachrymose trip is like taking a belt of absinthe after meditating. We're no sooner outside the Gare du Nord when a friendly Muslim cabdriver picks us up. He denies that any non-Christian houses of worship stayed open during the war, then rubs his crew cut and tells how he has a *real* mosque, how he stops work and goes to pray *every day at three*. At the end of this emphatic monologue at our hotel, he cheerfully rips me off—pocketing 100 francs for a 30-franc ride before I've adjusted to the currency exchange—and bows happily, saying, go with God.

We take a nap. Marshall and I collapse in the bed downstairs while Alex claims the one in the loft area. In a minute Marshall has his eyes closed and Alex calls for me to join him upstairs. "I'm feeling nervous. Can you be with me awhile?"

I climb the stairs. "What's up?" I ask.

"I don't know, it's just, how come we keep meeting the people we're supposed to meet? Elodie, and the nun, and how we find our way everywhere?"

"Luck," I say.

"Maybe it's more than that. Maybe we're on like invisible railroad tracks that steer us into the things we want. Like how we hardly ever hit dead ends? It's weird."

"I know what you mean," I say. "I've had the feeling for days that we're not so much trying to find things as they're trying to find us. Or something like that."

"Hmm," Alex says, unconvinced.

"Look," I go on. "Not to take credit away from our great detective work or anything, but the fact is that people who've traveled know how small the world is, especially places like Western Europe. All of Belgium and France could fit inside Arizona and New Mexico, and they're filled with people who've been in each other's business forever."

A voice pipes up from the bed downstairs. "Know what I think?"

"Tell us."

"It's like we're inside a video game, and God is playing us."

Alex and I look at each other. "Go to sleep," we both say.

The snoring commences almost instantaneously. Alex and I resume in a whisper. "Well anyway," I suggest, "maybe it's just being part of something that's bigger than we are."

"Yeah, but that's also kind of spooky."

"Well, don't let it freak you out. Can you sleep?"

"I have to go to the bathroom."

"It's in the hall."

"How do I know if someone's in there?"

"The hard way is to shoot a bazooka through the door and if there's a scream . . ."

"Never mind. I'll just sleep."

That's what he does. I attempt dividing my nap between them. Dead to the world, Alex scrapes a broken toenail over my belly. Downstairs, Marshall snores in my face. Finally I get up and take the telephone out on the wrought iron balcony to call J. P.'s estranged son, Olivier, whose number Shasha had given me in Brussels. Can he fill me in a little about his father's escape from the Nazis, or add anything to further our quest?

"It's imprudent," he says. There's the sound of silver clanking in the background. His mouth is half full with what I imagine to be a wedge of overripe honeydew.

"What's imprudent? To tell me where your father hid fifty years ago?"

"I am no longer of the faith."

"I understand that. Yet you must've heard something of his story."

"I have no interview for the press."

"I'm not press, I'm the second cousin of your father!"

"Thank you, good-bye," he says, his voice fading as he hangs up.

I look in on the sleeping boys. Marshall is hot, sleeping nude atop his sheet; Alex is freezing, shivering in his sweatshirt beneath two quilts. How long will I remember them like this? Seeing them sleep, I wonder what I've forgotten already, what irreplaceable videos I've lost. . . .

Musing quietly on the terrace, I almost welcome the sense of isolation. I make out a mysterious noise—the sound of tricycles coming down the street? many little children pedaling to converge from various side streets? But no, it's drizzle on the leaves of the vines framing the terrace. Another sound—a black cat padding secretively across the street, thinking no one can see it. As I used to be able to hear grass being mashed by a goat's teeth, I now hear the air filling my seven-year-old's lungs as he sits up in the next room, scratches both ears at once, yanks on his baseball cap, and is ready to face the day, fresh as a raindrop.

"I was asleep forty-two minutes. *Now* can we call Mom?" he asks, spying the phone on the balcony.

I tap the numbers and hand him the receiver.

"Yes . . . me too . . . I'm not going to get lost, I've got our address in my Nikes. . . ."

Hearing his side of the conversation I recall how a phone was brought to me at a banquet table in China when the connection finally went through; it was my boys itemizing what their mom was packing in their lunch boxes before they trudged off for school in the snow, fatherless at 7 A.M. Another time, in New Zealand, the hotel maid had already stripped my bed after I'd checked out when I abruptly fell ill in the lobby, I went back to shiver on the bare mattress and picked up the phone; the instant the connection to my sons was made I felt my blood strengthen.

Alex's turn with his mother: "Everything's wicked old . . . there are swastikas everywhere . . . no food anywhere. . . ."

In Tahiti once I received a piano recital from Alex, the musical tones flying over the Pacific. And a few months after that I called my answering machine from Chile to hear Marshall calling from a Boston restaurant, complete with the sound of canned violins playing in the background:

Dad when you get home
Wherever you are
Will you call me at my Mom's?
I don't feel very good
I have a pain in my side maybe you could
Rub it, a pain
Right in the heart.

Now they were with me. Watching Marshall take the phone again to say good-bye, I see in a flash of insight that what I'm doing on this trip is nothing less than taking repossession of my sons, saying: *You're not only your mother's stock, the scions of stolid Midwestern WASPs. You are also hiders in attics, hunted outcasts, pariahs and scaredy-cats and glorious eccentrics, caustic by nature and questioning by habit, and always on your toes. You are Jews, persecuted and scorned exiles, feverish with longing . . .*

Hanging up, Marshall looks tearful for a moment. Fortunately, Alex comes to his rescue. Revitalized by venting his full arsenal of grievances on his mother, he finishes applying his array of deodorants and is chipper enough to throw a full-body tackle on his sibling.

"Clobbered at the ten-yard line!" Alex sings. "We ready?"

◆ ◆ ◆

If anyone knows about this synagogue, it'll be in the Marais, the old Jewish quarter. It's a square mile filled with sights the boys have never seen before. A Jewish laundromat. A Jewish crazy person, cheerfully haranguing people in song like a *nudnik* character out of *Fiddler on the Roof.* A Jewish butcher shop where I strike up a conversation with the jolly proprietor while the customers wait with blank looks between the dangling chicken carcasses.

"Did any Jews manage to hide in Paris through the war?"

"Oh, no one! The Germans, they go from house to house, zearching, zhooting!"

"No Jews stayed at a synagogue?"

"They locked them all in a football stadium where after three days women were giving birth in the aisle seats, children were jumping to their deaths off the goal posts. . . ." He narrows his eyes at us. "Very bad place. Gives you chicken bumps."

We go to a Jewish deli that is like the Zabar's of Paris. But the proprietor is too much a "character" to be likable. He surrounds himself with two slobbering wolfhounds, and has a politician's slippery eyes, with practiced jive about his eight grandchildren. He gives us a deli man's perspective on the war, telling us that one of his hidden cousins lived on a diet of herring and marzipan for four years, another carried quince paste in his rucksack.

Next stop is a barber shop right out of the Depression. A black kettle sits on the coal stove and a vintage box radio softly plays some hard-to-catch old tune. Tacked to a blue pegboard are photos of 1930s movie stars with their hair in impossible pompadours. Six or seven of the glummest souls I've ever seen, waiting for haircuts, raise their eyes. The barber himself is like an old blind mouse, in a tie under his white barber's coat, shuffling about and poking his nose into the air to discern who's rung the bells on his glass door.

The anachronistic setting makes me bold. "Does anyone know anything about a synagogue in Paris that stayed open during the war?"

Silence. Using a jumbo black comb, the barber continues snipping with his little mouse nose in the air.

"Anything at all?"

At last the barber speaks. It turns out he and his wife are Protestant but have worked all these years in the Marais cutting the hair of Jews because "Jews are *de bon coeur.*" They say they remember a roundup when all the children were asking their parents, "Where are they taking us?" The wife says a Jewish neighbor, a jeweler, was locked in a van but managed to pick open the lock with his diamond tweezers. He was caught and deported anyway. "Under those conditions, how could there be a synagogue?" they ask, both staring at the coal stove, their aged faces beautiful in repose. "Six million," they sigh. "Six million."

The number of cars crossing the Mississippi each day . . .

Out on the sidewalk, we accost knife sharpeners from Transylvania, cobblers from Poland, tailors from Tunisia. We talk to a stutterer who had his mouth mockingly stuffed by the Nazis with wooden matchsticks, to a pianist who had his thumb shot off when he jumped from a convoy train. We hear about a Jew who survived by hiding in southern France with the Basques (*"très gentil, très sympathique"*), about a Parisian concierge who denounced his Jewish tenants and then stripped their apartment down to the light switches, about a Polish refugee who learned he could escape to China if he had Jewish relatives there, so he found a Shanghai phone book at the general post office and looked for any Jewish names to put down as reference. What was the SS going to do? Call?

But we're getting no closer to the synagogue. Impatiently, I yell my request up to a woman leaning out her window. Bemused, she says to try the little religious place on the corner. We sidle in among the crowded artifacts. Menorahs of all sizes share shelf space with bottles of blue Windex, plastic dreidels with boxes of baking soda. The frail purveyor's lips turn wet and trembly as he relates a story to us about being sick in a sanitarium when the French police came and took him right out of his bed on a stretcher. His Polish father smuggled a message to him from a concentration camp in the handlebar of a bicycle. "My son, don't be sad. Have courage. We will survive. Rip this letter up. *Au revoir.*"

Everyone has a story, the purveyor says. People don't talk about it because it hurts too much. *"Mir vel leben,"* he repeats. "We will survive."

Moved, I buy a tallis for Alex's upcoming bar mitzvah.

"Good boy, good boy," he says, stooping before Alex on arthritic knees and touching his hair.

"Have you heard of a synagogue that stayed open during the war?" Alex asks.

"Non, non, ce n'est pas possible," he says gently, wrapping the tallis in newspaper and handing it to him.

❖ ❖ ❖

And then in the cab, I realize I was ripped off a second time today. The shopkeeper charged me twice what I've seen these things cost elsewhere. Astonishment makes me rant.

"How could a fellow Jew do that?" I demand of the cabbie, a Sephardic Jewess with a mezuzah hanging from the rearview mirror next to a flat hand to keep the evil spirit away. *"Vel leben,* my ass! He'll survive, all right—by fair means or foul!"

"You're an idealist, eh?" she says, cocking an eye at me in the mirror.

"It's just . . ." I sputter. I tell myself to shut up, but her dark liquid eyes are almond shaped and I feel she might understand. "It reminds me of the time in college when I'd frequent this little Mr. Klein who owned a tiny milk store on Angell Street. My girlfriend and I felt sorry for him and we'd stop in to shoot the breeze and when he was certain of our friendship, you know what he did? Sold us sour milk!"

The cabbie barks out a short laugh that exposes her back teeth.

"You don't understand. He did it on purpose. He reached around back for one that was totally curdled and used our so-called friendship to pawn it off on us!"

"Serves you right," she snickers, and the boys snicker along with her.

"Sure, blame me for being an easy mark. But that's not the point. I hate to say it, but times like that Jews seem like we haven't evolved in five thousand years, we're still a haggling desert tribe, cheating and scheming and taking pleasure in besting everyone in a deal."

"You don't think it would have happened if he'd been a Mr. Jones?" she asks. Her laughing eyes are so slick with mirth they're impossible to fix. It's as if our Ashkenazi eyes are packed in water but hers are packed in oil. "Or a Mr. Abdullah?"

She's put me on the spot. Dry granular soap, I notice, has stuck to my cuticles. If it's true that prejudice is the poor man's sociology, the trick is to resist facile generalizations. But I'm not ready to leave the subject just yet.

"It's just . . ." Out the cab window a slope-shouldered, 300-pound bear of a guy wearing a yarmulke pinned to his kinky hair by a barrette and wiping his sweat-dripping chin with his Snoopy T-shirt is playing the clarinet to a klezmer beat. "I don't get Jews," I confess.

"What do you mean you don't get them?"

"I don't *get* them. How they can be so pious, but cheat you in business? How can they be so serious, yet act like such show-biz hams?"

"Maybe that's because you're trying to pigeonhole us, and it's not working."

"Yeah, Dad," Alex says. "That's where you screw up: trying to lump everyone together."

"Yeah," says Marshall heatedly. "Why does it make it all right for you to be anti-Semitic just because you're Jewish?"

"You're right," I admit. "It doesn't."

"Know what I think?" Alex says. "It makes it worse. Because if you hate yourself, why should they have any reason to like you? You got to give them something to like."

"How in the world do you know that?" I ask.

"Duh, Dad. It's how you survive sixth grade."

"I don't know," I say at last. "I guess I just expect more from the Jews."

"Ah," says the cabbie, winking at me in the rearview. "Ah."

◆ ◆ ◆

I install the boys in the hotel, but I'm still worked up. "How about we just order room service for you guys and I'll go for a run?" I suggest.

"I'll have a falafel with extra hummus and feta, please," says Marshall.

"Make mine gestapo soup," says Alex.

"You mean gazpacho?"

"That's what I said."

I lean to kiss him. "Ow," he says as I plant a wet one on his cheek.

"Can we have another Sunday school?" Marshall asks.

"Tell you what," I say, lacing up my running shoes. "If you promise not to fight while I'm gone I'll tell you a quick Sunday school story about something that happened once in Zimbabwe."

"Just so long as it doesn't have more of those fifties names," Alex scoffs. "Kip . . . McDougal . . ."

"I was staying at a safari lodge deep in the bush," I begin, ignoring him as I rummage for our candles. "It was very wild: lions sniffed around our tents at night. And it was very civilized: the head of the dinner table would tap his water glass with his silver bread knife each evening and say, 'Ladies, if you'd care to be seated . . .'"

"Yuck," says Alex.

"Yuck plus," says Marshall, blowing out the match.

"Well, it was a formal kind of place, out there in the bush. The colonial Rhodesians who lived on after black independence were diehards, the last of a breed. But there was one diehard in particular whom I didn't like on sight. She was so stiff and starchy I thought her face was going to break every time she brought her spoon to her mouth. She was a hardlooking blonde with skin that had dried out in the African sun—pretty but too upper-crusty for my taste. I'd made a point of avoiding her, but the final morning I found myself sitting next to her on the two-hour drive to the airstrip, and we fell into conversation. And there in the backseat of an open Land Rover, bouncing along the clay roads, we discovered we had a number of things in common. It turned out she was divorced the same year I was. She'd had her first child the same month I'd had mine. Her background couldn't have been further from mine—she'd been brought up very isolated in a farmer's cottage in Rhodesia, with a kitchen floor that consisted of fresh layers of elephant dung ('Ah, the smell of fresh elephant dung,' she sighed). But sitting there with our thighs slapping together over the rutted clay road we discovered we saw eye-to-eye on many important issues of life. We found ourselves opening up to each other. She told me that she loved her son more than anything in the world, and she was proud of how polite he was. She was especially proud that he'd stand whenever a lady entered the room."

"You saw eye-to-eye on *that?*" Alex asks.

"Well, yes," I say. "Because even though I don't expect you to stand, I'm pleased you've both learned to treat people with respect."

"You *are?*"

"Exceedingly," I say. "We sat there in the back of the Land Rover clutching the brims of our safari hats and we were beaming with pride at our children. It was a link we had."

"I get it," Alex says.

"Me, too," Marshall says.

"But now I'm coming to the part I want to tell you. I asked what her last name was and she told me it was Smith. She asked me the same and when I told her, for the first time in my life, my name didn't seem enough. I've always said Rose and left it at that, but I sensed that although she was too discreet to ask, she wanted to know what my background was, so I volunteered information I never volunteered to anyone before. I told her my name was shortened from Rosenzweig by my grandfather. For some reason I wanted her to know that. I wanted to tell her who I was."

"Your name was shortened from Rosenzweig?" Marshall asks, openmouthed.

"So was yours, butt-nard," Alex counsels him.

"So was *mine?*" asks Marshall, truly alarmed.

"Our name was shortened from Rosenzweig about seventy years ago," I say. "I've told you that before."

Marshall is suddenly pacified. "Oh yeah, I remember," he says.

"When I told her that, she nodded smartly, and told me that when she was nineteen she spent a summer hitchhiking by herself around Europe. One morning at a youth hostel two girlfriends she'd met asked what she was going to do that day, and she said she didn't know, and they invited her to come along with them to Dachau. She'd never heard of Dachau, and she went and saw the concentration camp. She'd been raised in such a protected, polite environment in colonial Rhodesia that no one had ever told her about the Holocaust, and there she was seeing it for the first time. And what she saw so horrified her that ever since she's read everything she could get her hands on about the Holocaust. She said that she'd grown up in the bush with lions and hippos and wildebeest and ever since that day, whenever anyone said to her that so-and-so was acting like an animal, she'd always stood up for animals. 'Animals don't have a Dachau,' she told them. 'They kill when they're hungry and that's all. They don't have a Dachau.'"

"Wow," say Alex and Marshall, forcefully enough to make the candles flicker.

"She told me something else. She said that once she had a boss whose name was Goldfarb and he'd changed his name to Gold and she thought it was sad that he didn't keep his people's name, that he didn't honor what they'd died for.

"And for the first time I thought about taking back the old family name of Rosenzweig," I say. "The name Rose seemed too bare without the -zweig, like it had been truncated. I felt like an elephant with his trunk chopped off, or a lion with a buzz cut instead of a large furry mane. I'd never felt that before, and it took this most unlikely Rhodesian lady in the back of a Land Rover to make me think of it.

"We continued the rest of the way to the airstrip in silence. I had a lot to think about. And I guessed she felt the same way. The whole time we'd been talking we never once used the word *Jewish,* but I'd told her who I was, and she'd responded to it. At the grass airstrip she was taking a little four-seater in another direction, and do you know what she said to me, as she shook my hand?"

"I don't know," says Alex.

"Me neither," says Marshall.

"She said: *'Shalom.'"*

23

THE SCOTCH TAPE
TEMPLE

*H*angover: my head feels like a rotten pumpkin being clawed by kittens. Alarms tweet on at daybreak from all over Paris: from steeples along the Seine, from the hotel's bedside tape deck with built-in clock. Heavily I convey myself to the shower where I try to put last night together. *After the story I went jogging . . . yes . . . then I stopped for a couple of drinks somewhere . . . right . . . asking people about the synagogue . . . then I couldn't find a taxi and had to run the whole way home, coming into the lobby to find the kids hysterical in their pj's with the concierge trying to comfort them, Alex white-faced with anxiety and Marshall swinging wildly from a coat rack, crying, "Dad's dead!" I was only forty-five minutes late but it'd been forty-five minutes of anguish for them, thinking I'd been lo-jacked. . . .*

"Yeah, but Dad?" says Marshall now, joining me in the steam. "Did you ever peel a kiwi with your fingers? Would a rock float if it had a hole in it?"

I marvel at how much better he makes the world seem. Like the biblical David soothing the tormented breast of King Saul, he has only to come into my view to make me smile. "I see you've recovered from last night," I say, turning him around to suds his shoulders.

"Kind of," he admits. "I dreamed I was being chased by geese in sunglasses and black boots."

I take a leap. "Were they like Nazis?" I ask.

"They *were* Nazis," Marshall confirms. But this sends him to a deeper place. His lip goes out in self-pity as he draws a line with his toe on the steamy glass wall.

"I cry sometimes," he informs me. "When you're not looking."

"You do?" I ask, astonished. "Why?"

"When I dream sometimes that all those kids were being killed, and then I wake up and say 'whew.' And then I remember they really *were*."

How can it be that a child has tears for the victims half a century later? But he does.

"You drink too much," Marshall adds.

"I *do?*"

"And drive too fast."

"I'll—try to take it slower."

"Thank you. It's just . . . I could never grow another dad."

My hangover lifts like fog from a harbor. Could David do *that* for Saul?

◆ ◆ ◆

Rue Tilsitt, one of the roads that ring the Arc de Triomphe, is the address for the Belgian ambassador, the Japanese embassy, and J. P.'s son, Olivier. Under threatening skies, Olivier receives us as correctly as a head of state tolerating a visit from Pygmies. In an Armani jacket with blue knit tie and blue striped shirt, he couldn't be more different from his father. A handsome man with manicured nails, tall and spiffy with dry palms, he's the picture of polish and parsimony. A high Parisian, if there is such a thing—like high mass or high tea. I whistle inwardly: from the likes of J. P. to this haut Parisian in one generation. And all he had to do was convert.

"*More* French roast," Alex grumbles, accepting Olivier's offer of muddy coffee as we follow him through an office of green marble.

Olivier is not in the diamond business. He's in textiles, president of a firm that handles PR for the leading French designers: Gucci, Yves St. Laurent, Givenchy. As we traipse from room to room—green marble to brown marble to black marble to white—it's all subdued chaos with stacks of press releases. His own quarters are even more subdued, with the hint of even greater chaos. Dainty as a fox, Olivier slides frictionless over the low-pile carpet in his ostrich-skin loafers and pivots his long sinuous frame into his chair, hands behind his head. The Arc is right out the window, like his personal possession.

As Olivier sits there sucking his teeth, we regard each other in a kind of silent power struggle, both of us weighing who has the higher valence: a somewhat bedraggled writer or a fancy fashion rep. Marshall breaks the silence. "Are you really J. P.'s son?"

Chuckling without mirth, Olivier pushes a silver chalice loaded with sugar cubes across the desk, lights up a Gitane, and blows a smoke ring toward the twenty-foot ceiling, where a plaster cherub appears to be blowing a bubble down at him. Then answers in the roundabout fashion he seems to favor.

"This building, like all the buildings on Rue Tilsitt," he tells us, "was constructed in eighteen sixty-five by Napoleon the Third, who intended to house his general. Instead it was turned into a hotel. I researched this when I first moved in five years ago. The landlord was a gentleman by the name of Baron Joseph Ginzberg. Jews!" he says, arching an eyebrow. "You are everywhere, and in all guises."

You and not *us*, I note. Like the wicked son. We bide our time.

"So to answer your question. What, just because I have a black onyx pen and pencil set I can not be J. P.'s son? Of course I am Jacov Pesach Morganstern's son. The question is: Why are you so interested?"

It's as good a time as any to tell him what we're after. He taps a polished fingernail on the silver chalice while he counterfeits mild interest in the subject.

"I know so little of his life," he says at last. "And of the time frame, even less."

"Do you know how his first children died?"

This he dismisses out of hand. "Not even," he says, fashioning a long gaze out the window.

Swinging his legs, Marshall accidentally kicks me in the calf. This one's going to leave a bruise. "Or about a synagogue that stayed open during the war?" I ask.

"I know only that they departed Paris on a steam train that went for days," he says with something like a sigh. "No one knew where it was going. One night the train stopped and he got out with all the other Jews trying to escape, and they were calling, *'Malek! Malek!'*—milk for their babies."

He recites this with no show of emotion. But in this opulent office above the Arc de Triomphe's soundless traffic, we can almost hear it: *"Malek! Malek!"*

"I know also that it was a ride so bumpy that his children, the beloved twins, yes? They were black and blue from holding the luggage on their laps. At some point the Germans came through and my father is pretending he is not nervous by continuing to read his newspaper; his hope is that they do not line up the passengers and order them to drop their trousers so they can see who is circumcised. And while he is hoping, one of his daughters says to him, 'Daddy, why are you holding the paper upside-down?' Which is rather a comical picture, if you think about it. Which I choose not to do."

Olivier removes a Chapstick from his drawer and, adopting a wintry smile, dabs it on his lips. "And there you have it, the sum and substance of my knowledge. I am afraid I am of limited help. I know nothing of where the train took them, for instance. It is all bits and pieces."

"That's all right," I say. "It's more poignant this way, to get

the history in tatters instead of all standardized and sanitized."

He considers this a minute, calmly stirring his coffee. It
seems to make no impression. "Yes? Suit yourself. You understand that any knowledge I impart is all I have from an entire
childhood of growing up with him. Maybe two or three words
on the subject per year. To know that a father at one time was
capable of holding a newspaper upside-down . . . it is not much.
He was not exactly what you call forthcoming, eh?"

"Was it because he was traumatized?"

"*Donc*," he says with a trace of exasperation. "He spent all his
love on his first family and had nothing left over for my mother
or me."

"But he was *your* father, too," Marshall points out.

"In a manner of speaking."

"I'm trying to frame a question, but I can't think of the
French word for *remote*," I say.

"I know very well the word *remote*."

"Is that what he was?" I ask.

"Put it this way," he says dryly. "We wouldn't have been his
first concern in a house fire."

I have been examining Olivier's throat, I realize. There seems
to be talc on it, or a makeup powder that smells pleasant. It's
confusing to smell pleasantness from a man I so immediately
dislike; odd to be receiving a gift from someone so close-fisted,
for in his own way he is more stingy than his father.

And then, just as I decide there's no point in continuing, he
volunteers the information we've been looking for. He dons a
pair of thin gold spectacles (suddenly I can visualize him wearing a yarmulke) and to our amazement, he takes the black
onyx pen and gracefully writes an address. "Go. Check. It is
the *shul* of which you speak. No one knows about it, not even
in Paris."

"How do *you?*" asks Alex.

He smiles. But it's a snide smile, the least attractive of all human expressions. I decide to pursue.

"Really, how?" I ask. "Have you studied the Holocaust?"

"Ppp," he sneers. "Why would I want to study such a thing? All those unhappy faces . . ."

"You don't like them because they were suffering?"

"No, I don't mind if someone suffers. . . ."

He stops himself, momentarily alarmed by his words. Then seems to decide something, and hardens his expression. "I mind," he says, "if they push it in my face."

For some reason it's Alex who's most offended by this statement. "How can you say that?" he asks. "These people lived through the worst event of the century—"

"Read your history," Olivier snaps, condescendingly. "The Holocaust was neither singular nor unique, merely a case of man's inhumanity to man, business as usual."

But this is too facile even for the twelve-year-old. He sees it for what it is—stock cynicism that passes for vision. "No," Alex says. "It's not usual to bury prisoners of war alive to save bullets, to poison the wells of land you're retreating from, to starve newborn babies to see how long they'll take to die. . . ."

Surprised by the boy's vehemence, Olivier dabs his lips again with the Chapstick. *"Maudlin, maudlin,"* he says, mock-patting his overheated heart.

"'Luh sair-pawng eh koo-vair day-kigh,'" Marshall says. "'The snake is covered with scales.' Let's leave."

But leaving won't be so easy, for Olivier has now taken the offensive. "The Jews got what was coming to them. You think it's coincidence that the history of this people is the tale of being kicked out of country after country? How long can you go on blaming the other guy? Besides," he says, curling his lips in a sneer of triumph, "I am weary unto death hearing about it. You people go over it and over it, and over it some more. Why are the Hebes so obsessed with the Holocaust?"

"Perhaps it is as one of your beloved cardinals said," I reply. "The Holocaust is to Jews what the crucifixion is to Christians."

He turns on me, his eyes dancing with fury. "There are already thirty thousand books on the Holocaust!"

"Someday there may be thirty thousand and one."

He sputters, giddy with rage, and I feel the most unlikely thing: pity. For as he attempts to light another Gitane with trembling fingers, I spy under the cake of makeup a pimple on his neck, red and raw. Aren't they the same neck pimples that the Hasids in Antwerp had? Doesn't he have the same fire in his eyes, hilarious with passion? Is it not them so much as himself that he truly despises? But pity is not what's called for right now. I try to locate the sphincter of my heart and tighten it against this man. Gird my loins, in Bible-speak . . .

I touch the packet of curls in my pocket and am imbued with clarity. Turning to the boys I say: "You know how you're always wondering which are the deadliest animals in the world? There, sitting across from you in living flesh, that's one of them now."

An ambulance wails past, making the sugar cubes rattle on our host's blotter.

"*Adieu, monsieur,*" I tell Olivier who seethes under his plaster cherub. "Thank you for the address."

❖ ❖ ❖

Outside the rain has started in earnest. We dash for a bus. Beneath the underwear ads, I am squashed against a hairy woman with the word *Impulsive* on her T-shirt over the nipples. The rain seems to have brought out the separate violent smells of mustard and mosquito repellent. I keep consulting the address Olivier wrote in elegant blue ink. The Raschi Shul is in the 9th arrondissement, say his directions. 6 Rue Ambroise Thomas.

"*Comme La Femme,*" says the back of the woman's T-shirt as she gets off. We follow.

This part of the 9th is teeming, a network of squirrelly little streets, filled with the bustle of not-well-to-do Jews hawking hair tonics and cheap trinkets—bad Israeli silver with dried orange glue squiggles where the turquoise has fallen off. In a downpour we walk past the Rue Ambroise several times before I spot the street, which curves around at a right angle from an archway. The Raschi Shul is in the middle of the block.

To call it unprepossessing would be doing it a favor. It's not one of your high-toned suburban temples with biblical scenes in soaring mosaics. This has grimy bare wood floors of stained pine strips, more or less covered by a ratty red carpet that's rotting from concentric circles of grease and curling up around the edges. The walls are cheap plywood paneling that have been shabbily marbleized, with electric wires tacked on with a staple gun. Fluorescent bulbs hang over all. The stale air is punctuated by a smell of disinfectant so sharp it could be urine.

We follow the sound of rain through the rooms. Upstairs is a function room floored in pitted linoleum; a sheet of transparent plastic is thumb-tacked across the ceiling to catch leaks. Downstairs is the sanctuary, where small white ceremonial towels are draped over the wooden seats to dry in the hot ammoniac air. The seats themselves are like grade school desks of several generations ago, connected stiffly to the desk portion. Under the lids are stored the Talmuds, mildewed old texts Scotch-taped together. Yes, I think, this is where the faith was maintained— not where the gilt edged leather-bound volumes are cracked open twice a year but here, where the pages are dogeared with thumbprints from people who work with their hands.

"Dad!" says Marshall from inside his time goggles.

"What?"

"Scotch tape!"

"So?

"Don't you get it, Dad?" Alex joins in. "All that Scotch tape from the journal. It's like a Scotch tape temple!"

But before I can register this I'm being high-fived by a hipster rabbi who looks like a California surfer wearing a prayer shawl over his very cool black leather jacket.

"A Scotch tape temple! You're all right, half-pint!"

Ouch, my head. My rotten pumpkin of a hangover returns as we learn our interlocutor is from Minnesota, not California—a rabbinical student passing through Paris on an exchange program. Turns out he's a RollerBlader on the side, not a surfer, and he's here to check out the secret temple that he, too, has heard about.

"J. P. Morgan, that's choice!" he exults, when Marshall fills him in. "And you're following his footsteps!"

"His tracks," Alex corrects him sternly. "Following his tracks."

The guy bites his nails and cackles heartily, grasping the nature of our quest instantly. "How can I help you, my children?"

What's with this joker? Is he for real, or just a figment of my hangover, the way pink elephants are said to be figments of the DT's? He's annoying, in any case. Yet I want to get the dope. Almost against my better instincts, I ask what he's heard about this place staying open during the war.

"The *entire* war!" he exclaims, spitting out a piece of cuticle. "Always had a *minyan,* story goes—mostly Polish refugees, Czech, Hungarian, Rumanian, no Belgians I ever heard of. But then again, what do I know? *No one* knows. It was top secret. Far out, *n'est-ce pas?*"

"How'd it manage to stay open?"

"Story I heard: Someone would stand on the lookout up above to warn people and they'd scurry out the back."

"Yes!" Alex says. "We were told J. P. was a lookout!"

"They all took turns sleeping, eating, the whole nine yards. Supposedly the Germans came in several times, found no one, split. Survival—name of the Jewish game! We may not always have the moves, and people may despise us unto death, but we survive!"

God help us: another self-exciting Jew. Who could dream up such a people? Yet what he's saying makes a kind of loopy sense.

"So now you ready for something *really* far out?" He rummages in his satchel, which is stenciled with the slogan RADREB. ("It's the nickname they gave me way back when: Radical Rebbe.") With a mad grin he waves a set of tefillin in my direction.

"Hold on," I protest, holding my head. "I'm a Connecticut kid. I don't know these rituals."

"Jews gotta do it every day," he says, gesturing me to turn around. And such is the force field of this crazy kinsman that I comply. I must say, it's not bad, kind of a cross between leather bondage and having your blood pressure taken, with a little of the apprehension of being fitted for a parachute. "Baruch for what's ailin' ya!" he says, and commences to mumble things I've heard, till now, only from the lips of very old people.

Do Jews confess? For some reason I'm moved to level with him. "I'm troubled by our people," I say.

A wink. "Go on, my son."

I struggle for the word. "We don't seem as . . . pretty . . . as I'd like us to be."

"Hey," he says. "You think we survived five thousand years being pretty? Does Mr. Tortoise survive eons puckering his lips to everyone? Stick with pretty, Darwin takes you out double-quick. Study the Shakers: dead in six generations, but sure put out some pretty furniture!"

I make to interrupt but he's not having any.

"You want longevity, come to the source. People of the book are a tough-assed people. Mean's in the genes! Don't be ashamed, it keeps the earth spinning through space. Me first, comin' through! Doesn't matter whose toes I stomp on, it's evolution time!"

"Dad's alienated from his faith," Alex tells him. "He questions his connection with his brethren."

"Then he wins the matching steak knife set! *All* Jews worth their membership cards are alienated! Half the Jews smoked by the Germans were alienated!"

"So you're an anti-Semite, too?" Alex asks.

"Me, I'm a skepto-Semite," he says with a smirk. "I'm skeptical of my people and would beg you do the same. *Everyone* should be skeptical of their little subset. WASPs, Muslims, planet'd be a hell of a lot happier."

I'm still a little annoyed, but more amused than anything else. "And the mystery of God? You got an answer for that, too?"

"You ready? God's not pretty, either. No way is *He* all sweetness and light. That's what people can't get their heads around. He's sweetness and light on a good day. Other days he's cranky enough to bite your arms off and gargle the blood. But bad shit happening doesn't mean there's no God. It means God ain't cardboard. The Hindus have it right: God has many faces."

Recalling the pitiful Olivier, I ask: "And people who disparage the Holocaust?"

He takes a pause, long enough to cock an eyebrow. "I see them as innocents," he says. "Their souls can't stretch wide enough to take in the cruelty of the world. Nuts I may be but my heart is moved—*moved!*—when I hear that kind of denial."

"Dad thinks guys like that are deadly."

"He's right. In today's world, it's deadly to be in denial." He takes off his yarmulke and spins it on his index finger while we think about this. "So where you following J. P. from here?"

"He took a long train ride," Marshall says. "Maybe to Switzerland?"

"Doubtful, peewee. By the time shit hit the fan, the good Swiss had put barbed wire across their entire border."

"Italy?"

"A section of it was 'Jewish Paradise' for a while, but that got rank, too."

"Well, I don't know," I say. "Back to Belgium, then?"

I'm slapped with the tail of his prayer shawl. "Holy hippalach, dude, get with the pogrom! Ever hear of the Pyrenees!?"

"Spain?"

"Spain was HQ for all major Jewish groups. Rumor was Franco's mother was Jewish. Whatever, for a time he gave us transit visas. If we could get the Germans to let us out of France, he'd pass us through. Bottom line: traffic jam in southern France. Jews waiting to bribe some SS man to let them cross over."

"Maybe that's where the beach hotel was where J. P. played pool with the Gestapo?" Alex speculates. "On the Mediterranean coast near the Spanish border?"

"Probably would have been the Atlantic side," offers the rabbi, thoughtfully gnawing on his thumb. "Mediterranean over there was swamp back then. Plus, on the Atlantic side were the Basques."

"Yes! We heard about the Basques helping!"

"Give this kid a pop-top Manischewitz!" He twirls his yarmulke into the air.

"Spain was like home plate," Alex explains to his brother. "Like safety, where they can't get you out anymore."

"I know *that!*" Marshall says impatiently. "But what I want to know is, how'd they make it out of *right here?*"

"OK, pipsqueak, watch this." Holding the strap of my phylacteries like a short leash, RADREB leads us down a passage at the back of the *shul* to a little metal door, hoofs a portable heater out of the way, unlocks the door, and ushers us into a dark space filled with trash cans. It's a janitor's storage room, not much bigger than a closet. Picking our way through dry mops, we come to a second door and are admitted into the rear of a run-down apartment building. We pass through a hallway of crumbling mosaics (shades of Moshav West Side!) and buzz ourselves out the front door onto the streets of the 9th arrondissement, ready to lose ourselves among a warren of wig shops.

Our RollerBlading rabbi extends the bitten nails of his hand, flourishing his yarmulke. "From this spot, the Spanish border," he says.

24

TIME GOGGLING

*E*ighteen hours later we arrive at the sleepy train station of Hendaye, a stone's throw from the Spanish border in the south-westernmost corner of France. We step through the very train station where J. P. and his twins must have come from Paris; it seems to have changed little in the intervening half-century. Despite a halfhearted attempt to modernize it with billboards for LoveBurgers and Levi's and a vending machine selling plastic doll combs and Aqua Velva, the station is forlorn to its very plumbing. Three or four young people lie on wooden benches, biding time. An old Gypsy in fancy shoes, with two leather bags planted on either side of him, sits with his knees drawn up to his chest, pondering his fate. Outside the station, all three of us step together on a baggage scale for a total of 141 kilos. (Marshall 20, Alex 43, me 78.) *The last summer I'll weigh more than both of them combined . . .*

Marshall's wearing his time goggles as we trudge to the administrative center of the city, which is closed for siesta. Nuns are just swinging shut the gates to their compound. From the interior of a church, a man and his daughter drag a ladder through the square; that aluminum scraping over pebbles is the only sound, and when they're gone, the place is deserted. We

sit, dusty and tired; it's so quiet we can hear a telephone ring behind a shuttered window.

Marshall passes me his time goggles. "They work if you relax," he instructs.

I see what he means. If you can allow your eyes to open gently—the opposite of squinting—you can imagine things no
longer there. The everyday sights fade away: no more metallic
road signs or gleaming bank teller machines. Instead I see the
blurry outline of an old Basque town with strange Basque writing everywhere. The Gestapo could show up any moment. . . .

In this frame of mind, I float over to the archway outside the
closed city hall where marriage notices are posted behind glass.
Scanning the names, I come across this: *Maurice Emmanuel,
chirurgien dentiste,* married two Saturdays previous to *Marie de
Courson, assistante dentiste.* The Jewish dentist marrying his as-
sistant! Was he related to Jews who came here during the war?
The whole drama comes home to me: how his parents or aunts
and uncles might have come here from some drizzling northern
town in Belgium, waiting here in the sun 200 yards from the
Spanish border but unable to cross, somehow surviving and
procreating so that a new generation can carry on the line under
the official stamp of the mayor of Hendaye. On a whim, I scrib-
ble down the newlyweds' address on Rue des Chevrefeuilles.

For some reason, this calls for a celebration. Still on French
soil, we walk into a dark male cave of a Basque bar where we're
the only ones not in blue wool suits, not in blue berets, not in
stiff but grimy white shirts buttoned to our necks. One of the
men limps over to me with a glass cane and the apologetic grin
of a drunkard. I count four teeth; maybe there are more. He
produces a slimy, vigorous handshake.

"I speak English very sad!" he announces.

"Oh no!" I demur with the overprotest this sort of confession
always brings out. *"Magnifique!"*

We have a conversation that's full of exclamation marks. The
language barrier makes us shout in each other's ears for some

reason. I tell him that I'm following the trail of my Jewish uncle, but he keeps losing the string of it. He's really quite tanked, but it's more than that. Something's organically wrong. He puts a hand on my elbow and strains to explain that he has abscesses in the brain. When I attempt to commiserate, he will have none of it, interrupting me again.

"You speak happy!" he bellows.

"No!" I bellow back.

"Happy. Happy good!" he insists.

"Well, thank you!" I say.

He takes a step back, bows deeply in a half-crippled, half-balletic arc, with his glass cane extended. "You are welcome!" he says.

Then asks me to buy him a drink.

The look the bartender has been throwing me the last two minutes, I realize at last, has been cautionary. Now it's too late. The bartender disapproves of my obtuseness, wiping the neck of a jug bottle with pursed lips.

"Make it a double!" I tell him.

This makes us intimates, my friend and me. He turns to me with an air of confiding important information. "I am Basque!" he says.

"Ah!" I allow.

"But the Basques, we are azole!"

"Azole?" I inquire. My mind races over the language, hunting for references to this strange word. Could it be related to the "Gazole" I've seen on signs outside gas stations, referring to petrol? In that case, could he be alluding to the allegedly in-flammatory nature of this ancient, generous people?

"Az-hole!" he aspirates vigorously. He points to the center of his backside.

"Ah, why do you say that?"

He studies this question for a minute. Now he's pointing to his head, where the abscesses are. "We are crazy!"

The bartender watches out of the corner of his eye as I take pains to disagree. They were very genteel to my people in the war, I say. I say this twice. They helped them evade the Nazis.

My new friend sighs mightily, with nothing new to add. "Well, I don't think the Germans are going to win!" he opines.

"Win what?" I ask.

"The war! I don't think so! They have not such a fresh army!"

"But . . ." I point out, struggling to find the syntax, "they *already* didn't win! They didn't win fifty years ago!"

He doesn't seem shocked by this information. "I am a little out-fashioned," he explains. But who am I to judge ill of that? I, who spend hours thinking about grade school?

He peers at his shot glass, layered with hours' worth of greasy fingerprints. "My abscesses . . ." he falters. I buy him another wine. We stand there beaming at each other for managing our way through this conversation. I fear he's going to aspirate again, collecting himself for another exclamation and filling this Basque cave with purple wine fumes. But he's merely amassing his breath for farewell. "Sorry I am so sad!" he says, raising his glass cane aloft in salute.

◆　◆　◆

The border is unforgivably ugly: a great bald highway bridge utterly devoid of mystery, nothing more than a widening of the road with four or five checkpoints. There's the usual truck mess: a refrigerated eighteen-wheeler from Ireland idles in neutral so that the air rumbles with lazy anger. Beyond, in the section of Spain known as the least desirable tourist destination in the country, warehouses and gas tanks extend to the horizon amid the pensive stink of diesel fumes. I feel the sensation I usually feel at borders: gypped.

"*Est-ce qu'il y a beaucoup d'*arrests *ici?*" I ask the French customs officer.

"Arrests, *comment?*"

"You know." I put my hands up to the sky as if coming-out-with-my-hands-up.

"Non, non." He waves me through impatiently. Why am I making trouble? But at the same moment he pulls over a Renault station wagon. A clean-cut couple in their late twenties is made to exit while a big brown goof of a customs dog jumps onto their seats and begins sniffing comically. You can see the man and woman are too straight to smuggle anything; you can also see how nervous this spot-check makes them. After an additional check of the trunk, the officer wearily waves them through.

I address the greenish pimple under the officer's bottom lip, resuming my interview. "Do many people attempt to smuggle here?" I ask.

"Non." He is guarded, or bored, or both. Or maybe I'm not supposed to be pestering a customs official who, with one hand behind him like a waiter, only *seems* servile. The hand is actually clasped to his holster belt.

Another customs officer comes over to see what's going on. "Is today a difficult day?" I ask him.

"Today not *difficile*. Some days, very busy. One thousand two hundred come-ins each day. Yes! Then very *difficile*. Today, *facile!*"

Bingo: this officer is from the nearby city of Pau, and he's a talker. The first officer, he says, is Basque. "Crazy, eh?" says the non-Basque from Pau. He makes a twisting gesture with his palms.

"Crazy," echoes the Basque, but he says it shyly.

I'm interested to find out why they perpetuate this myth about themselves. But mostly I want to know why the Basques were kind to my people. Are they softhearted folk?

Probably two burly guys in uniform are not the best people to ask. Both their faces grow expressionless as wood. "Pppp," sputters the Basque, as he rolls his eyes. It's a derisive sound, the way men in so many countries try to stop the conversation from turning to feelings.

"Pppp," echoes the non-Basque. I'm being dismissed.

"But I will tell you something," volunteers the Basque shyly, after his colleague walks away. "It was more difficult to cross fifty years ago, when they used a different bridge."

"Yes?"

"Yes." He mulls it over as another car drives up to his post. "That one over there," he says, pointing to the sinister vertebrae of a bridge that is closed down and barricaded beside the railroad tracks. This one's more like it—rotting plaster shows the brick beneath, with antiquated lights towering down as in a prison yard. I walk over and am standing there admiring it when the brown mutt waggles toward me. "Hi there," I say. An inquisitive creature, he's got a muzzle so overdeveloped that the rest of him seems along for the ride. Its snout sidles toward me, followed like an afterthought by the dog. And then I hear it: *sniffing.* The snout is all over my bag, my pants. *"Bah!"* I shout, heart pounding with unnamed guilt.

The guards look at me with new interest.

I decide to hitch a ride out of here. Good little yuppie children that they are, the boys are scandalized. *"Beg* a ride?" they ask.

"How do you suppose J. P. got around?"

Planting ourselves on a country road beside a river, we await transportation. Hitching is something I haven't done since my early twenties, when my generation turned it into an art. It feels electrifying to be doing it at my age—brings back all the bare-assed self-exposure of those days. A vintage green Volvo picks us up. Inside is an elegant older couple, white-haired and rainbow-hued, the man in turquoise slacks and his wife with a pink cashmere sweater around her shoulders. The song playing softly on the Blaupunkt is from my youth, the BeeGees' "Massachusetts."

"Nous sommes de Massachusetts!" I tell him proudly.

They don't seem to grasp this. A few shrugs and grimaces suffice for conversation. Where else but in France can you express so much with a smirk and a sigh—the communication equivalent of a baguette and cheese? But in a minute curiosity overcomes me: I have to inquire in my broken French if they've ever heard of J. P.'s hotel. I write it for them on the notepad I carry: "1940? Hôtel de la Plage."

"Ah!" says the wife in a husky voice. She reaches for my red Bic. *"Démoli en* 1978," she pens.

It turns out they know a lot more English than they first let on. The driver is the former police chief of a Basque village in the hills; he offers to drive us to the beach by way of Basque country. "Just a short tour, no problem, *ça va?"*

Why not? But they exude an air of propriety that the boys and I find inhibiting. We wind through hill country that is disappointing suburban sprawl, complete with glassed-in bus stops with J&B ads. The landscape has been sanitized into tract housing of fake shingles with air conditioners popped through. Fierce bony old men putter about their tiny subdivision gardens with hiking sticks and Velcro Pumas.

"What are Basques like?" I ask. "They tend to describe themselves as 'crazy.'"

"Crazy like the fox," the man says, gesturing us to close the windows against the road dust. "We are the oldest ethnic group in Europe. Our language is older than Greek, so old that 'ceiling' means 'roof of cave'; 'knife' means 'a stone that cuts.'"

"We preserve not only our ancient language but also our genetic differences," wheezes the wife, a bursar at a nearby community college. "Our shoulders are low, our blood is distinctive, our bones are like prehistoric bones. Perhaps it is possible we are the sole race which survives from Neanderthals who were wiped out by Cro-Magnon man? Hitler, you know, he was embarrassed by the Basques, because he wanted a pure race, and here was a pure race but dark like Jew people. . . ."

"We are Jew people!" I exclaim.

"We are mostly peasants, shepherds, fishermen, miners," continues the husband, not seeming to hear me as he lights menthol cigarettes for himself and his wife. "In addition to our own language, we speak also French and Spanish. But when outsiders come through, we pretend we do not speak French, we do not speak Spanish. This is our Basque cunning, that we pretend is crazy."

"It is to guard our privacy," the wife adds, taking a deep drag. "The Basques are a secretive and proud people. Very, very strict Catholics, with beautiful singing voices."

We're well inside Basque country now, winding past gnarled cedars beneath outcroppings of rock grottoes. I wish we could smell the minty air outside instead of this mentholated smoke. The grass is luxurious with brown ferns. Rock walls feature mossy flat stones, reminiscent of New England tombstones, facing outward. An occasional white house dots the landscape, big enough for three generations to live under one roof, with shutters that are dyed brownish red from the blood of cows.

"The Basques put up Jewish refugees from Belgium," the ex-chief of police resumes with a nod to acknowledge that he heard me before about being Jews. He took in everything—Jews, Massachusetts—without letting on. A secretive people, indeed, and just the sort I'd want as allies during a war, but I'm going to suffocate in this closed-up car. "You see, we also know about being a persecuted minority. We have a history of not mixing with the world. If people would come through, we would hide from them. So it was not such a stretch for us to hide Jews, too, in our cellars, in our grottoes."

I entertain a vision of Basques as the Jews of the Pyrenees, and look over to see Alex in the beret he picked up off the bar floor—like a Basque yarmulke. He has his eyes closed, looking either bored or car sick.

"Why didn't the Jews just cross the hills into Spain out here?" asks Marshall.

We pass a startled-looking shepherd, leaving him in a cloud of white dust. "The entire length of the border was a forbidden zone patrolled by police with dogs. Yes? Also, the hills get quite high. There is snow underfoot even in high summer."

"What about back in town?"

"The harbor was chained off with cannons on the peaks in case anyone tried to row across."

"We kept the Jews from starving," adds the missus, exhaling a long plume of blue smoke. "Everything but rabbit was requisitioned by the Germans. They were so hungry that when we gave them a mackerel they would make the feast last all day."

Alex opens his eyes wide. "That's what the pictures of fish were about in the journal!" he says. I give him the thumbs-up but hush him to keep the narrative going.

"Helping the Jews, yes, but also we had an interest: money," says the husband. "No one is a saint, you know," he tells us, going on to say that often Jews would leave their autos behind as they darted for freedom; the Basques would inherit them and any other worldly goods that couldn't go over the border.

"Very few Jews remain here. A few settled north in Bayonne where they own all the chocolate shops and banks, lending money only to each other," offers the wife without disapproval. "They are a tight community like the Basques."

The car, the conversation, the confinement, all add up to such a feeling of claustrophobia that when we spiral down out of the hills and are deposited at the shore of Hendaye—*"C'est là!"* says the ex-chief, pointing to the beach near where the hotel was—we feel like rejoicing.

Spain is so close it's palpable: in the way a teenager sits on his parked motorcycle with his feet on the handlebars, whistling up to his girlfriend with two fingers; in the way workmen tap stone into place with a piece of wood. With an excess of sloppy motions, potbellied policemen wave Fiat convertibles through intersections that would fare better with no direction at all.

"Bonjour, messieurs," calls a woman from across the road, shaking a bedspread from one of the balconies overflowing with pink geraniums, *"il fait beau aujourd'hui."*

"Oui, très beau!"

It's one of the world's blessed spots, plain to see. Did war ever come to this place? Hard to imagine. On the *plage*, long-legged women jog along the wet pools of hard sand, old couples stroll hand-in-hand with their cuffs rolled. The surfing shops and churches are both doing brisk trade—bells peal out over the crashing waves. This is La Côte Basque, also known as La Côte d'Argent, and it's easy to see why the Gestapo could relax enough to play billiards with their prey.

But the feeling's deceptive because J. P. was betrayed here, if the family story is to be believed. We find our way to the location the ex-police chief indicated, in a lot between two Victorian mansions. There stands its replacement, a giant green-and-white condo complex with thirty identical steel intercom buzzers at the front door, along with thirty identical steel mailboxes. I call up to one of the tenants spray-washing his dishes in an open window on the third floor.

"Savez-vous si ceci était un hôtel du Gestapo?"

He aims the spray at me out the window.

Now comes the detective work: going back through time to find out what this site looked like before the condo monster took its place. Hendaye this afternoon is a summer beach resort in full flower; the little souvenir kiosks have a relaxed air, the shopkeepers chatting with each other as they crank down the shades against the late-afternoon sun. I'm interested in a device Alex has found, a time machine in the shape of an ordinary postcard tree, featuring local shots of *la plage* last winter (unrecognizably covered with snowflakes) and *la plage* many summers ago (the surfers have flamboyant mustaches that turn down at the ends). Spinning the postcard tree, we feel we're traveling back in time; it's halfway between a Jules Verne contraption and a Tibetan prayer wheel. Around it goes, until it stops at a postcard showing a row of buildings on the beach, with the last lot only a gaping hole. With a jolt we realize it's the site of the Hôtel de la Plage, caught in the instant after it was demolished.

"I'm telling you: tracks," Alex says contentedly.

We're pleased with ourselves, but we still haven't gone back before 1978. From a birdcage in an open window, a parakeet squeaks its single note as we walk by. Marshall spies a realtor's office across the street that features a giant aerial photo of Hendaye in its picture window. "Look, Dad. It must have been there a long time."

"Right-o," I say, idly contemplating its faded appearance.

"No, Dad, *look!*"

And then I get it. I run across the street to examine it more closely. There, from a seagull's height, looking down on rows of houses lapping back from the shore, and surrounded by the deep shade of trees felled long ago, there is the roof of a third Victorian mansion on the beach. Marshall takes out his loupe and makes out letters: *DE LA PLAGE.*

Alex picks up Marshall, planting a kiss on his brother's cheek. We've seen it with our own eyes: another lost hiding place, made visible.

◆ ◆ ◆

It's been a long day. We install ourselves in a hotel room in time to see an ocean sunset that's almost volcanic in its pink intensity. From the balcony the shoreline is a crescent wash of rouge that a slim-ankled girl steps on, with precision, all along its length. I toast her from afar with my scotch.

"Marshall's sulking," Alex reports.

I leave my perch on the balcony to find Marshall. "Alex thinks I don't know what you were talking about with the Rhodesian lady, but I do," he says, lying stiffly on his bed. "You were talking about not hiding anymore."

"You know, some people might think seven's too young to take this trip," I say, helping him into his pajamas. "But you're getting the whole thing."

"But how come I don't have any hiding places in *my* life?"

"What do you call all these places we're finding?"

"Yeah, but they're someone else's. I don't even know what mine are supposed to look like."

"And you may not know for years," I tell him with a smile.

"But it's possible you have some right now you're not even aware of."

His face registers delight as he climbs under the covers. "You mean I could have some but I don't know where yet?"

"And the rest of your life will be spent trying to figure out what they're doing there."

"Oh goodie! But can you give me a hint?"

"I don't honestly know, Marshall. It's something you're going to have to find out for yourself."

"It's a growing up thing," Alex counsels from the other room where he busies himself with a drawing. "A coming of age thing."

"Is it, Dad?"

"Yes," I say, kissing him good night. "You'll know it in the fullness of time."

"'The fullness of time,'" Marshall says, rolling over the phrase in his mind as he turns over in bed. "That's a good expression. Did you make it up?"

But I can tell a stall when I hear one. I blow him another kiss, close the door, and go to watch Alex trace J. P.'s pictures of fish into his drawing pad.

"So do you think you might?" he asks, erasing the gills and blowing the eraser bits off the tablet.

"Might what?"

He looks impatient. "Change your name back to Rosenzweig!?"

The fins are lacking something. I add spots and wiggly stripes till it almost resembles a mackerel J. P. might have feasted on.

"I'll have to get back to you on that," I say.

❖ ❖ ❖

After Alex is asleep I have no choice but to concede defeat. The trail's cold. With no more information, we've gone as far as we can. Idly toying with the time goggles, I feel I've ducked my destiny, and am halfway between relieved and bereft.

Bereft wins. So I rouse myself, desperate for a clue. How

would a Cossack barrel through at this point? What would Mr. Pinanski counsel? How would they proceed in Kick-Kick-Connecticut? What about in Grimm's? Is there anything my magical media pass can manage?

And then it hits me: a newspaperman in Idaho who, for his column, would make cold calls on the phone and interview whomever picked up . . . the person we heard about in the Marais who managed to locate Jews in Shanghai out of the phone book . . . I look in the yellow pages under "Jews." Not there, of course, but then I look under *"médecins—psychiatrique."* None seems to practice in Hendaye (though there are many in tony Biarritz up the shore). So I go to the white pages for names that might be candidates. No Steins, no Grossmans, no Levys. There's a Cohen in a neighboring town several miles from here, but no one's home. And here's a Schwartz, Anne— but her line's busy. And a Klein, Joseph. But of course Klein could be German. There's a click as the receiver is answered. But *non, non*—Joseph Klein vehemently denies he's Jewish. In any case, it's the strangest call he ever got: an American madman calling at 10 P.M. to ask what religion he is.

Remembering the name of the dentist I found outside the mayor's office this afternoon, I put on the time goggles and call the newlyweds.

"Allô?"

"Allô? Pardonnez-moi, Madame Emmanuel, parlez-vous anglais?"

"Hmm, I mean to say, a leetle."

"Good. I am wondering if you or your husband is Jewish."

"Pardon?!"

"You see, I'm an American Jew tracing my uncle who hid in Hendaye fifty years ago. And I'm looking for other Jews in this area to help me follow his story."

"But I am sorry, this is hasty, my husband is not home right now."

"I'm sorry to bother you, *madame.*"

"It is not a bother, it is just, I do not know who really you are. You startle me. . . ."

"But is it possible," I say, scratching an itch under my goggles, "that you yourself know the story of the Jews in this area?"

"No, I am sorry, I do not know who is your uncle. Or you? How, please, do you come to call us?"

"The listing outside the mayor's office, actually."

"I see. I think . . ."

"Not to startle you. But I have so little time to learn so much."

"You sound *sympathique*. But it is . . . awkward to me. You understand? My husband will not be home for two days. But so . . . can you tell me . . . you are doing this for what reason?"

"To show my children what happened to their people."

"I see. I think . . ."

"To teach them what the world's capable of, both good and bad."

"Yes . . ."

"I know no one here, *madame*. I'm just a stranger, grasping at straws. . . ."

"*Ah, je suis désolée—*"

"It was silly to hope you'd heard about a Jew who played billiards with the Gestapo. . . ."

Pause. A gasp. "Yes, I know this *histoire!*"

"You *what?*" I say, ripping off the goggles. "How can that be?"

"Yes, it is a rather famous *légende* among the Jews of Hendaye, a man with twin daughters. I know because he was a friend of my father-in-law's."

Tracks, I think. But all I say is: "Then it's true?"

"This I cannot say. But the *légende* is that this man, your uncle?"

"Yes?"

"Lived in a hotel for weeks with the Gestapo . . ."

"Yes, we found the site today!"

"He played billiards with the commandant every night. They put a glass of schnapps for Elijah. He played for his freedom."

"Whoa, slow down, this is a lot to take in."

"The Gestapo, you see, was interested in him because he was rumored to have diamonds at his disposal, no one knew where. The commandant said that if he won he would get these diamonds, if your uncle won he would escort him over the border. But of course he did not. He betrayed!"

"Did he sleep with the Gestapo commandant's wife? Is that why he betrayed?"

"This I do not know. But the Gestapo I think need no excuse to betray anyone."

"Do you know what became of him after?"

"He take his children and escape for the Free France in a wagon of hay, I think. No, in the back of a milk wagon! Yes, it was a horse-drawn milk wagon because it crashed and they got cut from all the milk bottles."

Malek! I think. *Malek!*

"My father-in-law received a postcard from him written with Hebrew words to get past the censor. 'Uncle Chorbin is coming to visit.' *Chorbin* is Hebrew for 'soon trouble,' yes? 'Make sure you visit Cousin Vayivrach.' *'Vayivrach'* is from the Bible: 'And he fled.' He was telling my father-in-law, you understand, to flee at once. He has the postcard right here, framed as an art object."

"Do you know where my uncle sent it from?"

"Let me see, I have to take it out of the frame . . . turn it over . . . yes, it was the Hôtel des Fleurs in Tournon d'Agenais. I know not where this town is. . . ."

25

KNOCKED OUT

Where was I? The last thing I remembered was jamming on my skates and hurling myself onto the ice to join my friends playing hockey. Then black lightning—a negative of the bright afternoon—and now there was this lady peering down at me as I lay with my head in her lap: "Say, Handsome, you've got to tie your laces if you don't want to trip!" I couldn't wait to tell my friends I'd been knocked out, but the lady, whom I recognized as the mother of my Dutch classmate Hotdog, said that was enough skating for one day, and that I'd better show her where I lived.

She said her name was Harriet or Marge or one of those grown-up names that reminded me of black lace bras. Her car smelled intimately of cigarettes and cats and something else I couldn't put my finger on. Harriet or Marge was chattering away as I directed her to turn left and right and right again. "Car's a mess, I broke a jar of mayo in back last week, fell right out of the bag and you know what a mess that was to clean? But I've been on jury duty most of the week and haven't had a chance to get the smell out," she said pleasantly.

I liked Harriet or Marge. She'd become a complete American. Unlike my mother, who needed to concentrate when she drove, she was able to do something else at the same time, like extract the last cigarette out of a pack of Parliaments, crumble the pack, and nimbly toss it into the cavity behind the front seat. She told me she subscribed to a newsletter about contests and so far she'd won a Flintstones key chain, a hockey puck signed by the Philadelphia Flyers (she was a big fan of ice sports, that's why she was at the pond that morning), a GE black-and-white TV, a customized bowling ball, and a chance to sing "Barbara Ann" with the Beach Boys. Contest winning was a science like anything else, she told me. She spent two or three hours filling out coupons each week; no more because she didn't want to burn out. Her philosophy was: "Scared money doesn't win."

Though this was a lot of information for me to take in after falling on my head, I wanted to ask her how I could join a contest and especially about that "scared money" part. "Turn right here," I said, "up the hill." But Harriet or Marge changed now, recognizing who I was. Coming up the steep driveway, she seemed to imagine that we fancied ourselves better than every-one else, living high and mighty while our neighbors lived mostly below us. "That isn't the reason!" I felt like saying. We lived here because other people had jellyfish coming out of their radiators after a hurricane, and my father thought it prudent to be up high. And now maybe she thought I'd been wearing figure skates instead of hockey skates for the same reason, and maybe it served me right to trip on them, when the truth was I didn't even want figure skates because they always seemed delicate and Jewish compared to the knockabout hockey skates worn by all my friends. Bringing me inside, she was still nice to me and my mother, but she wasn't her chattery self, and I could see she was nervously looking around at the rugs and plants and sets of burgundy hardcovers with gold lettering and wondering, maybe, if that made us think we were better than she was. Just because she spent two or three hours a week filling out coupons trying to win things we didn't want or already had?

My mother was sincerely grateful that Harriet or Marge had rescued me and even offered in Flemish to make her tea but

Harriet or Marge declined, and after that I used to see her at the drugstore sometimes but she never called me Handsome again or even said hello to me, as if she'd never stroked my head in the first place, or wished she hadn't.

◆ ◆ ◆

In truth, her whole family was bad news. The husband, Happy, who'd found work as a part-time lobsterman/housepainter, coached the sneakiest Little League team and was the only person ever to get thrown out of a game. He was razzing the opposing pitcher by waving the water bucket rag at him and grinning malevolently even after the ump, Mr. Lawless, warned him not to. Twice. The final time, Mr. Lawless tore off his ump's mask, so we could see how red his face was, and jabbed his finger and roared, "Hap, you're outta here!"

This was a dire pronouncement and both bleachers fell silent. The parents of Rowayton Little League didn't take sportsmanship lightly. In the school gym the principal gave long convoluted talks about how the winning team must always cheer the losing team, and so on. And here was a coach pulling a patently unsportsmanlike move. "I mean it, you're outta here!" Mr. Lawless repeated.

Hap knew that if he wiped that jeer off his face he'd be admitting he was wrong in front of all the parents, who included a number of his housepainting customers. In the silence of the ballfield, his problem was how to get off the field and still save face. This he attempted to do by continuing to grin while saying his name. "I'm Happy," he kept saying as he shuffled backward along the third base line to the outfield fence where his Plymouth was, like a bad vaudeville comedian who wouldn't turn his back on the audience for fear of getting booed. Not until he started his engine did Mr. Lawless, with a sigh that signaled "good riddance to bad rubbish," allow the game to go on.

None of this, however, changed the fact that Happy's son, Hotdog, had become the most popular kid in fourth grade. Girls seemed to find him cute and he was widely admired for cheating. He lived in a three-story suburban slum house that gave off an aura of crookedness. Leaves rotted in its sagging gutters. A rusting dumpster sat perpetually in the yard. I was inside the house only once, and had misgivings about being invited. (Hotdog didn't have much choice; we were assigned a homework project together, tracing Roman gladiators.) I was scandalized by the dirt. Fuzzy black grime adhered to the baseboards. The refrigerator was sticky with the juice of rancid tomatoes. Now that I was on his turf, I chose that moment to remember from my obsessive reading that the name *Hartog* was a loaded one; the housekeeper who may or may not have betrayed Anne Frank's family was named Hartog. More problematic still was a secret cupboard in his father's den that held the "stash" I'd heard Hotdog boast about in the boys' room at school. Here it was in the flesh, and Hotdog was showing me its contents: a bottle of Canadian whiskey, a gold-plated car distributor, and a series of girl dolls, one inside the other, Russian nesting style. But these dolls weren't wooden Russian dolls, round and clever, with glossy handpainted outfits. These were cheap mass-produced dolls meant for ridicule, with the mean odor of rubber. They had greasy green hair over malevolent grinning faces—probably where Hap had learned to make his pitcher-rattling face—and they were topless.

"Titties," Hotdog snickered.

I snickered back, but I felt prissy, like I ought to snicker and mean it. We repaired to the TV room. The afternoon sunlight slanted onto the screen, bleaching out the cartoons, but Hotdog and his little sister didn't seem to mind as they took turns trying to hang snot on each other without the other's knowledge. After about a half hour of trying to find this engrossing, and not having begun our homework, I put on my hat, thanked Hotdog for his hospitality, and said I had to be going.

"What do I care?" he replied. The sister commenced dancing around and singing a Pepsodent commercial. Then she stepped on a broken light bulb and went up to Hotdog to show him her wound, but he greeted it with an armpit fart, at which point she sat down and began to squeeze the bottom of her foot with her thumbs and to squeal when something oozed out.

Hotdog made the TV louder so he wouldn't have to hear her squeal. "Haven't you left yet?" he asked me.

But I hadn't left yet because I couldn't find one of my blue-and-white leather gloves. It wasn't in any of my pockets. It wasn't under the cushions of the couch, though when I lifted the cushions to look, the sister stopped her sniveling and dived for the broken crackers and pennies within. Hotdog ignored my efforts to find it; he just made a hissing noise when I accidentally blocked his view of the TV, but it didn't take me long to ascertain that my glove wasn't anywhere in the TV room or in the kitchen, where Harriet or Marge exhibited a similar dearth of sympathy, sliding a tray of minute steaks into the broiler, a Parliament dangling from her lips.

Neither Hotdog nor his mother cared enough to understand that this was my glove, one that my mother had specifically gone out and gotten for me. It wasn't just a mitten; it was a glove with separate sockets for each of my fingers, so that my glove and I had established a close working relationship with each other, and here I was abandoning it like a child to a den of wolves, never to see it again or, worse, to find it one day in Hummiston's lost-and-found bin wizened beyond recognition, like a toddler kidnapped at age two who shows up with a jail record at fifteen.

Even though I remembered taking it off inside the house, my last hope was dashed when it wasn't outside in my bike bag. I took a final glance toward the upstairs TV room, half expecting to see Hotdog sticking his head out the window, waving my glove as a sick joke, or at least to see him and his sister pulling each other's hair. But there was nothing. The house had my glove hostage, to make its peace with its new family, the tittie dolls. I had to leave.

Plum-colored winter twilight was collecting in low spots between the trees. One hand, in its glove, was warm; the other was
cold. This was the year a pet duck of mine had died, and some
of that grief seemed to spill over onto this incident. Not only
that, but I'd buried a bird the day before that may not have been
fully dead. I'd been waiting for it to die fully but finally I tossed
the trowelful of dirt over it anyway, the soil pulsing with its
helpless heartbeat. I was such a fake and a phony! What right
had I to feel superior to anyone? I still hadn't heard back from
J. Edgar Hoover and knew by now I probably never would, but
that hadn't stopped me from declaring him my pen pal to my
classmates. What a liar I was! And a bird killer to boot. Remorse
swarmed up from both sides of the road to remind me that I
was a person who'd committed terrible acts.

The frozen cattails, dense on either side of the tar road, were
tragic as they rattled against each other in the dying light. The
potholes crushed in with pieces of sandy tar—unspeakably
tragic. How could anyone fix this road? All the roads in the
world were in varying states of disrepair, and who had the time
or energy, who had the lightness of heart, to fix them all? Think
of all the broken light bulbs in the world. Who could sweep all
the broken glass? How fussy, how tedious, how tragic it all was!

As I turned onto the last road to my house, I paused for a
minute on the little wooden bridge with its assortment of minnow bottles. The sun was disappearing in the distance, one of
those luminously bleak winter sunsets with gray chickadees dip-
ping across it, and I felt moved to make a gesture. Wasn't there
something you did for a fallen comrade? Weren't you supposed
to salute and play taps? I didn't know what taps was, but I could
make some gesture of respect. I lifted my hat off my head to put
it over my heart.

And my glove fell out.

I never went back to that house. Some years later it burned
down. The whole town turned out to watch flaming mattresses

being tossed out of the upstairs TV room window and falling to the yard, where they burned like torches. It was rumored to be an insurance scam, but it was never proved.

◆ ◆ ◆

Like the gladiators in the homework assignment we never finished tracing, Hotdog and I were to be locked in combat one more time. It was in fifth grade, a pivotal year for many reasons. My younger brother looked like he was here to stay. Though I did my best to join the circle of family warmth by singing him "Drill Ye Tarriers Drill" at bedtime, even camping out for a time in his room made unbearably cozy by the night-light, there was no avoiding the conclusion that I'd been fired as the son in the family, and I soon went back to my own bedroom, two flights away from everyone. At the same time, I sometimes glimpsed the possibility that there were more Jews around than I knew. The Rowayton School secretary who consoled us when we were sent to the principal's office was a kindly woman by the name of Mrs. Israelson—could *she* be, maybe? And a kid whose bushy-headed father was buying up buildings on the waterfront? But we didn't signal each other, as secretive as the few kids whose parents voted Democratic instead of for Ike's boy, Nixon.

Fifth grade was also becoming my year for drawing pictures. I drew monsters with wavy lines through their triangular heads, and gave the drawings wild names like "Don't!" It was the only year I ever felt any connection with crayons—they were like colored fireworks shooting off my fingertips—trying to please my teacher, Mrs. McDougal, who wore mysterious sea-green sunglasses around the clock. Unable to see through her lenses to tell whether I was succeeding, I tried harder—forcing the artwork out of me the way you force forsythia to bloom before its time. One art period I was consulting a book on World War II for inspiration and was so affected by the black-and-white photos of uniformed men lying crumpled on the ground that I felt compelled to go up to Mrs. McDougal's desk and ask her about them. What fascinated me was that they looked as if they didn't particularly mind being dead; they looked in repose, and it made me wonder if crossing the line from life to death was less a huge yawning divide than a crack in the sidewalk, no big deal to step over. Or was it that these soldiers were simply unaware of the enormity of what had befallen them? But how could you not know—be the *only one* not to know—about the most major thing ever to happen to you? I'd discussed such things with my mother, who seemed so intimate with the subject, but with no one else. So to ask my teacher "Are they really dead?" was really to ask her to go into a place of secret grief with me.

Mrs. McDougal didn't lower her lenses to look at me straight on. But I sensed that she was peering at me with eyeballs that were pale and intelligent.

"I'm afraid so," she said.

A thrill went through me that was almost sexual. Death was real. That meant World War II was real, too—the camps, the stories, the whole kit and caboodle. My mother's carryings-on weren't mere hysterical ravings. There really was something called death that one could reasonably be afraid of. I walked back to my desk stunned that she'd shared such an intimacy with me.

But mostly fifth grade was shaping up as my year for marbles, a serious endeavor in those days. I was one of the acknowledged masters along with Hotdog, who by now had picked up the grade school knack of accumulating power in direct proportion to how much he withheld use of the word *hi*. He was also, by universal acclaim, class stud, having once dared to dance with the most unattainable girl in the school, Lynn Williams, whom I adored from afar.

Hotdog never came out and said so, but he'd made up his mind that I was a freak. Not only had I made a wussy declaration of affection to someone whose body he'd waltzed with utter nonchalance, he also couldn't fathom what would compel me to draw stupid pictures and then go to the trouble of giving them even stupider names. He never asked me; he must have assumed that if I were simple enough to want to do such a thing, no explanation I could give would make sense.

Hotdog and I squared off under the watchful invisible eye of Mrs. McDougal. We were in the fenced-in area of the school yard, and few kids were actually attending because all of them had already been eliminated and couldn't bear to see the bitter end. Our marbles were sixty feet apart. I made my move to a position right behind the latch of the chain link fence, thus forcing him to come closer. I was capable of more daring strategies; indeed, you didn't get to this stage of the tournament without displaying an ample supply of guts as well as caution. But just at that point, I wanted to lure him closer where I could get a look at him. Then I'd shock him to his bones.

It was an uncharacteristic strategy for someone as reckless as me. The move had concision, craftiness, even had a kind of communion, because I was investing the latch of the chain link fence with the power to hide me, and we had a relationship, the latch and me. I liked it; it liked me. A very clean move, played with my prize marble—white with blue swirls through it, like clouds in reverse.

But Mrs. McDougal suddenly blew her whistle. My prudence had made her lose patience. I couldn't tell if her patience had been wearing thin awhile or she just wanted to wrap up because recess was coming to a close. But she yanked the whistle from her neck, screeched it, and said, "Come *on*, Danny!"

This was unheard of. No bystander, not even a teacher, had the right to comment on a game in progress. Her shrill outburst shattered my faith in myself and suddenly made me see what I looked like: a meek hider. I was a conniving sneak relying on low cunning instead of being a brave swashbuckler like Hotdog. I was cowering in my hole while Hotdog was fighting the war out there in the open, his face in the wind, his chin to the waves.

I felt a blast of red-faced shame for the world. Was it possible that the world would allow virtue to stumble and tittie dolls to carry the day? And worse, that the world didn't even *recognize* good as good and bad as bad? I had assumed that thoughtfulness and good taste would somehow lead me automatically to victory. Now what came crashing home to me was something I'd already sensed but not yet formulated: the second rate often got the prizes. Scared money *didn't* win, you weren't *supposed* to be discreet, good guys were at a disadvantage. That's why people like Yudl and Velvl had to run for their lives in the war: honor handicapped them. They thought too hard! They cared too much! In the game of life, decency did you in.

Wiping my bitten nails on my shirt, I looked around at the extra kids who'd gathered, sensing kill. Lawless was noncommittal. Lynn Williams was unreadable, her queenly eyebrows half raised in anticipation. This thought inserted itself from the stupefied depths of my brain: Wouldn't Harriet or Marge be glad to see me lose? Against every instinct, I nudged my marble forth.

Two inches. That's all I moved. To an undiscerning eye like Mrs. McDougal's, there still looked to be no way he could get me from sixty feet. But I knew how magical moves happened with regularity. You'd wake straight up out of a dream some nights, reliving an amazing shot made that afternoon. And so it was this time. I knew it before it happened. Hotdog, who thought pictures were useless things unless you were making obscene stick drawings of ex–dancing partners, was unthinkingly chucking his mongrel marble at me from halfway across the school yard; a one-in-a-million shot, and just the kind that was guaranteed to happen.

The rest of it was predictable enough to be anticlimactic; still, I was riveted to watch his marble span the sky. It bounced twenty feet away. It hurtled toward my marble, hit a gum wrapper and was knocked off its path, hit a bottle cap and was knocked back on its path. It smacked me dead on. I was knocked out of the tournament.

I kept up a brave front the rest of the day and only later, when

I climbed the stone ledge behind my house and spotted my mother through the kitchen window making tuna fish, did I burst into tears.

As is often the case when you lose something you came close to winning, people were rather cold. Mrs. McDougal was remote. Lynn Williams was inscrutable. Hotdog went on to a stellar high school career as a wide receiver and a driver of convertible Mustangs, lifting his index finger off the steering wheel without changing his expression as he whipped past to signal his recognition of the fact that you were marginally alive. I bit my nails more furiously than ever, understanding that the world was a trickier place than I'd given it credit for being. We weren't dummies here, on this planet. We were complex and sly and filled with angles. Was I up for the challenge? Yes, but not in the arenas I'd selected so far. I made a life change. I gave up drawing. The next year, I started writing.

26

HANDS TO THE FLAME

*O*h no!" I exclaim. "Did we leave Marshall back in the Basque bar!?"

"I hope so," Alex mutters.

"Or at the Spanish border!? Oh no! We have to go back!"

Alex shakes his head at the brainlessness of our game. And he's right: it *is* hard to pretend Marshall's missing when his excited hiccups keep emanating from the floor of the rented Citroën.

We drive up hills of red roses and through fields of sunflowers all facing the same direction. This is Free France, the section the Nazis allowed the puppet Vichy government to rule for part of their occupation. Ancient family estates are surrounded on four sides by cornfields, the stucco of the mansions crumbling off to show the bare pink bricks beneath like grand old ladies lifting their skirts to flash pink panties. For hours we travel in the heat on narrow roads lined with sycamores, the three of us content in our own worlds: Alex in his blue beret reading *The Third Reich*, Marshall on the floor picking out German words on a road map, and I taking notes with my memo book propped against the steering wheel so that every jounce in the road makes me honk the horn.

And before the day's out we're far away, up in the hills north of Toulouse where J. P. put himself after his run-in with the commandant in Hendaye. We park our dusty Citroën in the little town of Tournon d'Agenais, which is like the stage set of a pre-Roman village, small stone houses presenting nothing but their shuttered exteriors while birds wheel everywhere through the deserted streets.

At the public square, a group of old-timers are playing *pétanque*—a kind of boccie or *boules*—eight or nine men and two or three women who are indistinguishable from the men. A hunched-over farmhand shuffles forth holding a tarnished steel ball the size of his palm, while a dwarf brother with a funnel chest waddles back and forth with a sound related to breathing. Marshall's being chased around and around the car by someone's farm hound as we try to communicate with a robust old chap whose home-rolled fag is stuck to his bottom lip.

"Pardon, où est l'Hôtel des Fleurs?"

No response. The fag is not insolent as it would be in America; it simply signals disinterest.

I explain to him that I'm looking for my uncle who lived here during the war.

No response.

"Il était juif."

"Ah! Bon bon bon bon!" The cigarette is dancing now as he leads us with a vigorous limp to a hotel called La Petite Tulipe and pounds the door for us.

"But this is the wrong place," I protest. "We're looking for the Hôtel des Fleurs."

No one's there. He insists we be patient, they will explain everything. A bell tolls from some medieval church nearby—*clank!*—and a moment later the door opens onto a beaming innkeeper. Our guide imparts a few words to him about *"le juif"* and leaves. "Sorry if we have the wrong place," I say, "we're looking for the Hôtel des Fleurs."

"We just changed the name!" says the fellow, mopping the

sweat from his fat brow with a kitchen rag. "I am very content!"

"We wanted to speak to the owner."

"Monsieur Deak was the owner, yes! Of course now he is dead many years. I married Monsieur Deak's daughter! Would you like to meet Madame? She is in the kitchen, making cassoulet. A three-day business, eh, this cassoulet. I have heard the story about the Jew who was, I believe, a milkman?"

"No, he arrived here in a milk truck."

"Yes! and cut up from the bottles! But he himself was, I believe, a jeweler?"

"Close enough."

"And was at first too scared to come out from under his bed, your uncle? Stayed three days in the attic smelling the cassoulet wafting up from the kitchen? So my wife, you will wait for her? She will be very content, too!"

"What's cassoulet?" asks Alex, getting his famished look.

"A ragout of white beans, goose, lamb, *lapin,* I don't know what else," he says. "Madame does not impart to me the secret details. Come! Come in!"

"*Ingang!*" Marshall chirps, practicing the sound of German words, which seem to have caught his fancy. "*Achtung! Wunderbar!*"

We're escorted to seats on a little balcony overlooking terraced fields where Monsieur beams at us between swabbings of his napkin. We are angels in his ray of love. He includes us in his vision of the olive trees, the vineyards, the little wading pool covered with green scum. "We do not see many Americans. One, two a year. English, sometimes. But Jews! I am very content!"

Gesturing over the valleys, I ask him what they grow here.

"We grow grapes, also, how should I say, plums with crooked backs to boil."

"Prunes?" says Alex.

"Yes. Also corn, and cows for milk, big cows, one thousand

kilos." He raises his elbows and puffs his cheeks so fat that he squints. "Also peas, green beans, peaches to delight the mouth! Oh, my wife will be so content!"

But she's not, as it happens. She's withdrawn and suspicious, with teeth imprints through the brownish lipstick on her bottom lip. Only a Frenchwoman would wear lipstick to make cassoulet. Keeping her head down with a stern expression, she picks a spot of dried goose liver from the front of her apron as our host explains what we're about. The muscle under the sleeve of her upper arm is beating as she picks. Pick pick pick! Her husband doesn't seem to notice as he beams at us, but the missus is definitely put out. What could she be suspicious of?

"Is it possible," I venture, "to see the room where J. P. stayed?"

But this demolishes any pretense of goodwill Madame may have wished to project. "Not possible," she says, as Monsieur throws her a surprised look. "It is being painted."

"We don't mind," I say, but it's a lost cause. *"Non!"* She flutters her apron and finds a new speck of goose liver.

Marshall clues me in. "Dad," he says out of the side of his mouth. "She thinks we've come back for the goods."

The goods? Preposterous! But the more I watch her stern picking, the more I think Marshall's on to something. Could she really think we've come back after fifty years to stake some sort of claim, that we're going to find something J. P. left behind or demand something back?

"We want nothing," I assure her. "We are here only for *l'histoire*."

"Ah, l'histoire . . ." She reluctantly recounts a story that in a nearby town, a Jew came back five years after the war, looked on top of the armoire, and there was his box of diamonds, untouched. He blew the dust off and *voilà*, nothing was taken.

"Of course not, *madame*. But I have a question, if you don't mind."

"Not at all." This said without undue pleasantness.

"Why do you suppose Jews came to this spot in the first place?"

"To the hills? Because they were less likely to be occupied."

"And did he choose well?"

An intake. *"Ah oui, monsieur.* They had complete freedom to come and go as they please. Went to school here. Very content. Nossing bad happen. All good."

"Ah, bon. So you have a room for us to rent? And a restaurant for eating?"

Now that we're on a commercial basis, everything is fine. *"Bien sûr, monsieur!"*

When she smiles, her teeth are brown.

◆ ◆ ◆

"Dad, can I ask Aude for another sip? It makes my chest tingle!"

Our waitress tonight has been the owners' frisky nineteen-year-old daughter, Aude, who sits with me now that the cassoulet has been dispatched. There are only two other people in the dining room, a blowsy elderly couple with a Lhasa Apso who keeps wandering on his leash between bites of his master's duck confit, his nails clicking across the white-tiled floor. Periodically Marshall runs in from the terrace to take another sip of Aude's after-dinner Armagnac through a straw and to open another fortune cookie.

"Redecorating will be in your future," he reads, and skips back to join his brother on the terrace.

"You were saying?" I ask Aude.

"I was saying that even here in Free France the Jews were in peril. There were many betrayals in the people-smuggling business: double-crossers were paid five thousand francs for each Jew they denounced. Any hotel rooms that could be found were frequently three times as expensive as normal."

"Not these rooms, surely?"

"Not these," Aude says with a smile. I admire the matter-of-fact way she smiles before she answers a question. And the sheen of sweat on her hairless arms. She's probably quite plain but, being French, her face is never at rest long enough for me to tell. I'm enchanted by the way she shakes her hair, the way she speaks with her fingers outstretched, and her pronunciation that is like the native cuisine, all booter and eggz and crème.

"The Milice were the neo-Nazi French police," she goes on, "an auxiliary to the Gestapo, with license to kill Jews and Resistance. Their radio shows were so popular they damaged sentiment for de Gaulle. But they were cowards: When the Resistance killed a member of the Milice, they didn't retaliate against the Resistance, who had guns. They went after unarmed Jews who could be killed with impunity."

"You speak English like a pro," I observe.

"I worked last summer at McDonald's in St. Louis."

Alex joins us. "Dad? Marshall's drunk."

"OK, just a minute."

Alex goes back to the terrace while Aude resumes speaking. "But to think that our hotel hid your family! You must be very agitated in your mind, how you say, excited, with your imagination. . . ."

"We are," I assure her. "But our room has been redecorated. It's all so new, there's no way to imagine what it was like fifty years ago. And your mother—"

Aude dismisses her with a wave. "My mother is neurotic. But it is all here, *l'histoire*. . . ."

"Dad?" Alex says, coming in again. "Marshall's so drunk it isn't funny."

We adjourn to the terrace. Sure enough, Marshall's got his T-shirt down to his ankles and is making up nonsense gutturals. *"Imbleng! Achblang!"* Seeing me, he holds up a big V sign with his eyes closed and falls into the wrought iron balcony, laughing. Aude puts on a lampshade and begins dancing with him. "Oh Marshall, Marshall . . ."

"L'histoire?" I remind her.

"I shall show you. Come!"

We skip down the hall in teams of two, Aude dancing Marshall on top of her fleur-de-lis sneakers. She opens a door onto a dank little room with a balcony over the garage. "Here is old!" she says triumphantly. She's proud enough of herself that she gestures for me to take a picture of the three of them here, putting up two rabbit ears behind the boys' heads when I click the shutter.

But something about this site doesn't feel right: I get no resonance from it. "Your father said something about an attic," I say. "Is there an older section near the roof?"

Aude disappears for a moment to steal a skeleton key from her mother, and admits us into a dark wing with a dingy orange carpet that smells of mold. "This part is condemned," she says. Covered in plaster dust, the bare light bulb's on a timer that clicks off, spookily, in two minutes. Working a rusty lock, she lets us into a bedroom that's like a mausoleum to the Beatles era. Tacked to the wall are fan mag photos of George and Ringo in Sergeant Pepper garb.

"Further back," Alex says. "We have to go further back."

At the rear of the room is a door with its windows painted gray. Behind it is a staircase. We climb two flights of wooden stairs so rickety the banister nearly comes off in my hands. "Careful, guys . . ."

At the top is a sealed-off room constructed of a hodgepodge of building materials: part cement, part brick, tar, tin, glass, and shingle. Opening the door, Alex and I exchange a look. It feels *inhabited*. Hanging on a rusty nail is the train of an old wedding dress, made from an American parachute. And behind a little pile of coal in the corner is the skeleton of a cot.

"*Bingacht!!*" Marshall shouts. "That's German for BINGO!"

"It is?"

"He's just identifying with the oppressor, Dad," Alex tells me. "It's a subconscious reaction to all the scariness he's been exposed to."

Well, well: Alex is showing the first signs of grown-up compassion for his brother. And well, well again: could this be the cot under which J. P. and his daughters hid for three days, smelling the cassoulet wafting up from the kitchen? But how could they breathe up here in this heat, right under the roof? Did he communicate in sign language with his daughters, afraid to make a peep? Did he while away the hours by teaching the stuttering one English, whispering her favorite word, *apricot*, falling in love with the adorable little thing her mouth did when she tried to pronounce the word? Am I going crazy, extrapolating these things from a few thin curls in my pocket? Or am I only doing what William Blake suggested two centuries ago— divining the world in a grain of sand?

The room is scented strangely, but I can't place it. Finally I realize it's the same unexpungeable reek of secrecy as the interior cells of the Atlantic Wall: the smell of dust that's been roasted and chilled over many seasons and flavored occasionally with human sweat. Mopping my face I wonder, are all hiding places really one and the same?

Marshall is too inebriated to participate, but Alex is scouting the place for evidence, using his beret to slash through cobwebs. Any evidence will do: a postcard written in code; the letters *J. P.* carved into the gray painted sash of the door with a belt buckle; a Jewish star scratched into the window pane with a diamond; maybe even a diamond itself. . . .

But there's nothing. No date, no plea for help, no vow to take revenge upon bloody oppressors. Access to the roof is barred by a sawhorse, but we push it aside to stand next to a satellite dish on the orange tiles overlooking the town. *"Tire! Super! Gagne!"* comes a cry from the square below where the old-timers have resumed their game of *boules* after dinner. *"Ingung! Bluchtung!"* says Marshall. Using his loupe wrong side out as a telescope, he slips on a tile as his brother catches him in a puff of dust.

"Hey, you switching to the German team?" I ask him. "Is it too scary to keep identifying with Jews?"

"The Jews got cooked!" he explains simply. And teeters

again; the loupe drops down the tiles and smashes on the sidewalk below.

◆   ◆   ◆

"That's enough, that's long past enough. No more alcohol for you from now on," I tell Marshall. We're on the street walking past the game of *boules* when the dwarf farmer with the funnel chest calls to us, pointing to a hag stumbling from a doorway with a miniature collie.

"Sophie, she knew your uncle's children. A schoolteacher . . ."

Whatever she was then, it's all too obvious that she's now the town drunk. She's in her seventies but looks 100. *"Bonjour?"* She smiles vaguely. She looks disoriented, her lips puckered in the middle as if she's been blowing a trumpet.

"Can you translate, Aude?"

How do you translate decrepitude? She's a wreck, with triangles of puttylike gunk between her false teeth. Veins radiate over her legs and face like a network of peach twigs. But for all that, she manages a straightforward gaze. She's very quiet, with a lingering regard, as she sounds her words carefully through bottle-sucking lips.

"She says she remembers the twins," Aude reports. "They were not in her class, but she would see them; one borrowed a pencil from her, very gentle, very shy."

And then she tells us about the morning of July 3, 1944. Members of the Resistance were meeting at the café down the road. They didn't bother concealing their bicycles, since the Germans rarely came through this area. But that morning they did come through and, at the sight of so many bikes, suspected a meeting. They attacked the Resisters, who ran into the fields. "In the fields there is blood, blood in the road . . ."

Sophie wipes her hands smartly to signal "enough!" Done with the dirty business.

I turn to Aude. "Your mother told us everything was safe here."

Aude crushes me with a contemptuous look and finishes Sophie's story for her. "The young men and women, they are massacred, all of them: twelve. And to make matters worse, the Germans come back in half an hour. A Jewish doctor, Dr. Weissman, is taking care of the wounded in the fields. When he sees the Germans, of course, he is only human, he begins to run, and *bam* he is shot dead. While my grandfather, Monsieur Deak, he walks slowly with his cows and him they leave be."

The town drunk nods and picks up the thread of the story, which Aude translates. "The Germans go through the village looking for more Resistance. So handsome, the Germans! Like movie idols, with shiny black boots and clear blue eyes, while we are all in rags. They go to a house where a mother has just given birth to a baby, wrapped in burlap. Howling with glee the soldiers kick the baby along the floor like a soccer ball, making a goal through the door where they bash its skull with the butts of their rifles."

Seeing the look on our faces, Sophie spits vehemently on the ground. *"Ça c'est rien!"* she sputters. She stares passionately into the eyes of her collie, and goes on.

Our young translator looks stricken. "She says that is nothing," Aude continues. "The mother of this baby is weeping. They tell her to be quiet but she screams curses at them. This so enrages the Germans that they slit open her belly while she is alive and dance on her till her bowels explode, then they throw her body on the street with instructions for no one to bury her."

Squirming, I look over at my boys. Alex is fingering his gums, so upset that he's betraying no emotion but a kind of luxuriant sulkiness. Through his drunkenness, Marshall's eyes are registering shock slowly. I'm reminded of the time he received a tetanus shot as a six-month-old: he was gurgling happily in the doctor's office when the pain hit and his eyes locked onto mine. Wasn't I supposed to protect him?

I half move to cover their ears, but they both pull away, need-ing to touch the flame one minute more.

"When the Germans are finished," Aude is translating the old woman's words again, "they come to the schoolhouse and ask who are the Jews. They hear rumor, you understand? That there is Jews here. And the headmaster, he says *non*, there is no Jews in this school."

"Did they believe him?"

"They are interested in his manhood, which they stab with red-hot wires."

Behind us, one of the *boules* players holds up fingers that can only be called agricultural: four on one hand, one on the other. *"Cinq!"* he says. *"Cinq* wires!"

I didn't even know the players had been listening. They seem to be hearing without listening, having lived with these stories in their bones all these years. They lean toward us in the dusk, gnarled as apple trees. And then it dawns on me that these old-timers playing *boules* in the dying light are the Resistance fight-ers who survived. Bent and aged, wearing flannel caps and suspenders over potbellies, they probably have a thousand years of pride and defiance between them. But they don't seem sad in the least; the dwarf is measuring the distance between balls with a ruler.

Aude is frisky no longer. She scratches one fleur-de-lis sneaker against her knee to squash an itch and resumes inter-preting. "They assemble all the schoolchildren in the gymna-sium, point the guns at your uncle's daughters. 'They are Jew!' But everyone defends: 'No, they are not Jew!' Nobody, nobody breaks the faith. If there is one person . . . but nobody."

Sophie blows her nose into the butt of her palm, unable to continue.

Alex has his mouth open, Marshall's beyond tapping his Morse code, and seems to be breathing with his skull.

Aude resumes. "The teachers they are crying and screaming.

Especially one teacher protests, wonderful teacher, so righteous, a saint—Sophie."

We look at Sophie wiping her palm on her sleeve as Aude continues.

"'Me, I am the Jew,' Sophie tells them. But they do not believe her. So they hang her too low so she won't break her neck but only strangle slowly, then when she still refuses to tell they push sand down her throat with a stick and leave her for dead."

Neither of my sons can bear to look at me, but I clear my throat, obliged to break the tension by saying something irrelevant.

"Sophie, this saint," I ask Aude, "does she come from around here?"

"Not so far, from the Camargue, the delta of the Rhone to the east of here."

Sophie gargles something, spits happily, roughs up her collie's fur playfully.

"She says the Camargue is very beautiful," Aude translates. "There are many egrets to make your American seagulls look like bums. Also flamingos, pink. And pelicans, which was her name in the war—"

"Her name—?" I catch my breath as the medieval bell begins clanking from somewhere around the corner. "*This* is Pelican?" I want to feel triumph but all I can taste is bile in my mouth. The boys are too busy processing their own doses of poison to be elated.

"Yes. She says it was your relative who gave her that name. Also because it was the name of the street he came from—"

"Pelikaanstraat! Yes! The street of the Antwerp diamond exchange . . ."

Leaning against a tree with his eyes closed, Alex has his hand up to interrupt. "Also pelicans are mythical birds," he says. "The mother pierces her own breast to feed her young."

It's the most sour triumph I've ever experienced. I want to holler but lack the air. Picking on a tuft of her sweater—she is her mother's daughter after all!—Aude is too gaspy to continue. Pelican speaks in English that is surprisingly fine.

"I have lost my brain cells," she says. "I should not be believed. The Germans are a cultivated people, they could not do these things. You must not believe me: I drink five liters of wine a day. I eat only raw eggs. I have lost all my teeth from the vomit."

As if to prove it, she wiggles her dentures at us with the triangles of putty.

But I know she is gospel. "What happened to my uncle's children?" I ask her softly.

"This I cannot say."

"The Nazis found them?"

"They find, yes. The children, they turn themselves in. They see all the, how you say, horror and they step forward to say, 'We are the Jews.' But what happens next at the camp I can not say."

"A camp? A concentration camp?"

"Yes, they are going there prisoners, with their father."

"Where was the camp? In Germany? Poland?"

The medieval bell finishes clanking as she delivers a one-word answer to all our questions. "Rivesaltes."

27

PISSING IN THE DARK

I hate this so much
I hate this so much
I can't stand this.
Am I gonna die? Am I gonna lose my brain cells?
Am I gonna lose my teeth and have to eat
Raw eggs!?

Puking, Marshall is crying words into the toilet bowl outside our hotel room.

"Just relax," I say, as he spasms up another ounce of clear gut juice, the other fluids having already been wrung forth. "Get all the poison out."

Aude is still with us, trying to be helpful. Holding his head, she looks at me sympathetically as Marshall moans into the porcelain depths: "I've run out of Mommy."

"What do you mean?"

"There's no more Mommy left in me. I wish she were with us."

His fingers grip the cold toilet rim, kneading it for comfort as he cries. "All that sand down the teacher's throat," he says, "do you think that's why she turned into a drunk? Because it made her too thirsty?"

Aude raises her eyebrows. But before I can answer, Marshall resumes moaning his litany:

> I wish I didn't drink that stupid Armagnac.
> I wish I didn't eat that salad.
> The home dressing was horrible!

Aude, who used to work at McDonald's, tries correcting his terminology. "Do you mean the *house* dressing?"

But I understand at once what he means. "Oh, Marshall," I say, stroking his sticky brow. "Are you homesick? Is that what it is? You want to go home?"

A hollow sound from inside the porcelain: "I want to go *home*-home." And pukes again—*bleccch*, like another German word—splashing me with transparent misery.

Aude avoids looking at me. Even this stranger knows that *home*-home means his mother's house.

Lifting his head from the toilet bowl, Marshall looks around blearily and asks: "What was that awful stuff tonight that we ate in Belgium too, that *lapin* stuff?"

"*Lapin, lapin,*" Aude says, knitting her brows and pursing her lips. "How do you say, it goes hop hop hop."

"Hop?"

"Yes. Jump and leap and hop, with a little fooory tail."

"Deer?"

"No. Smaller. A little animal, why can't I think? Hop hop hop."

She makes little dancing gestures with her fingers over the toilet rim. Then she raises her eyebrows at Marshall expectantly, looking like a curious little . . . bunny.

"Rabbit!" Marshall roars.

"*Oui, oui!*" she says. "With the foot that is good luck."

"Rabbit!" he roars. And churns up even more misery from the bottom of his gut.

Thanking Aude, I excuse her from the scene.

"But it's not *your* rabbit, Marshall," I say soothingly, cradling his head and wiping the curds from his chin. "Your rabbit is safe at home."

"My rabbit died."

"What are you talking about?"

"Mom told me, when we called home. She died two weeks ago. A dog barked at her in her cage and she shook and shook and shook . . ."

◆ ◆ ◆

In the other room after Marshall passes off to sleep, Alex blames me. Because that's easiest.

"Dad, how could you!?"

"How could I what?"

"Let him get so drunk!" he says. But what he means is: Let him eat rabbit! Let his rabbit die! Expose him to this awfulness! If what they'd been dealing with a few nights before were the facts of life, these were the facts of death, and I was responsible.

"You idiot, Dad!" Alex screams, pummeling me—the first time he's ever raised his fists to me. It's only because I'm larger that I can pin them, cradle his head to my chest. Where he sobs at last.

"We're never going to get remarried to Mom, are we, Dad? We'll always be divorced, won't we?"

It reduces to this. It always has. It always will.

"I'm so sorry," I say.

I can do nothing but be a witness to Alex's despair. All I'm allotted is to watch him get the poison out of his system the way Marshall's done, sob and sob about what a klutz he is, about how he's no good at anything, he hates being Jewish, he wishes he were dead. I'm helpless, sitting there in my puke-wet clothes, watching his tears drop on the blue knee of his pajamas and soak into the fabric, turning it even darker blue, spreading the blue around.

How could I, indeed? They're both getting the inoculation of evil, now, and it stings more than anything they've ever known.

Looking at his sketchbook, which I see is filled with drawings of torture and gore, I frame the kind of question a father can ask his son only a few times. "Alex, am I too hard on you?"

"Ahuhno . . ."

"I'm sorry if I am. Is this trip too hard?"

Alex wipes his tears. "It's just . . . all those people who were killed, they were just like us, weren't they? They weren't just, like, out of a history book. They fought with their brothers and sisters and teased each other and all that stuff, didn't they?"

"Maybe even cracked each other's toe knuckles."

"And then they died for real, six whole million. . . ."

The number of phone calls fielded by the IRS prior to April 15 each year . . .

He struggles to express himself. "You know, death wouldn't be so hard to take if you knew what it was, or you thought it was doing some good, but when the death is *killing* you . . . I mean, when it's death by *dying* . . ." He takes a breath. "Do you know what I mean? I'm not saying it very well."

"You're saying it perfectly. Go on."

"It's just . . ." He slobbers a final sob, the tears raining down his chin. "I was lying about Becky, Dad. I never asked her out. She's a slut, Dad. She let a boy take her to third base."

"I'm sorry. I'm sorry about this whole mess. It'll seem better in the morning. You want me to give you three stars for today? Would three stars help?"

He doesn't even answer me.

◆ ◆ ◆

When I collapse in my room, my eyes are so tired that the bridge of my nose seems to pulsate in time with my breathing. I'm in such a state of alertness, listening for more tears, that I'm straining the muscles in my ears. But both boys are sleeping quietly.

An oppressively hot night. Trying to rain but it can't. I know without looking that envelopes are sticking together, that the night table drawers are too swollen to open. It's like living in a cave, with no breath of air to shake a few raindrops loose. The neighborhood resonates like a stage set. You can hear every sneeze from one end of the stone street to the other.

the boys being chased by farm hounds until Alex stumbles and goes down, reaching out for me but being gnashed away

calling to Marshall who's lost in a train station but it comes out: Malek! Malek!

seeing their ID cards blow off in a hailstorm of diamonds

Clammy with anxiety, I turn over and my worries turn with me, to greet me on the other side—

waiters with swastika bow ties turning in Jewish hiders

skeletons from the Atlantic Wall laughing at us with teeth stained blue

Christmas carolers coming through with machine guns, smashing heads of children as they sing

Trying to sleep in this inn where J. P. hid from the Nazis, amid imagery that's twisted Grimm's into Hieronymus Bosch, I admit to myself that I'm Jewed out at last. Jewed to the gills! I'm so sick of subtlety! Of acuity! The curse of Jewish brainpower! I can't take the alertness anymore! It's the alertness of the weak and frightened, of small darting animals in the woods, breathing with their entire bodies. Their fervency has gotten under my skin. My ears are overflowing with biblical hyperbole. It's all been passing out of them into me: the dates when their mothers died, the details about their babies perishing. From speaking to the stutterer, I've begun stuttering myself. From talking to the pianist who had his thumb shot off, I've begun to feel thumbless. Now at last I understand why I'd laughed at Little Henry as a child and made fun of my palsied aunts. Grief is contagious!

And now it comes to me: how the Nazis could do it. I mean, you go to the archives for five minutes and your eyes fill with tears. But look at it for five hours and you start to fidget. Now imagine that you're an ordinary German soldier stationed in the thick of it for five weeks, for five months. Day in, day out, all that carnage—you start to resent *them* for exposing you to it. Even though you're the one perpetrating the carnage, they're screaming and carrying on and you're sick of it because for you it's just a job you're inured to by now, but to them it's fresh horror every day. They're going through it with their skin on fire, pulling their hair out, bleeding red blood—can't they just die quietly? How heartless must they be to keep subjecting you to it? Any more crying, and you swear—*take that, sniveling Jew!* Now you're hitting them. Die silently, you think to yourself—or at least die in a new way, because you're so sick of watching them die the same way, so many every day. You think up novel ways to break the routine of death, club 'em with a rifle butt instead of shooting them in the head, anything to put a little spice in this rat race of killing. To escape the ennui of anguish you cause more.

I take a deep breath, suddenly aware that I've been wheezing. The medieval bell clanks two, clanks three, as flat a sound as a hammer hitting a plate. This is timekeeping at its most rudimentary, entirely without resonance, just banging out the hours left . . .

you j★st lie ther★
t★ll it ends
and y★u j★st get s★ck of it

Dank with a combination of red wine and Roquefort, I watch the heat lightning and feel like choking.

"Dad never gets lost." Alex had said it almost wistfully, back in Antwerp. But I *do,* Alex. I'm lost right now. Lying awake in this medieval stone village with the anxiety raveling up and down my Adam's apple like a broken zipper, words come unbidden into my head, words I didn't even know I knew:

For the sin which we have committed before Thee under compulsion or of our own will, And for the sin which we have committed before Thee by hardening our hearts

What was this? The prayer of atonement from the Yom Kippur service? Verily I had much to atone for:

For the sin which we have committed before Thee unknowingly

And for the sin of ridiculing Yudl on water skis

For the sin which we have committed before Thee by unchastity

And for the sin of wearing a radio earphone to High Holiday services

For the sin which we have committed before Thee by sinful meditation of the heart

And for the sin of wanting to burn everything Jewish in my house

For the sin which we have committed before Thee knowingly and deceitfully

And for the sin of laughing about the Low Salt Holocaust Diet

For all these sins, O God of mercy, forgive us in the twilight, in the waning of the day, or in the blackness of the night!

◆   ◆   ◆

I hear a scream.

"Dad! *Daddy?*"

I make my way in the dark to Alex's bed, where he sits trembling so much he makes the frame shake. Reaching for him, my hand becomes sticky from his cheek. It's blood, everywhere: on his chin, on his lips, all over the pillowcase. His nose has erupted, bleeding spontaneously in his sleep.

"Daaaaad!"

I lead him trembling to the bathroom where Marshall was vomiting just a few hours earlier. "Ho, kid, it's OK, splash some water on your face," I say, cleaning him up. The nosebleed seems to have subsided, but he's trembling too much to take a leak. The hand holding his penis is jiggling piss all over the seat.

"Alex, Jesus, get a hold of yourself!" I yelp, helping him aim it more center till I hear the plash.

"Dad, what's happening!"

"Nothing, Alex, you're just scaring yourself."

"Dad, where are you!?"

"I'm right here beside you. C'mon, kid."

"I mean where are *we?*"

"We're in France, Alex."

"Daaaaad!" The sound reverberates through the stage-set neighborhood. "Call a hospital, *quick!*"

"Jesus, Alex, get a grip. . . ."

In the dark I steady him at the edge of the toilet, his voice half an octave higher than usual.

"Dad, do you remember that Woody Allen movie you made me watch one time? Where he says I lubbb you! I luff you! He loved her so much he needed a whole new word to express it?"

"Annie Hall," I say. "What about it?"

"That's how much I hate the Nazis. I hubb them. I haine them. I despiiie them!"

"I know what you mean."

"It makes me so angry I could kill a dog. Blood comes to my eyes. . . ."

I take the opportunity to piss, also. Hearing the clatter of urine against the inside wall seems to soothe us both in some primitive way.

"How could that old lady talk about how they looked like movie idols? Admiring their shiny black boots like that! It's like, how come the victims feel bad instead of the guys who did it? How could their eyes be clear and my eyes feel like they have blood in them?"

"I don't know, Alex. Maybe that's part of being a bad guy, that you don't feel the pain. And maybe that's part of being a victim, that you not only suffer the pain but the guilt as well."

"But *why?*"

"Maybe the only way victims can come to terms with it is to assume responsibility for it."

"For getting hurt in the first place? But that doesn't make any sense. Why didn't they feel mad?"

"Maybe it was easier for them to feel guilt than to feel anger.

Maybe it wasn't until years later that it became safe to feel the rage."

"Do you think that's why the Israelis hate the Arabs so much?"

"Could be. That's the thing about rage, it's hard to aim it right."

"But what do you *do* with this rage, Dad? What do you do? Do I swallow it? 'Cause if I do, I'm going to choke, I swear I'm going to choke."

I groan inwardly for all the hours I passed in my room, all the arctic suffering that brought me this unhappy insight. "You keep it off to the side of your mouth," I say. "Keep it there like a mint."

"A mint of rage? But it won't dissolve, it'll stay there forever."

"That'll be your strength," I say.

"But . . . can't we smash something with this anger?"

"If you do, you'll just be another hater in the world. No, all you can do is surrender to it and let it pass, let the rage wash over you, just breathe it in and out."

"That's it?"

"That, and fall in love with a good person. I don't care if she's Jewish or German or a humpback whale. Just add to the quota of love in the world to help balance out the hate."

And now is when the heat breaks, the thunderstorm erupts, the rain beats against the windows of our room. Anyone outside in the downpour, bequeathed a glimpse of me clutching my inconsolable son through flashes of lightning, would see a look on my face as lonely-mean and vulnerable as that of the wild dog that skulked into the forest of the Ardennes. *That's it?* I'm asking myself. This is all I've got to give him? As the rain pounds our ceiling and the thunder rolls up and down the walls, I feel so inadequate as a father and as a man. Standing there before the toilet, it occurs to me that I've always been pissing in the dark with my children, not knowing with any certitude where I was going or what I was doing, just shooting from the hip and hoping it wouldn't be too messy. Was this the way to raise two sons? Or was there no other way?

How could I?—take them on such a trip? What kind of father would shove his sons' noses in the most terrifying experience of the century? Have I bequeathed Alex my rage, as my mother bequeathed me hers? Was another of my precious Reasons that I wanted them to contract my suffering? By taking them here and watching their reactions and even going so far as to take notes on them, am I different from a Bengalese beggar who breaks the knees of his children so that strangers might better pity them? Has my old childhood recklessness come full flower? But it was one thing when it was only myself I was being self-destructive about. Here I've put two young souls at risk. . . .

And given them the nerves, as Shasha had warned. Alex is still shaking the way I imagine Marshall's rabbit did. A dog barked at it in its cage and though it was perfectly safe it shook and shook the rest of the day and died that night, literally scared to death. Have I, finally, brought my flesh and blood too close to the ogres?

Pardon me, O awesome King, for exposing these innocent lives to heartache of such magnitude. . . .

28

THE LITTLE HELL

I wake up late, syrupy with dreams, as though I'd drunk a potion the night before. In my sleep, I'd been granulating the corpse of Hitler in a Cuisinart, then gone to the ends of the earth to scatter the remains—on a dirt road in Patagonia, on an ice floe in Siberia—but I knew in my dream that wickedness has a way of reconstructing itself from its ashes, of knitting itself back together. . . .

So disoriented am I, getting dressed, that I can't figure out what's amiss as I force the prong of my watch strap. I'm so confused I can't make out the time. Then I realize I have the watch on backwards so it reads 3:45 instead of 10:15. It seems a metaphor for my quandary.

The shower helps me metabolize last night's anxiety. Two quotations come to mind: Alan Dershowitz recounting a friend saying that the Holocaust makes it possible to contemplate the destruction of the human species as a "satisfying close" to the history of our epoch. "That species, the one that committed *that,* has lost its worthy status. Humanity has desanctified itself."

And I recall the words of a medieval chronicler who broke off his work to say, "I am ashamed to tell all that the Cossacks did to us. I am ashamed to tell it for fear of blaspheming the name of man which God created in His image."

Not pretty thoughts, either one, and I find myself looking forward to Marshall's arrival in the shower with me. But he doesn't show. When I towel dry and come into his room, he's still in bed, surrounded by mounds of Kleenex.

"How are you?" I ask.

"My throat killed all night. My head was spinning and my nose was stuffocated. I was up six times because I was wicked drunk."

"Other than *that* how are you?" I ask with a smile, hoping for his normal rally.

"I just wish we had a delete button," Marshall says gravely. "We could take all that stuff out of our heads."

He looks limp as a wire that's been blowtorched. His eyes are colorless.

"Sorry about your rabbit," I decide to say.

"It's OK, Dad. That's life."

I expect Alex to bray from wherever he's holed up: "Life! That's a good one! His bunny bites the big one and he says that's life!" But Alex is silent. Where is he anyway?

Down by the scummy little pool, as it turns out. "What're you doing?" I call.

"Trying to wash yesterday off."

❖ ❖ ❖

The day confounds us with its normalcy. Aude and her family have gone for a day trip somewhere and have left us food on the terrace. Silently breakfasting on avocado mousse to the hoarse choir of locusts, even the most delightful of summer sensations fails to cheer us: feeling the different currents of air temps, from smoky-cool when the air darkens under a passing cloud to brazen-hot when sunlight recurs, darned by blue dragonflies. Beauty is wasted on us: I have an urge to try to keep the summer from blooming, to pounce on each flower before it sprouts.

As we drive off in our Citroën I feel like having an accident so I won't have to deal with the grim task ahead of us.

"Where we headed?"

One word: Rivesaltes.

◆ ◆ ◆

We reach the other end of southern France by late afternoon. The boys are so hungry we take a seat on the sidewalk outside the train station of Perpignan. Aude and her mother left us bags of hard-boiled eggs and baguettes with ham and Roquefort that drips onto our laps. On the eggs Aude has penciled caricatures meant to take the sting out of last night—Marshall grinning like a Tasmanian devil, Alex juggling a couple of dictionaries, and me with a long flowing beard. We should be amused. But we chew hard and swallow joylessly.

The sun of southern France is shining warm and fresh, the world so pulsating with green that if I were a dog I'd roll over and scratch my back in the grass. But the wind is blowing Styrofoam peanuts and I'm needled by the sense that things are a little off. Like that billboard there: at first I think it says Paranoid when really it says Polaroid. And like that man there, the one in the brown corduroy suit, running up the handicap ramp. Something's wrong: his sleeves are too short, his jacket doesn't fit him right, *something*. Then I see: he's trotting to keep up with two gendarmes to whom he's handcuffed.

"Are you tense, Daddy?"

"A little, Marsh. I don't know why."

"Maybe something bad's going to happen."

"I'm sure everything'll be fine," I say.

"C'mon then," he says, pushing me with two hands, his entire body angled from the sidewalk like Sisyphus at his labors, "it's not going to stay light forever!"

◆ ◆ ◆

Finding the small burg of Rivesaltes a few miles away, I locate a bistro in the town square and park the boys at a video game while I order a drink. The place is nearly empty. An old farmer with two black teeth accosts me.

"*Comme ça!*" he bellows, showing me how to pour water into my pastis.

"*Comme ça?*"

"*Comme ça!*" he roars, giving me a hearty clap on my shoulder.

My, what a friendly bistro. The patrons are all beaming at me so much I begin to relax. The big-boned man at the table behind me seems Australian—no, German—but the jolly kind, with a porcupine mustache bristling with beer suds. The bartender with bashful brown eyes and ringlets of thick curls is about my age; there's a generational click between us as I find myself wondering what I wouldn't wonder at home: if he's Jewish. Smiling with my first contentment of the day, I take a sip of pastis and feel my anxiety thaw like water trickling down a glacier, and think that this is one of the joys of the world, to stop in to a strange bar and feel instantly at home.

"*Ditez-moi,*" I say, to any of my new friends within earshot, "*savez-vouz où était le camp de concentration dans cette région-ci?*"

It's as if I'd pulled a stink bomb out of my pocket. Muttering with surprise, the old farmer withdraws his hand from my shoulder. The bartender's bashfulness is edged with bitterness as he brushes the curls out of his eyes and recedes to dry some glasses with a raggy towel. As if on cue (did my gaffe set off a silent alarm?), a TV clicks off from the room behind the bar and out struts the woman who owns the joint—pretty but tough. Wearing a red bandanna and picking a gold tooth with the prong of a fondue fork, she looks as if she'd enjoy scratching my eyes out.

Behind me, the jolly German self-consciously throws himself into his sausage; I can hear the double-time click of his fork and knife. Two motor scooterists saunter in and immediately sense that something's up. They look at me quizzically, then ask a question of the owner. She barks some curse in an accent I can't decipher, pointing her chin at me. They glare, pivoting toward me on their stools with their knees open, the Gallic male posture of hostility.

To lessen the tension, the bartender brings a tray of green felt to the two scooterists, but they wave the dice game away, still glaring.

"No?" I say, in English. "No one's allowed to mention what happened here fifty years ago?"

But this is pushing it. The atmosphere is so charged, it's no longer safe.

"C'mon kids," I say.

"But we're in the middle of Double Dragon."

"C'mon!"

❖ ❖ ❖

"Geez, Dad, what'd you do in there?" Alex asks as we drive off.

"I asked if they knew where the concentration camp was in this region."

"Well, maybe you have the wrong country."

Maybe I do. This is France, not Poland. There were no Treblinkas in France, everyone knows that.

"They knew," Marshall says.

"Why?" I ask. "Did they seem guilty to you?"

"Not really," Marshall says. "But J. P.'s journal doesn't lie."

This, however, is all our resident skeptic needs. Alex pounces on the journal and waves it in the air, causing pawn receipts to flutter from its pages like moths.

"You know what?" he says. "I bet the whole journal is a lie! I bet J. P. put in just enough true stuff to trick us, to get back at us for bothering him! C'mon, Dad, you said it yourself! If there *had* been a camp in France, wouldn't we have heard about it by now from someone besides the town drunk? You know what I think? I think we should find a motel with a pool that's not mucky for a change. The tracks were fun but this is getting ridiculous."

Marshall places the journal protectively on his lap. "Ask that old lady," he says.

I stop the car by the dusty curb and roll down the window. *"Pardonnez-moi,"* I say, "I hate to bother you but we're from America and were wondering if *vous savez où était le camp de concentration . . . ?"*

She shuffles forward in bedroom slippers that are half off her feet. Places her scrubbed fingers on the car window. And her eyes fill with tears.

"Le camp des juifs," she says.

We catch our breath while she hauls a blue kerchief out of the pocket on her billowy dress, swipes her eyes with peasant dignity, and gestures to the boys. *"Beaucoup de juifs, comme ça."*

"Many Jews, like them?" I translate.

"Oui! Les enfants, les vieux, et les petits, comme ça." She blinks at the boys again. Then she points to her necklace.

"They wore jewelry?"

"Non." She makes her face into a mask of brutality. *"Les allemands . . ."*

"The Germans . . ."

She makes the gesture of ripping off the necklace.

"Took their jewelry."

She nods, continues to mime.

"Their rings, their bracelets . . ."

She leans so close to the window I can smell the sardines on her breath. She shows a nugget of gold filling between her molars.

"Their gold teeth, they took them, too." She closes her eyes emphatically. Shakes her head.

"Where did this take place?" I ask.

She points to the ground, stamps her foot indignantly. *"Ici!"*

"Right here, on this spot?"

"Non!" She makes a circling sign to indicate: around here, this vicinity.

"But where? Is there anything left so we can see what it was?"

She gesticulates, over the fields there, to the north, not so far. Just there!

"But we don't know how to get there. Can you come with us, to show us?"

"*Non non, mon mari . . .*"

"Your husband wouldn't allow it?" We are, after all, three strange men. "*Merci,*" we say. "*Merci, madame.*"

She straightens up, lifts her fingers off the window. Her lashes sparkling in the sunlight, she bows her head slightly as we drive off. In the rearview mirror, my last glimpse is of her extracting a hand mirror from her pocket and touching the side of her hair.

I'm exhilarated, and frightened. The car motor sounds powerful, as if it's rushing us to our destiny, whether we like it or not. I feel love for the old lady. Is this odd? And I miss her fingers. Her fingers were so clean they now strike me as almost tragic. The scrubbing she must give them, to get the soil out! I feel reverent toward her, toward her scrubbed conscience. She's the only one we've met in Rivesaltes who's owned up to what happened.

"She was like holy, wasn't she, Dad?"

"Just what I was thinking, Marsh."

We leave town in the general direction she pointed us, driving down long straight roads that cut through old vineyards. Alex turns on his Walkman in the backseat while Marshall thumbs through the last of the journal's clay-stained pages, but the only clues as to the camp's whereabouts are ambiguous doodles— scribblings of diamonds and bats. Not that I entertain any illusion that there's much to see, even if we find it. The most I'm hoping for is a couple of boards lying around, maybe a pile of cement—anything at all to prove in this final case that J. P. wasn't just being poetic.

Most of the afternoon the sun's been hidden, but at this hour of sunset it glows, the size of a centime going down behind rolls of green hay. The stones on either side of the road hold the light, pink and gold, the shade of blush champagne, what the French call *"la cuisse de nymphe émue"*—the inside thigh of the aroused nymph. This is the color of southern France at its best, but the landscape itself is uninspired: flat all the way out to the Pyrenees in the background. And the farther we drive, the more desolate it gets. To the east, past a train line that goes straight north, seagulls beat their way along greasy salt marshes. The vineyards look scabby, covered with the gray film of diesel exhaust. Tufts of needlelike grass take their stand at the edge of the road, defying the tar. The word *villous* comes to mind. *Scabrous. Scurfy.* Wayfarers pass through en route to somewhere better—either the beach resorts of Spain's Costa Brava or the wild cliff grottoes of the Pyrenees. We haven't seen any other cars since leaving the bistro. I'm a little spooked by how isolated we've become; wonder how long it would take for someone to come across us if we got a flat.

"Look, some kind of . . . thing!" Alex says, taking off his Walkman. "Is that anything?"

It's a dilapidated chicken coop with claptrap fencing. "Good call, though," I say. "Keep trying. Keep your eyes peeled."

Another few minutes pass. I can almost hear the effort behind the boys' eagle eyes. "What about there? In that field . . . ?"

"No, that's an outhouse."

It's approaching nine o'clock. Not going to stay light much longer. In the distance we make out the shell of a small brick building. "Like a guardhouse!" Marshall says.

"Don't get your hopes up," I caution as we head for it.

The distances are deceiving: It's farther than we thought. But when we pull onto the shoulder in a reddish upsweep of brick dust, I open the car door onto rusty barbed wire.

"Uh, I don't like the looks of this," Alex says. "Can we go find a motel now?"

It's a simple two-room structure, but the walls are in such a state of decay that we can hardly tell what was once inside and what out. Broken bricks lie scattered about, putrefying into piles of dust. The wood's cracked and splintery. In one corner, there's a moist mound of sawdust about eighteen inches high, almost like an anthill. Seeing some remnants of white in the mound, I put my hands in—it's perfectly dry inside—and pull out a clotted ball of paper. Unraveling it, we discover the ball is made up of long individual strips of paper, as though shredded.

"I can't believe this," I say, staring.

"What?"

"Look at the typewriting: '... *und wieder fort* ... *nach über-haupt* ...' It's German!"

"Uh, this is getting seriously creepy," Alex says. "I vote we get out of here."

"But I don't see how these could date back to World War Two," I say. "There weren't such things as paper shredders back then, were there? Didn't they come in recently, like with desktop computers?"

I'm perplexed, but Alex is looking pale. "Dad, I read about shredders in school. I hate to tell you, but they started making them in the thirties."

"You sure?"

"Positive. I don't think we should be here!"

"But still," I say, "how could paper have survived? Unless maybe the sawdust preserved it?"

There's our answer. The sawdust acted as a preservative, embalming the paper these last fifty years. I make an effort to breathe down to the bottom of my belly.

"OK, congratulations, we have our proof," Alex says. "The French had a camp. J. P. wasn't putting us on. Let's leave."

But just then Marshall makes a sound of stifled panic. "Oh my God," he breathes, pointing over a rise behind us. "Something back there!"

We've been so closely focused—the clots of paper, the antiquated typewriting—that we've paid no attention to what's farther away. At Marshall's bidding, we scan the horizon. And there it is. Gleaming in the sunset, wall after wall after wall ... an entire colony of ruins like an alien cityscape.

Quickly we consult the journal. And there are J. P.'s doodles just as we're seeing it, row after row of barracks with ratlike creatures flying from their black insides.

Marshall is gurgling with dread. "Oh my God, Dad!"

Alex has instinctively taken my hand. "I don't think we want to go there," he says.

"We got to!" Marshall shouts.

The seven-year-old can handle anything. And with tact, as well—not making the less brave among us feel ashamed. He's giving us room to make up our minds, gazing at the debris in the distance, entranced. But I want to make sure the twelve-year-old doesn't start trembling again. "Do you think you can hack this?" I ask him.

"I don't know," he says.

"Listen, I'm freaked, too," I tell him. "We signed up for a big ride, but this may be more than we bargained for. If you don't want to do this . . ."

"I'm cold," he says.

"Want my sweater?"

"Thanks."

Putting it on seems to make him stronger. He stands up a little straighter.

"What do you say, want to call it a day?"

"No, I think we ought to check it out," he says. "We've come this far. . . ."

"You sure?"

"It's bigger than we are. Let's get it over with."

I look into his eyes. "OK."

We get back in the car and ease onto the weedy track behind the structure that seems to lead to the distant buildings. It's rutted with disuse. Stones leap from the tires. Small shrubs slide and bang against the chassis beneath our feet. I'm concerned about the time. It's hard enough to negotiate this path in twilight; I don't want to think about what it'll be like to come back in the dark. We drive in silence. In only a few min-

utes the sun is going down in the Pyrenees, the sky lit up pink
as a teacup.

This is no tourist trap, with cola for sale in plastic cups and
signs pointing out the rest rooms. This is the monster, untouched, left to decay in the wind. What stuns us first, as we
step out of the car, is the scale of the place: barrack after roofless
barrack as far as the eye can see, each with a number painted in
black on the orange cement walls: 20, 48, 88. We pick our way
over the rubble of broken concrete and clumps of earth. Everything's surreal: vines grow tough as twine, snails are glued to the
inside of the walls, rats squeak angrily that we're trespassing on
their turf.

In the flat distance, we're startled by the sound of a train yowl-
ing across the land. Its proximity convinces me that they must've
laid a spur to the main train line across Europe to Auschwitz.

J. P. survived this. I am chilly with awe.

"Lookit over here!" Marshall says. He's pointing to a white
tiled edifice with a chimney. Four intact compartments make
up its furnace.

"What was it, Dad?" he asks.

I don't know. And I don't want to share my theory that it was
a crematorium. Surely they didn't have those here, did they?
This was just a concentration camp, wasn't it?—a place where
they detained Jews until they could ship them to the death
camps, not a death camp itself. Though the journal does show a
gallows . . . and over here is a contraption that looks similar, the
wood so softened by rain I can push my fingers halfway
through. Bullet holes honeycomb the walls; scrounging in the
dirt, pouncing on anything that gleams, Marshall has already
collected a handful of eight bullet casings.

I, myself, don't want to touch anything. As an effort of will, I
reach down and pick up a clod of earth. What a strange texture,
as if bones have been mixed in with shards of brick, a little like
the cremated ash of my friend Kip who died after his bar fight.
But my friend's ashes had a clean feeling. His body had been

purified, scorched of its mortal sins. This is the filthiest soil I've ever rubbed between my fingers, dense and light at the same time. It's stained to its fiber with perversion.

Alex reads my thoughts. "They didn't kill people here, did they, Dad?" he asks.

"I'm not sure."

If they didn't actually exterminate them, certainly they helped them die. We pick our way through what looks like a tiny exercise yard, mean and foul. Past a shithouse—no other name will do—a shack containing a rough wooden board with holes so close together the inmates must've had to rub shoulders as they were defecating. In the corner, a long '60s-style car seat sits propped against the wall. So modern-day lovers have come here, too—a thought that doesn't fill me with hope for the species.

But the truly obscene thing is the color of the barracks, that creamy orange-pink, a lurid sherbet shade. It's more than fake jollity, it's mocking. It's the Nazis laughing at their catch, taunting them with the color of Creamsicles and cotton candy, saying isn't life fun? This is the same mockery that made them dig swimming pools for the officers at Auschwitz and erect merry-go-rounds next to the siding where Jews were loaded onto boxcars. Whoever chose this color also tossed candy to the children in the pits before machine-gunning them, also chased naked grandmothers into the gas chambers, heckling and mimicking them.

With a cindery taste in my mouth I acknowledge that this is the most evil place I've ever been in.

And suddenly I know: this is where the curls of hair are from. The twins had their heads shaved in this spot. With my hand in my pocket the way my great-uncles fingered their diamonds, I squeeze the cellophane tight to divine, rightly or wrongly, the rest of what I need to know:

. . . A cow was wandering around. . . . J. P. figured if a cow could get *in*, couldn't he get *out*? Sure enough, he located a hole in the barbed wire . . . waited with his bald-headed twins in the shithouse for the moon to be hidden behind clouds. . . .

. . . A German shepherd arrived straining at a leash . . . pulling two SS guards, a father and son, both with generous warm eyes and civilized smiles . . .

"Some will get away," consoles the father, a pep talk. "Don't blame yourself. You can't be perfectionistic and kill them all at one time."

"But I've been doing such a good job, Poppa," protests the son. "I've been killing them all up!"

"I know you have. I'm proud of you. You do good work when you put your mind to it. But you must adhere to protocol and call me kommandant."

"Thank you, Herr Kommandant. You're doing a good job, too."

"It's because I love you that I'm doing such a good job," says the father, urinating in the inmates' water trough. "Because I want the world to be clean and fine for you."

Suddenly the shepherd sniffs at the wall of the shithouse.

"Kommandant! What's this? A little Jew pig?" The son unsheathes his bayonet, almost as big as he is. "Is someone *here?*" says the son, gouging his bayonet again and again through the cracks in the wall. "Is someone *here?*"

Presently he hits pay dirt. There is the rich dark gloss of blood on the point of his bayonet. "Ho ho," says the son. "Bull's-eye!"

The door of the shithouse flies open. Out stumbles a bald-headed child, cradling her dead sister in her arms and stuttering "Ap, ap, ap."

The son trembles with excitement. "Look, Poppa! They come in pairs!"

The father looks on proudly as he buttons himself up. With his own bayonet, he skewers the dead one out of the live one's arms and tosses her away. "Did you know that Jews are good dancers?" he asks his son.

"I never heard that," says the son. "But I am willing to see."

With well-placed chops the father slashes off both live legs above the knees. "Dance the hora for us," suggests the father.

The bald-headed child prances on her stumps. "Apric—" she pleads. "Apric—"

"Jews *are* good dancers," says the son. "They could use a more becoming hairdo but they are good dancers."

It begins to rain. "Come," says the father. "We mustn't let our boots get wet."

"You're right, Poppa," says the son.

They begin to walk away, leaving the live one dancing on her stumps.

"Please!" says the father, an afterthought: turning back to shoot her through the head. "Remember to call me Kommandant."

That shot shakes me out of my delirium. Marshall's eyes are closed. Alex is looking at the snails fastened to the concrete walls. I know he's thinking about the escargots he ate in the Ardennes. He turns to me with a nauseated face. "Dad, uh, let's get out."

Across the flat plains the neon of Perpignan is shimmering 15 kilometers away. The rats are screeching louder now. Soon their eyes will start to glow. We do our best to hasten over the stubble of bent nails toward the car, but the straggly vines seem intent on slowing us down, clinging to us as we push them aside.

Then I trip, sprawling flat out with my chin in the dirt.

"What was *that!?*" I yelp, leaping up from the ground. The journal's flown from my hand, scattering bits of brightly colored ribbon.

"Dad, you OK?"

My boys have their hands on me and a look of wild concern.

"I thought I got an electric shock. There couldn't be live wires around still, could there?"

I don't know whether I'm losing it or what. But my ankle, where I was zapped, is numb. What *was* that? Marshall retrieves the journal and shakes the new clay from its pages.

Back in the car, my heart's still pounding. Both boys climb in front to keep their hands on me. Mercifully, the car starts right up. We start to inch forward but darkness is gathering now all around our headlights, and I can't get my bearings.

"Are you sure this is the way we came in?" Marshall asks.

No, it isn't. Somehow we've been turned around. In no time we've come upon a section of the camp not visible before. Ramshackle but still intact, this was the officers' compound, built better than the barracks. It's shaped like a V, with an annex off each side. In the center, behind a broken staircase, a black swastika looms ten feet high on raw concrete. Just like the one on the cover of the journal.

My face flushes.

"Very interesting," I mutter in a hollow voice, "but we'd better go now."

I gun it down the dirt trail, pebbles drilling the car's manifold, but a minute later slam on the brakes. In the feeble glare from the headlights, I see I've stopped inches from a three-foot-deep trench.

Reversing through the dust we've raised, we soon are back at the swastika. Now I figure it out. The officers' compound is like the hub of a wheel, with spokes of dirt roads laid out in military formation. But I'm stumped. Which dirt road do we try?

"Dad?" It's the voice of my trooper, my intrepid seven-year-old, frightened, wheezy. "Can we fast-forward this to tomorrow?"

To my surprise, Alex comes to his rescue. "Don't worry, little brother," he says, taking the beret off his head and popping it on Marshall's. "Dad won't let bad happen."

How I wish! I have no choice but to choose another trail at random. As we jounce along the rutted path, the weeds between the tracks conceal a small boulder that with a thud scrapes the underbelly of the car. I'm growing the sickening feeling that we've fallen into some kind of trap.

We caught three more, Herr Kommandant.

"What time is it, Alex?"

The boys lean forward, their eyes round with dread. My mouth is utterly dry. We can't be lost. There's got to be a way out. If worse comes to worst, we can always wait till sunup to see our way clear. Then immediately I correct myself: there's no way we're going to spend the night in this terrible place.

Some late arrivals for you, Herr Kommandant.

"What *time*, Alex?"

"Nine fifty-six."

OK, if I just keep going in this direction, maybe it'll open up. Marshall's bullet casings are rolling around on the floor in back, tinkling with every lurch of the wheel. We're not caught, I refuse . . .

And just as I'm thinking this, we slam with a soft thud into a dirt embankment. No damage done. I push open the door to peer behind me as I back up.

"Keep being brave, kids, we'll be out of this in a jiffy. . . ."

Back up just a little, and then, my heart drops. Down we slip, the right rear tire sliding over the lip of another trench. I step out the door onto the sound of crunching glass under my feet, thinking, It *is* a trap! It's a great big maze to trap Jews stupid enough to come back fifty years later! Look at this kike! His people escaped half a century ago and he rents a car and delivers his children right to the front door.

These are the three I was telling you about, Herr Komman- dant. . . .

Loops of rusty barbed wire are clutching at my pants cuffs as I strain to rock the car free. "Alex, come out here with me. Marshall, you sit in the driver's seat."

"But I can't see over the dash!"

"You don't need to. Just reach down with your foot and give it some gas. Ready?"

With Alex beside me and Marshall in the driver's seat, we heave. Nothing happens. "You've got to press the accelerator, Marshall!"

"I can't reach!"

Suddenly he makes contact with the pedal. The wheels spin frantically, spitting dirt. The car lurches forward, stalls out, slides back. "Well, damn it, don't waste the battery!" I shout, yanking free of the barbed wire to snap off the light.

Blackness wings out on all sides. An enormous silence, peppered only by the sound of Marshall's raggedy breathing. Asthma of the soul. He's caught it from me.

Never have I felt so inconsequential. The earth and I have no point of contact. We have nothing in common; it's not a planet I'm familiar with. The very ground, demented by hurt, is hurting us back.

So this is where our beloved Tracks have led us?—to the same place it led my ancestors, a wasteland with no false ceilings, no trapdoors, not even any trees to run behind or grass high enough to crouch in? This is what the world looks like without hiding places—a Nazi dystopia of rubble and rats, the eternal revenge of Brothers Grimm. For J. P.'s family, this was the end of the line, the place that put an end to all the hiding places. The barn lofts and wine cellars were all for naught when they got here. And for us, too? What were Heart's Island and the rest of my secret places? Just childish fantasies, as useless as the magic wishes I'd hoarded for the black night I'd really need them, which was never more than now.

Marshall bursts out crying. "Daddy?"

"Don't worry, we'll get out of this soon."

"No, Dad. I just saw a soldier. With a gun."

"You're tired, Marshall, you're upset."

"No, Dad! He just ran behind that mound there."

And then, like a nightmare, I see it too—the tips of rifles be-hind an embankment. Have we entered a time warp? And then—my brain shoots sparks, my heart tugs at my stomach—two real-life soldiers in real-life uniforms and real-life boots scurry for cover from one embankment to another. And two more drop from the blackness to the ground, aiming their rifles at us.

"Uh, Dad?" Alex is saying. "Uh, Dad?"

Marshall cowers under my jacket as he burbles a litany to himself, like a nursery rhyme. "Dad won't let bad happen, Dad won't let bad happen. . . ."

More soldiers are slithering out of the trench behind us, as six more trot directly for us across the open ground with their hands on their holsters. There must be fourteen altogether, coming from all directions. I glance at my car and realize there's no way we could make a dash for it even if the car weren't stuck. They've got us. Nothing left but to surrender, to raise my hands as far as they'll go.

And then, I remember. We've done nothing wrong. Instead of raising my hand, I stretch it out straight as far as it'll go. To shake.

"*Bonjour.* We're Americans. I'm Dan, this is Alex, Marshall, Americans all . . ."

The kids put out their hands to shake, also. *Bonjour, shalom.*

I reach into my pocket for identification but pull out some sort of laundry list instead. "Claudette two times, Rochelle . . ." *Get out of my life, J. P.!*

Of course Dominic, the leader, is French. Of course he's friendly. A quick reading of us tells him that, of course, we're friendly, too. The world's not inside out. My watch is not clock-ing the '40s. They're having a military training exercise, that's all, they're sleeping here for the night. I notice Dominic's nails, bitten to the quick. They're all so young.

I've never shaken so many hands in my life, but I insist, I want to make sure we're all on the greatest of terms.

Alex is having a grand old time with his new friends. "Oh, is that a Famus? I've never seen a twenty-gauge automatic before!"

You take a kid to Europe to learn the lessons of World War II and he becomes a munitions expert.

Marshall, meanwhile, is cleaving to my side like a duckling. I feel certain he's wishing he still sucked his thumb, because if ever a seven-year-old were entitled to, he's entitled now.

Yes, Dominic is telling us, this was an "internal transit camp" where Jews were detained before going on to extermination camps. Known as the little hell before the big hell, it was inhabited mostly by children who were given one meal a day, a spoonful of chickpeas and a piece of bread, before going on to Auschwitz.

"Up, up, hooray!" say the soldiers, boosting our rental car out of the trench. And with much merriment and more handshaking all around—Alex is even exchanging addresses with someone who wants to be his pen pal—we're out.

◆ ◆ ◆

The grass on the dirt trail is thinning out, thinning out, and then: blacktop. How we Americans do love blacktop. With a gasp of relief, we hit the open road, reach our stride at 70 mph, with the tar stretching wide and smooth before us, the lights of Perpignan winking like an oasis as we fly to them.

Sitting there in his big brother's beret, Marshall's breathing has returned to normal, but he's awfully quiet. I need to open him up a bit to get the pressure out. "Sorry I barked at you, kiddo, about wasting the battery."

"That's OK."

"Were you blown away, seeing the soldiers?"

"I thought they were Germans from World War Two. That they had a secret underground base all this time."

Not so far from what I was thinking, myself. But I flash on

something else, as well: what it felt like to come out of the Tunnel of Terror when I was five with my uncle and aunt. Is this really the world out here, or just another chamber of the concentration camp? Yet it doesn't matter. I know my fellow journeymen, my sons, are real. They're the end of my doubts.

"Alex," I say, "one question. Why'd you say *shalom?*"

"Well, you know," he says, genially sucking on a gumdrop one of the soldiers had passed out, "you learn fast in a crisis."

"But why *shalom?*"

"I don't know," Alex says. "It just popped out of my mouth."

A mystery.

And here's another mystery: how soon we're among the bright lights of Perpignan. In no time we're there, in the thick of the desperately cheerful yellow and red Catalonian flags flying from billboards and taxi antennas. It's a comfort, these flags: what it means is that the world was not homogenized by fascism, did not come under the sway of that giant black swastika. All types, all colors and creeds, are welcome.

"Do we get a star for tonight, Daddy?"

"Double stars. And you know what that means?"

"Double treats?"

"You got it. So start ordering."

Alex gets *frites* and ice cream from a wandering vendor, Marshall settles in with an Orangina. I treat myself to a bottle of Jack Daniel's—none of this pastis crap but good solid Loudmouth Soup—and swig it from a paper bag, college style. Thus we sit on a park bench, each with his own thoughts, soaking up the flamenco guitar at the corner. It seems like a festival but it's an ordinary weeknight. Cars putter by blaring Spanish rock. Indochinese saunter by—some from Saigon, some from Kampuchea. Young Frenchmen have big dogs—Alsatians, shepherds—while their elders have little bitty poodles and schnauzers. The hookers whistling, the punks panhandling, the garbage trucks squealing their brakes—I am basking in this blessed cacophony. . . .

Still rattled to our bones, we collect ourselves. I take a breath and close my eyes to hear the boys talk: a genuine grown-up conversation without me, by God . . .

"Did you believe how huge it was?" Alex says. "And why they didn't burn it, that's what I don't get."

"Maybe the devil lives there," Marshall says, "and they're afraid to burn his home."

Alex doesn't scoff. "Maybe that's why Dad got shocked on his ankle," he says. "It was the devil shocking him."

I hear Marshall toying with his bullet casings. "If it *was* the devil, though, he was only playing with us. Because he could have shocked us worse."

"He was just reminding us that he was there," Alex agrees.

"But I don't know why he was shocking *us*. We didn't do anything wrong."

"Don't you *get* it, Marshall? J. P. didn't do anything wrong, either. *None* of those six million did anything to deserve what happened to them. Isn't that right, Dad? Dad?"

"Shh, he's trying to sleep."

"He's not trying to sleep, he's trying to meditate."

"With Jack Daniel's?"

"Whatever."

But I *am* having a meditation, thinking, *the number of children spilling their breakfast cereal on an average Saturday morning, the number of yards of dental floss used during the career of an average dental technician, the number of calories in a month's worth of moo shu pork, the number of bubbles in an acre's worth of grasshopper spit* . . .

. . . and then the voices of my sons float back into my hearing again, dovetailing with my thoughts . . .

Marshall: "And that's why it's up to us to make friends with what happened."

Alex: "How can we make friends with what the Germans did?"

Marshall: "We just do, that's all, and also with the Jews for having it happen to them. 'Cause if we don't, we'll be just as bad as the Nazis. Right, Dad? Won't we, Dad?"

But I'm content to sleep, to meditate, whatever I'm doing— to breathe in the miracle of not being in a concentration camp—and let them roll it over in their minds.

"Not *as* bad."

"Not *as* bad, but *almost.*"

"You're right, Marsh. Got to hand it to you. *You gorgonzola.*" I hear Alex grab him. "Ow, Dad, tell him to stop!"

"Up, up, hooray," I hear, as Marshall's upended onto soft grass nearby and his shoe comes off. "Just two more toes, Marsh. I'm almost there!"

"Stop or Dad won't give us a double treat tonight!"

"He already promised he would. So what treat would you like?"

Upside-down, Marshall considers. "We all sleep in the same bed."

"All together, in one bed?"

"Can we, Dad? Please can we?"

I open my eyes to vast richness. My sons are staring at me with eager faces, under a moon so neatly halved it looks cleaved by a paper cutter. The night air is so clear, I can count the number of times the pigeons flap their wings in the streetlight. The lowly skunk cabbage in the grass beside us is a wonder, its purple resiliency, its quirky fleshiness; I'd think it was comical, if I didn't feel so much like getting on my knees and worshiping it. Even the broken twig in front of my eyes is iridescently complex, with an inner tube of green sap, a lattice of spiderwebs like spun crystal. And in all this vast and layered richness I realize that the love I have for my sons is more pure than any love I've ever felt. My view of them is less complicated than my view of anything else in the world. Maybe because of the whites around their eyes, I think. I've never seen whites so white, so alert and calm and trusting.

If anything should happen to them, I think again, my molecules would dry out. I'd die, yes, but also I'd survive. Like J. P., I would *have* to survive. And that's one of the 400 Revelations I'd sooner not have learned.

"Can we, Dad? All sleep together? In the same bed?"

"Absolutely," I say. "But there's one thing we have to do first."

◆ ◆ ◆

It's a little past midnight when we get back to Rivesaltes. The bistro is empty. My troublesome pals are gone: the jolly German, the old farmer with two black teeth, the hostile motor scooterists. No one's there but a young bartender with short hair, perhaps the little brother of the long-haired one from earlier this evening, scrubbing the copper bar top with Comet cleanser, going round and round with a brush that's smaller than his hand.

"*Fermé, fermé,*" says the bartender, waving us away as we open the flimsy glass-paned door. But something tells us to walk in anyway. The boys make a beeline for Double Dragon, which has been unplugged, while I stand before him at the bar.

"*Fermé,*" he repeats, his voice rising. The expression on his face is frightened, and I wonder why.

And then it occurs to me: It's the same bashful bartender from a few hours ago. Unbelievably, he's shorn his curls. The scissors lie on the portable dishwasher behind him, wisps of brown ringlets lie on the floor. Why would he do that? To disguise himself? To make himself look less Jewish, after I'd troubled the waters? Or maybe he shaved it to *stop* hiding, because it seemed to him he'd been hiding behind his facial hair for years.

Or maybe, as Alex would say, it had nothing to do with us. Maybe he was due for a haircut and this was his night for it, *c'est tout.* That must have been it.

Still, as Marshall would say. *Still* . . .

The TV from the back room is playing *Lifestyles of the Rich and Famous.* I can't dismiss the notion that the act of cutting his curls seems to make sense, in an almost biblical way, though I can't say why. The poor guy wears an expression like a cornered rat—fear that could turn nasty and make him grab the scissors against his intruders. But I must speak anyway, and be done.

"Nous l'avons trouvé."

"Vous avez trouvé—?"

He pretends not to know what I'm talking about, but I know he does.

"Le camp des juifs," I say slowly. *"C'est très grand. Et très mal."*

He turns away at once, takes three dice, and tosses them in the tray with green felt. I put my hand on his wrist, skin to skin.

"I regret to embarrass you," I say in English, certain that he can understand me. "But you must not be ashamed of this camp. You must not be afraid of this camp. See it, see it, and make your peace."

He doesn't look up, but he doesn't pull away, either. His bottom lip is trembling.

"Bonne chance," I say, leaving.

◆ ◆ ◆

In the king-size motel bed, I'm assigned the middle spot, with a boy in each arm.

"Once upon a time . . ."

"Oh good," Marshall says, snuggling in close and clasping the journal tight. "Tell about the holy lady."

"I will," I promise. "Be patient."

Alex checks his home telephone number on his wrist, a nightly ritual, and adjusts himself into my shoulder with correct solemnity.

"Once upon a time there were two American men named Alex and Marshall," I go on. "And they were all grown up and strong in their bodies and in their minds. And they had five daughters each, and they told these daughters that before they were born there'd been a terrible war—"

"The most terrible war of the most terrible century," Alex reminds me.

"The most terrible in history," I agree. Lying there with my two favorite people tucked in my arms, I go on. "And the two American dads told their daughters that in their own child-hood, back when they themselves were kids, they once took a trip to see where it happened, and to find the places where some lucky people survived—"

"Those who *did* survive," Alex reminds me. "Because not many people did."

"Not many at all," I agree. "And they saw a bartender who cut off his curls, and they saw a German message that had been preserved in sawdust, and they saw a holy lady whose breath smelled of sardines—"

Stirring, Marshall says, "Yay!" very sleepily, and rolls his head to bury it deeper into my armpit.

"And she pointed the way to a terrible place where the earth was hurt and tried to hurt them back, but at the last minute the earth did not succeed in hurting them because a group of sol-diers with bitten nails turned out not to be their enemies but their friends.

"And they saw all these things, these strong American men. With their own eyes. And they told their daughters.

"And their daughters believed them."

Marshall's asleep. I know because he gives off a scent the way a baking apple starts to smell good when it's ready. I pry the journal from his hands and kiss the top of his head.

"As for you," I tell my older son. "I just want to say I'm proud of you, for the way you helped your brother when he was scared at the camp."

"You mean how I refrained from being my usual caustic cyn-ical self?"

I reach across and pinch the bridge of his nose. "No," I cor-rect him. "How you managed to be your courageous, compas-sionate, and thoroughly original self, with reserves you haven't even tapped yet."

"With reserves I haven't even tapped yet?" he asks, reaching across and pinching the bridge of *my* nose.

"Yes," I say, punching him in the arm. "You're not that bad a guy. For a Red Sox fan."

He smiles. Then his smile gets serious.

"Well, I believe it, you know," he says.

"Believe what?"

"'Dad won't let bad happen.'"

My smile gets serious, too. I put the journal beneath our pillow for safekeeping.

"That's quite a responsibility," I confess.

"Can you hack it?"

"Honestly? I don't know, sometimes. The world's got a lot of bad in it. I don't know if anyone can be protected from anything."

"Do you not want to do this anymore?" he asks. "We could turn around and go home anytime."

"Well, we've come this far. . . ."

"Really? You sure?"

"Yes," I say. "It's bigger than we are."

He looks me in the eye. No trace of either his or mine turning inward, going astray. "OK," he says.

◆   ◆   ◆

We fall asleep holding hands, the three of us. We've never done this before, and I have a pretty good notion we'll never do it again. But for this one night only, holding their hands with the journal beneath our heads, I'm conducting something better than a charge of electricity: a charge of humanity.

I love life, I think.

Because it keeps us company . . .

29

NIGHT GLOBE

*I*n pursuing writing, I made peace with my mother. With uncharacteristic patience, she showed me how to use a thesaurus, looking up the word "lost" in back, then thumbing through the front until I found a trove of words, a vein I could mine for variations as subtle as she was, and then some. All those different categories, each with a dozen synonyms: "Vanished, bewildered, forgotten, wasted, irretrievable, wicked . . ." The mix of her breath and all those words made me feel so rich that even years later, when I reached for my thesaurus, I would smell sour strawberries and exhale in wonder. "Write!" she'd tell me, when I was doubled over with rage at nothing I could put my finger on. "If you're angry or upset or impatient or mad, nobody wants to hear it. Write it instead! *Channel* your anger!"

It lofted me above the rage. The object of my rage—whatever it happened to be—became a thing of aesthetic interest, rather than something I wanted to blow up with a cherry bomb. In fact, it even gave me a vested interest in protecting the thing, because by the simple act of focusing attention on it enough to write about it, I was growing to love it.

Writing also helped me tame the strictest teacher in the school. Ill-tempered Mrs. Wilson had serious boxy shoes and different color stockings, one deeper brown than the other, over bulldog knees. She was a chin-grabber who took no guff from the likes of me. After the first week of sixth grade she peered at me wrathfully and said I wasn't the student my sister had been the year before. The next week I flicked a fountain pen at Mc-Dougal, meaning no harm, but it stained his head through the red flat-top he got at the beginning of every school year with a line of navy-blue dots. Mrs. Wilson had had enough. She squeezed my chin and ordered me to "turn over a new leaf."

So I did. Writing stories for Mrs. Wilson was different from tapping out babyish ones on the portable Remington, or penning summaries of Zorro for Rothschild. This was big-time. We had an exercise where we had to use each week's vocabulary words in a sentence. I went so overboard that I ended up writing entire paragraphs around each word, textured mini-stories that hinted at much larger stories behind the vocabulary words. Mrs. Wilson wrote EXCELLENT! READ TO CLASS! on the tops of them with red pencil, underlining so hard that one time she ripped the paper.

I wasn't a hider in this game of making up sentences. I was the captain. Sentence making was my ship; when I yelled "Come about!" Hotdog had to jump. Writing was better than having fingertip fireworks; it was like taking dictation off my brain, just copying down the words that appeared like magic behind my eyes, so easy it was almost cheating. I imagined I had an invisible power tool like a drill press screwed onto my school desk; I inserted paper and it came out fully written. Written words formed themselves into adventure stories about people I'd never dreamed of but who had a life and a logic I couldn't refute, and I was almost as spellbound as the rest of the class when I read them aloud. Writing was as effortless as somersaulting downhill, as lurching on a trolley cart through Heart's Castle and being completely safe.

Other good things were happening. Maybe they were the long-delayed rewards for standing my ground with Manny the bigkid, or for not losing my glove in Hotdog's house, but I finally got a letter back from J. Edgar Hoover. Well, from his secretary, saying that Mr. Hoover was out of town but that I could rest assured my letter would be brought to his attention on his return. Thereafter I could claim to be his pen pal with a degree of legitimacy, even though I was sufficiently cynical by now to understand that this was as far as it would go (and soon enough, that a cross-dressing G-man might not be a savory pen pal in any case). More glorious still, my Little League team won the championship. On the day of our win I was part of a triple play at third base with McDougal on second and Lawless on first, all of us in our blue-and-white uniforms, that was written up in the newspapers I delivered the next afternoon, with special instructions to all my clients to turn to the sports page. As for ogres—I still wasn't convinced they weren't hiding in buckets of pine cones, but I operated as if they weren't, which amounted to the same thing.

Things were looking up on the social front, too. Lynn Williams picked me first at dancing school. The foxtrot was girls' choice and Miss Hunnibell selected Lynn to start it off. Lynn looked around, found no one suitable, meandered over to my side of the ballroom, and, with a sigh of exasperation, resigned herself to selecting me. My knees felt like bicycle tires punctured by glass. That night my crush went into overdrive as I spent the first in my life tossing and turning on account of a female. So besotted was I to have her within reach at last that by next afternoon I'd befriended Lynn's younger brother, Treat, and invited him to my house to play a game I made up called Vice Versa.

"How do you play that?" he asked.

"Anything I say, you have to say the vice versa of it."

Treat was in fourth grade. He was so overjoyed to be invited to a sixth grader's house (as overjoyed as I was to have been chosen to dance by a seventh grader) that he was willing to go along with anything.

"OK, first thing: What if I had your dog?"

Treat thought for a minute and then made the inversion. "What if I had *yours?*"

"What if you married my sister?"

"What if you married *mine?*"

Rapture. I never had Treat over again. I'd heard the words I longed to hear, words that brought me so close to my fantasy that I never needed to go near it again. Over the next few days I took pains to let Treat down gently and we sustained a mutually respectful distance the rest of our childhood. Treat grew up to become a chisel-jawed movie star, but even as I sat in the dark watching his face 40 feet high as he beat up bad guys in *Prince of the City* or seduced women prettier than any who ever graced our dancing school, his granite features summoned up for me only the innocence of a little kid who inadvertently solved the yearning of an older schoolmate, releasing me at last to go on to further crushes, some of which were even reciprocated.

◆ ◆ ◆

It was a victorious time. At summer day camp in Darien my new girlfriend and I were co-captains of the Olympic-style team Macedonians. I was the final runner in the long-distance relay race that ended the weeklong competition. My runner brought me the baton first and I had the solitary glory of bringing it the final mile. As the finish line came into view, I could hear the man at the loudspeaker spotting me far away, not at first making out who I was and then announcing my name over and over as I came running in, the entire camp cheering and my girlfriend covering me with kisses. David bearing the head of Goliath didn't hear hosannas as sweet as those that rang in my ears that day. Later that evening, after sailing with my father, the jib halyard accidentally went up the mast and my father asked me to shimmy up and get it. He was inviting me to put my dare-devilishness on the line, and afterward he felt such rare uncon-flicted pride in me that he bought me a chocolate soda at Hummiston's. "Brave boy," he reported to Mr. Hummiston, and I glimpsed how bravery could become one of my colors. It was different from the recklessness I'd exhibited till then. This was *considered*, and that made all the difference.

Even my rage was becoming useful, welling up in my blood as a source of strength. For the final two weeks of summer I went to a Jewish sleepaway camp where I fell in love with a girl from New Jersey named Bobby Siegel. Being from a lobster town, I assumed her name was "Seagull," and it enhanced the romance. Contrary by nature, I spent the fortnight reading a biography of Hitler and discovered what a brilliant military strategist he was, a fact I didn't mind sharing with my fellow campers. Word got around. One afternoon during rest period a giant blubbery counselor showed up in my bunkhouse and taunted me for my choice of reading material. The entire bunkhouse including Bobby Seagull was watching but I kept right on reading. He called me a Nazi lover. He asked me if I wanted to put his relatives in the oven. All of a sudden I snapped. I jumped up from my bed and screamed in the counselor's face till my veins stood out. I felt so savage that even though he was twice my size, I could've pounded him into the ground. He seemed to shrink as I swelled more. When I stopped screaming, the bunkhouse fell into amazed silence as he skulked away. I lay back down and pretended to continue reading the biography, but there were pinpricks of stars in front of the words.

Ever since that day I knew that strength wasn't the most important component in a fight. Rage was. I never got in fistfights. They scared me too much. But I knew that if I were in a pit in Poland waiting to be shot by a ring of Not-sees, I'd have it in me to jump up and rip out their Adam's apples with my teeth. I was twelve years old and it frightened me to know that about myself.

❖ ❖ ❖

But it was at the beach that the summer's real triumph occurred. The ultimate rite of passage for Rowayton kids was the Test, which consisted of swimming the length of the beach four times, thereby winning the right to swim to the raft without ask-

ing permission. This may not have seemed like much to an outsider, but it was meeting Rowayton on Rowayton's terms: Being
allowed to swim to the raft meant that we were good swimmers,
with all the weight that signified in a seaside community. In the
Rowayton culture of preadolescent boys, passing the Test meant
what being able to join the men on a hunt meant to a caveman
culture, being consecrated as a junior member unto the faith.

The Test was administered under the kindly gimlet eye of the
town's chief caveman and lifeguard, Art Chace, high priest of
the beach. Bronze-muscled and gentle-voiced, Art was village
elder and Atlas all in one: the incarnation of every authority figure I'd ever had or was to have. He had white hair on his golden
chest and totalitarian powers. With a few quiet syllables he
could ban you from the beach for a whole summer, but he was
a benign disciplinarian who'd smile a small shy smile that meant
that even though you were a kid, he had respect for you.

Art never said when it was someone's time to take the Test;
like the best rites, it was something you came to on your own.
One morning shortly before school began in the fall, I decided. I
didn't mention it to anyone at breakfast, just rode my bike to the
beach and told Art I was going to try. Then I was in the water. It
seemed like I was doing the sidestroke for hours, sawing seaweed out of my way. Then I was on my back for hours. Lashes of
acrid-tasting waves swept down my throat and made me want to
throw up. I was doing the crawl, the most spastic of my strokes,
flapping and stabbing like a crab, holding my breath, pulling
through my cramps. Then back on my side again for the home
stretch. It was crude, but I made it. Even from a distance I could
see Art smiling his small smile of respect. Walking toward him
along the beach, I made a secret gesture: I turned my head to the
right and shrugged my shoulder as if to wipe water off my chin.
But what I was secretly doing was kissing my shoulder.

Out of the mellifluous haze of my childhood past, I vaguely
recollected that I'd made the same gesture before—hadn't I
done it when I'd gotten Kimberly's father to come baby-sit my

little sister and me, and when Mr. Heart had taken me to the secret place behind the trapdoor of his Castle? I'd never paid attention to it before, but I understood now that that small instinctual move was the most profound and sacred thing I'd ever done. I was kissing myself for doing right.

Passing the Test didn't mean I was in the clear, that I'd no longer need hiding places anymore. Real life wasn't like fairy tales in that regard: you didn't emerge from a struggle to find your life was clear sailing. You sallied forth a while, then a new struggle presented itself and you ducked back into hiding, and when you ventured out again it was with a more boldly defined set of hopes and fears before you needed to slip back into the shade. I wasn't a hero. But I wasn't a hound dog, either.

So with this bit of self-knowledge I was ready to leave Rowayton School and hobnob with kids from South Norwalk in the public junior high. I wasn't cured of myself and sensed I'd probably never be, experiencing my life as a kind of liquid strangeness, the same as anyone else did. I was still afflicted with vividness, still felt fugitive in the homes of my pals, capable of being too easily impressed and too easily wounded, *susceptible* would be the word—not wary enough, with an obscure sense of not belonging, just like everyone else, Jew and non-Jew.

But I could pronounce the word *Connecticut* and I felt at home there.

◆ ◆ ◆

To clinch my victory, I had a bar mitzvah. I was afraid it was going to be just the Hebrew equivalent of the Test, but in this jubilant time I felt more spiritual than ever before or since, and I decided to make my devotion semipublic by doing a good job. I studied hard, not put off by the fact that the temple was a distance away, and that the ceremony itself was scheduled to take place in half of a high school gym, walled off to mask the sounds of someone practicing jump shots on the other side. Nor did I opt to take the easy out favored by some Reform Jews and learn the text phonetically. I wanted to do it well, and even broke tradition in the temple by deciding to learn to chant the music. When I asked the rabbi to teach me, he seemed to blush a little, and promptly made it his business to find out where a record of the chants could be procured. After paying the $4.99, I received the 33-1/3 long-playing record and every night when I finished my clarinet practice, I'd chant along with it, trying to be a grown-up in a world where being grown-up mattered.

I had only a month from the time I received the record until my bar mitzvah, but I was determined. On the Sunday afternoon one week before the ceremony, I sat on the nubbly red fabric of the Castro convertible and slaved at the songs. I vowed I wouldn't leave my room until I'd mastered them. The sun was going down. Sometimes I came achingly close to memorizing the final chant, only to have the tune to a middle one disappear in my mouth. But unlike the times when I'd left gluey fingerprints on the windshields of flubbed airplane models, I didn't allow myself the luxury of getting frustrated. It seemed childish and beside the point.

At last the final chant took: I grabbed my bike and rode around for a while in the dusk feeling as though my chest and belly were indestructible, like one of my army tanks. I ate three pieces of pumpernickel bread, not worrying that they were going to spoil my appetite before dinner. The celebration the following Saturday was more moving than I'd hoped due to the presence of one surprise guest—my old psychiatrist, Dr. Blaine. In the midst of my chanting, I saw him sitting in a folding chair on the shellacked floor of the gym, and my eyes welled up. To keep from bawling in front of everyone, as soon as I'd finished chanting I pretended for the remainder of the service not to see him and, in the way some men stave off premature ejaculation by reciting baseball statistics, I started taking my pulse surreptitiously up there on the bema, and measuring how fast it was racing against the new birthday stopwatch my parents had given me.

Later, at the reception in our cardboard palace, Dr. Blaine

wasn't there. I felt that he'd seen my tears and had charitably decided not to inflict any more emotion on me. I never saw him again. But in the pile of presents I amassed that day there was a special one from him, a globe of the night sky that I treasured the rest of my childhood, that I brought to my various college dorms, that I eventually moved into the bedroom I shared with my wife. It was a beautiful blue-black night globe, with the constellations in white, and though I never tried to learn the constellations, I found myself staring at it over the years, and I always remembered trying to hold back my tears as I chanted my Hebrew while someone respectfully held off shooting baskets on the other side of the wall. It was one of the nicest gifts anyone ever gave me; it spoke of setting your sights high and letting your imagination soar beyond your present circumstances, and when my wife was moving herself and my children out of our house, I knew what I wanted to give my firstborn to keep on the table by his bed to show him where things were in the dark.

30

STOPPING *MIT* THE BOO-HOO

Ah, children, ah, dear friends, don't be afraid of life! How
good life is when one does something good and just!

—*The Brothers Karamazov*

You're here to see Mr. Morganstern?" asks the nurse back in
Brussels.

"No, a Mr. *Morgan.*"

"J. P. Morganstern? He signed himself in using his full name.
Are we talking about the same gentleman? Sweet, unassum-
ing?"

"Definitely not."

"I'm sorry. My mistake. We have two Morgansterns here.
You must be referring to the noisy one: rather forward? Always
waving his false tooth around?"

"That'd be him."

"Who had a cerebral accident?"

"*Cerebral accident?*" we ask. "You mean, like a stroke? When
did this happen?"

"A month ago, maybe."

"Impossible," I say. "We saw him a month ago and he was
strong as a horse."

"Shortly after that, then. Was there anything unusual about him when you saw him?"

"Oh yeah," the boys say. "Oh ho yeah."

"But objectively, yes and no," I clarify. "I mean, I don't know that we're qualified to say."

"You're family?"

"You bet we're family," the boys say. "Don't we look like family?"

The nurse stares at us. She's worried-looking, puffy-faced, a British nurse in a Brussels nursing home who's not sure she approves of either the forward Mr. Morganstern or these three ragamuffin Americans who've popped in unannounced, saying they've been on an overnight train since yesterday from southern France.

"He can't talk, you understand. He hasn't spoken in weeks."

"We understand."

"He may not comprehend a word you say. . . ."

"We'll take our chances."

Wearing bits of each other's clothing—Alex in my sweater, Marshall in Alex's beret—the boys and I are led down a eucalyptus-scented corridor to have our audience with J. P. He's resting in a plaid lounge, gaping at *Married with Children* on a large-screen color TV—such an improvement from his small black-and-white model that he probably figures he's made a good deal, and all he had to pay was a few brain cells. He's more curled up than before but somehow not a whit diminished, still capable of jabbing you in the ribs to draw your attention to something, poke and grab, buttonholing God. When he sees us he grins like an old eagle with his tongue lolling in his mouth, his paper hospital skirt stretched over his knuckly knees. I can see his upper thighs like soft baby skin but pickled—gray-pink and gristly. And up above, what was that? Was he wearing a diaper? And was that Desenex I smelled, for diaper rash? With one huge soft testicle swanging free.

As I kneel before him he reaches for my hand and grips it like a vise. I'm startled again by the strength in those knobby fingers. The boys crowd in close around him, like a huddle. Alex places the journal carefully on J. P.'s lap. Marshall removes his beret and puts it on J. P.'s head. I hand him the cellophane of curls, which he indelicately stuffs in the pocket of his robe, then looks up at the boys with a line of spittle coming off his lip, which is twisted into the echo of a smile.

"*Nu?*" say his shoulders.

We have so many questions to ask him. Is his apartment dim because he never got used to the light after being in the wine cellar for three months? Did he sleep with the Gestapo guy's wife? Why did he choose the name J. P. Morgan in the first place and what compelled him now to take back the old name? How did his son Olivier become so estranged? What were the ribbons in the journal about? Who the hell were Mimi and Babba and Rochelle? How did he finally make it over the Pyrenees after the concentration camp, and once in Spain was he home free? Did we parse the poetry from the truth? Can such a thing ever be parsed? And what about all the leads we neglected to follow or couldn't even see? Why was there a wedding dress made of an American parachute in the attic in Tournon? Might the old janitor at the German nunnery in the Ardennes have had a saga of his own to tell us?

But questions are only questions—they have limited usefulness in a world where answers don't do any good. We got a piece of the story and, for the time being, that's enough. *We* are the story now, it's time to tell him something of what *we* know. Wishing myself luck (it's going to be a leap but a leap is what's called for), I take a breath and this is what I say to J. P., not quite sure whether I'm speaking my thoughts aloud or somehow transmitting them silently.

"We found your places. Not all of them, but a few. We sat in them, breathing the air. Some have changed beyond recognition. Some are the same as the day you left them. In no way was it a *conquest*, as you said, any more than a mountain climber can say he made a conquest of Mount Everest. Everest sometimes suffers climbers to ascend it, and the true climbers are not made arrogant but made humble by it. And similarly, some of your hiding places were kind enough to let us visit them in silence and humility."

This is the voice I've wanted, the voice from my heart I've been aiming for for so long. J. P. tilts his head and looks concerned but keeps grinning his skull-like grin, wagging my hand to continue.

"One of your places, the last one, tried to hurt us," I go on. "It could have been traumatic for the boys. But it's had the opposite effect. It lanced the boil. They faced it down and it purged them and maybe they'll be better people for it. Something I never expected from that place. Me too, maybe. Time will tell.

"I've come to see something else I never expected. I've been thinking about your children a lot, even going so far as imagining that I've felt vibes from them. But the truth is I don't know anything about their lives *or* their deaths, and maybe it's right that I don't know. They're not meant to be known by me, any more than the Unknown Soldier is meant to be known."

He's sitting and watching me, nodding his head with his tongue out, and I'm not sure if my thoughts are wounding him or angering him or even getting through at all. Making chewing noises and sneaking an occasional glance at the TV but still keeping his iron grip on me, he pumps me to continue.

"Maybe you think I'm carrying on like an idiot, but you're like my priest, or my rabbi, I don't know who you're supposed to be like, I only know I have to tell you . . ."

I struggle to formulate the concept.

"See, I love my kids so much, but no more than you loved yours. I lost the home movie of my kids, but if I could see it again, I'd see they were just ordinary kids, no more special than anyone else's. They're regular kids!—like all the others in the world. That's the heartbreak, that's the gasping shock of it all, that the kids who perished were every bit as alive as mine are, as ordinary and precious, and what's amazing to me is that somehow that's not a sad thing to acknowledge. On the contrary, for some strange reason it's a hope and a consolation. . . ."

And when I convey that, the most remarkable thing happens: The memories come flooding back to me as if they were just waiting to be released. All the old home movies: a clip of Alex and Marshall jumping from sand dunes; a close-up of their laughing faces when they were thumb-wrestling in the backseat; a panoramic shot of them sitting in football helmets at a lemonade stand at the bottom of the driveway, the sort of typical red-blooded American kids you pass on the street every day; then getting into a lemonade fight, Alex pouring a Dixie cup down his brother's back, Marshall chasing his brother like a tiny piston all over the newly cut grass with a Dixie cup of his own.

And mixed in with my movies is a stray, from someone else's: a boy and his father standing in a killing pit ringed by Nazis. It's the instant before they're about to be machine-gunned with the rest of their anonymous Eastern European village; the father is speaking very quietly to his son, pointing to the sky before the bullets ring out, and I realize my love is nothing extraordinary, it's what all parents feel. Sometimes we look at the sunlight bouncing off their hair or the water pouring sleek off their throats and we say, "Thank you, God," and it's the only prayer we have. . . .

Pour les enfants, I think. *Pour tous les enfants* . . .

"You're tiring him out," the nurse says. "I'd better bring him back to his room."

Still J. P. doesn't lessen his grip on me, nor I mine on him.

"You know, I used to think that I cling to my kids to make up for all the parents who had theirs ripped from their arms. But the fact of it is, I can't truly love mine unless I love the others as well—"

J. P. chokes on his drool, chuffing it forth. Time's running out. What am I trying to say?

"It's not enough to love your own children," I say. "The Nazis loved their children, but that didn't stop them from doing what they did. Our children are given us as a key to loving *all* the world's children, the Hotdog children and the Olivier children and the Adolf children, too, the lost ones and the living ones, and even those who *used* to be children: the world.

"It's the only way to undo the Holocaust, to the extent that it can be undone at all."

The nurse releases the brake on his wheelchair and spins him around. But J. P. brakes the forward motion with a foot on the floor and, grinning that skull-like grin, looks at me with his shoulders raised:

About time you got it, the shoulders say.

And off he goes, wheeled out the door with the dusty beret happily on his head. Alone in the plaid lounge, the boys and I nod to each other, smiling shyly. I push Alex's shoulder, he pushes Marshall's, the three of us making tentative contact as if we haven't spent a month in each other's faces. At the same instant we hear from down the hall the unmistakable sound of a hand being slapped. And a cry from the nurse:

"Enough with the goosing, Mr. Morganstern!"

◆ ◆ ◆

For a final celebratory dinner, I give the boys their choice of places to eat, anywhere in Brussels: three stars, four stars, the sky's the limit.

It's a wonderful place, this kosher McDonald's, and by unanimous decision we decide to take our trays to the outdoor tables, and stepping outside I feel my heart swell like at a baseball stadium when you emerge from the interior and there's the open air and springtime green and young athletes in clean uniforms and you feel your heart lift in your chest. You see a runner stealing home and he dives headfirst into the dirt and when the dust settles the umpire screams, "Safe!" So do I feel safe on this final stretch of our trip, approaching home.

"Let's say it's a Jewish holiday, though," says Marshall.

"Which one? Sukkos? Purim? We haven't done Passover for a while."

"Yeah, that one."

"So be it," I say. "Happy Passover."

I look around at the blue and white decor and see that the boys are expanding at the rate of the universe. Alex sneaks a secret smile at Marshall, and Marshall sneaks one back at Alex, and witnessing this I can almost taste the love I feel. An old lady with a white bun sits at a nearby table, stirring and sipping her cup of tea. A Hasid seated on the other side wears an opaque expression as he rests his bones, dabbing the root beer foam from his lips with a paper napkin as delicately as a woman touching up her lipstick. It feels like a stolen moment: The rain's washed the city clean and the voices out here are alive, giving and sending, a kind of grand dissonance as tiers of golden light illuminate the boulevard.

Alex tries to lift me up. So surprised is he when he succeeds that tears fill his eyes.

"I can't believe it! I just picked up my dad!"

"Hey, welcome to the future, kid."

Here in this temple al fresco of McDonald's on our very own Passover, Alex closes his drawing pad, a relic that's as vital now as J.P.'s journal. Marshall takes off his time goggles and, thinking no one's watching him, slips them in the trash can. *Good for you,* I think. *You've used them well.* And finally I realize why I've taken this trip, the most obvious reason of all—I've been offering my children something I never got: a center, a core with all the vowels intact, no asterisks necessary. Suddenly I'm irradiated with hope, bumped to a higher plane. I haven't felt such clarity for decades: Conjuring my childhood I stand shoulder high in water and see those starfish again, at my feet. My whole life is see-throughable. I'm exalted as when I was a child, sanctified by grasshopper spit.

The Hasid is astonished when I sweep by to kiss him on his grizzled cheek. But it's like kissing one of my sons. *"Mir vel*

leben," I could say to him. "For better or for worse, we will survive." But what I decide to say is "Great fries."

The dumbfounded look on his face morphs into a wide grin,
exposing a single poppy seed between his two front teeth.

He understands: If we aren't family, who is?

◆ ◆ ◆

The boys take my hands for the walk back to the home base of
our old hotel, the Metropole, each humming his own song past
the secret passageways, the trapdoors and false ceilings of buildings we'll never explore. Their watches go off in sync as they
babble about how they're going to take their children to Europe
someday, how they're going to . . . I'm not even listening, no
longer curious to know what they're discussing. It's not my
business anymore. I'm so exhausted I just want to get to the hotel and plunge into a bottomless sleep. The sky's broken open to
reveal one of the great sunsets of all time, like the inside of a giant diamond flattened out against the sky, and as I push open
the door to our fourth floor room, sunshine floods in from the
bank of windows, burnishing the room with orange-strawberry
light. We climb through the windows to stand on the little balcony. The sound of a police car recedes sourly as the sky pleats
itself into bands of green and pink, and I'm emboldened in a
flush of triumph to think: We did it! They said we couldn't but
we did! They said it was a goose chase but at least we glimpsed
the geese! We stitched our small family into the greater fabric of
things. We found a way to travel back in time, developing antibodies and seeing with our own eyes. No one got lo-jacked . . .
no one got left! out! We even managed to stop *mit* the boo-hoo.

And more. We paid tribute. We did not forget them.

"Kiss your shoulders, boys," I say.

"Why?"

"Just do what your father tells you."

They do so. And their eyes are opened, too. "The light!" they
exclaim. "Do you believe this light, Dad? It's like, I could eat it!"

They do better: they come forward and enclose me in a hug.

I soak up calm, power, goodness . . . whatever I need to leave them out here, climb inside to bed, and begin the rest of my life without them. Then, half a century after the Holocaust, I hear two young voices make their announcement from the fourth floor balcony to the populace of Europe, yelling it down from the top of Gestapo headquarters:

"We're the Rosenzweig boys! Jews from America!"

ACKNOWLEDGMENTS

I've been blessed to enjoy the support of many people who've believed in me and openheartedly bolstered my labors. I'd like to express my deepest thanks to my editor David Rosenthal, and the ten-year-old stickball player within; to my editor Ruth Fecych, whose deft touch is as graceful as it is masterly; to my agents Charlotte Sheedy and Regula Noetzli, who have been passionate on my behalf; to my cousins Jack and Ruth Kaufman, who planted the seed; to all the relatives in this country and abroad who tactfully endured my hours of interviews; to my dozens of contacts in Europe who led me through the maelstrom; to Toby Rossner of the Bureau of Jewish Education of Rhode Island, for putting up with my numerous questions; to Facing History and Ourselves, for their careful guidance; to Lee Teverow of the Athenaeum, Providence's jewel of a library, for gamely tracking down my bizarre research requests; to Skip Burns, who first put to me the immortal words, "What do you most want to write about?"; to Malcolm and Clarice Grear, for offering me salvation during Dark n Cold; to Lyle and Nancy Fain, who first told me how to rent bikes in Belgium; to Nick and Nancy Sander, for high-class digs in the Big Apple; to Bente Hoesgburg, for unceasing encouragement; to Addison Parks, for all those philosophical talks; to Johnnie and Bill Rodriguez, who were a sounding board for this tale over the years of its many reincarnations; to Monique Raes, wherever you are; to my godfather, Walter, for his droll willingness to share his knowledge of Yiddish; to Bonnie Friedman, whose exquisite literary taste was a beacon; to Andy Hoffman, who first revealed to me, in an ordinary-looking coffee shop, what it was I'd got by the tail; to Shpiz, who kept reminding me that the strength of a text is measured by how strong are the pieces you leave out; to Miles, who managed to square pi for me, right there in my sunporch; to my brother, Ron, and sisters, Renee and Cecily, for their insight and generosity; to my parents, early champions and late drinking pals; to the big boys, Alex and Marshall, for being there; to the little boys, Spencer and Jeremy, for giving me so much more than déjà vu; and above all to my wife, the lovely and elegant Shelley Roth, who led me to my truest voice.

A READER'S GUIDE

Reading Group Questions and Topics for Discussion

1. After their horrible adventure in the ruins of the French concentration camp, Alex experiences a wave of terrifying, uncontrollable anger. "That's the thing about rage," Daniel counsels him, "it's hard to aim it right." What does he tell Alex to do with his rage? Where has Daniel aimed his own rage up to this point in the narrative? Do you think his methods of rage control will be altered by this journey?

2. How does Daniel explain his lifelong compulsion to hide? Discuss his assertion that hiding places are "not merely dark holes of concealment," but "places of revelation."

3. The Europeans' response to Daniel's improbable quest is at times dismissive, at other times downright humiliating. Where do we see Daniel struggling with his own uncertainty and naïveté about the process of following J.P.'s tracks? What methods do Daniel and his sons employ to keep plowing ahead? Why do you suppose so many people do end up helping them by supplying clues along with hospitality?

4. Daniel explores what he calls the "native sense of estrangement," or the idea that by virtue of being human, no one ever feels entirely accepted, no matter how confident an exterior he or she presents. How does he reach this conclusion? Where in the narrative do we see the theory convincingly exemplified?

5. Daniel interprets his cousin Olivier's comment—that the Holocaust was "neither singular nor unique" in an inhumane world peppered with genocide—as a full-blown

denial of the Holocaust. He goes on to label Olivier one of the "deadliest animals in the world." What do you think? Is there a significant difference between the camp that still doubts the veracity of the Holocaust as an historical event and the camp that sees the Holocaust as a horrifying event with parallels in Africa, Asia, Latin America, and elsewhere?

6. Who is Mr. Pinanski? What role does he play in Daniel's coming of age? Why do you think Daniel tells us about him?

7. Daniel's story is forthcoming about his stormy relationship with his highly emotional mother, but we learn very little about his relationship with his father. Is this fact significant? What does the memoir reveal about Daniel's take on responsible fathering? Can the book be read as a manifesto on parenting?

8. At the end of the memoir, Daniel asks, "What kind of father would shove his sons' noses in the most terrifying experience of the century?" How does he answer himself? Do you think he is fully at peace with his reasons for doing so? Does he have different reasons at the end of the journey than he had at the beginning? Does he have any regrets about putting "two young souls at risk," as he describes it?

9. What does the rabbinical student in the Parisian *shul* mean when he jokes that "all Jews worth their membership cards are alienated?"

10. Daniel describes his childhood as permeated by a constant and consuming sense of anger. What are his theories about how he acquired this anger? What is his "asthma of the soul?" How did anger inform and shape his friendships with other children growing up?

11. From J.P. and Schloime to Daniel himself as a teenager, we see characters "metabolizing" the Holocaust through humor. What do you think of this approach? Can you think of

a media outlet in which it would be appropriate? What about a stand-up comedy sketch? Do you think there is a commonly agreed-upon social etiquette concerning Holocaust discussion in general? If so, how is it decided and by whom? Have you ever felt uncomfortable due to a reference to the Holocaust? What was the circumstance?

12. Daniel believes in injecting his children with "an inoculation of evil." He theorizes that "by being dosed just a bit with the world's evil, they'll build antibodies against it." By the end of the journey, how do you think Alex and Marshall have fared under their father's treatment? Has their exposure to evil changed them? If so, is it a change for the better or for the worse? Has Daniel revised his original ideas about what his children need from him? Do you agree with his ideas?

13. The fracture of family brought about by a recent divorce constantly informs Daniel's trip with his sons, both in his mind and in theirs. Does their attempt at regeneration through an arduous quest work?

ABOUT THE AUTHOR

DANIEL ASA ROSE is the author of *Flipping for It,* a novel cited as a *New York Times* New and Noteworthy paperback, and *Small Family with Rooster,* a collection of prize-winning short stories. His essays, stories, reviews, and travel pieces have appeared in *The New Yorker, The New York Times Magazine, Esquire, Playboy, Partisan Review, GQ, Condé Nast Traveler,* and elsewhere. The winner of one O. Henry prize and two PEN awards, he is currently the Arts & Culture editor of the *Forward.*